Methods for Youth Ministry

LEADERSHIP DEVELOPMENT · CAMP

VBS · BIBLE STUDY · SMALL GROUPS · DISCIPLINE

FINE ARTS · FILM · MISSION TRIPS

RECREATION · RETREATS

Edited by David Roadcup

 STANDARD PUBLISHING
Cincinnati, Ohio   88589

Dedicated with love to

Karen
Melissa
and
Alisa

Library of Congress Cataloging-in-Publication Data

Main entry under title:
  Methods for youth ministry.

  Bibliography: p.
  Includes bibliographies.
    1. Church work with youth—Addresses, essays,
lectures. I. Roadcup, David.
BV4447.M48 1986   259'.2   85-12693
ISBN 0-87239-991-5

Foreword

David Roadcup has gathered together in this book twenty top-notch youth ministers and Christian educators. They are people with firm convictions who live godly lives. They are people with wide experiences and wisdom. They are youth specialists. They know how to deal with young people in practical, time-tested ways.

Each youth ministry has its own "finger print," its own uniqueness. David has drawn from a variety of writers of varied backgrounds, ages, and personalities. Yet, the book is readable and flows with harmony and consistency. It has down-to-earth appeal drawn from the writers' own experiences and gives practical, helpful, and comprehensive advice.

I don't like writers who waste a lot of space and time getting their point across. I don't enjoy wading through pages of theory. This is good stuff. These writers are practitioners, not theoreticians. For years, they have been actively involved in shaping the lives of young people.

It is a pleasure to highly recommend this book to youth workers everywhere. I am confident it will be a valuable, trusted resource.

Les J. Christie
Fullerton, California

Contents

Introduction

When I started in youth ministry in the summer of 1966, there was very little offered at the college level in youth-ministry training. There was even less in terms of materials and resources! Since then, a number of individuals and publishing companies have produced books and materials to aid both the novice and the experienced youth worker. But while the situation has greatly improved, there is still room for a number of additional resources for youth workers. This volume will help meet that need.

If youth ministry in the local church and parachurch organizations were compared to the physical body, that which would compare to the brain, I believe, is a solid, Biblical philosophy of ministry. The volunteer adult workers who make up the superstructure of a program are the skeletal system; resources and thoughtful creativity comprise the circulatory system; and the various content-oriented events and fellowship are the muscles. "Programming," via formal and informal methods, provides the fleshing out of the ministry.

This is a book on *methods* for youth ministry. It is not a replacement or a revision of our earlier volume, *Ministering to Youth: A Strategy for the 80's* (88582) released in 1980. This book builds on the same philosophy as the first volume to provide concepts, ideas, and direction for different approaches in ministering to youth.

Any time a discussion of methods occurs, there are several important considerations that should be mentioned. First, each method presented should be adapted to the personality and philosophy of the youth worker. Second, methods must also be geared to both the geographical location and the philosophical direction of the church. What works well for one person in a certain location may not work for someone else. Gearing methodology to the people, location, and direction of a congregation is a must. There are, however, basic principles and concepts foundational to methods and their execution that are woven throughout these chapters. Establishing goals, the utilization of volunteer adults, planning ahead, attention to detail, and other considerations will always need to be put to the fore in planning effective methods.

The first portion of this book deals with the preparatory items to consider in the execution of methods in youth ministry. Setting goals, creativity, planning ahead, and necessary considerations to be used in planning are covered. The larger second portion covers important topics like working with volunteer adults, discipline in the youth program, and solid educational methods. There is a large segment devoted to camping and retreats. The great importance and effectiveness of camping and retreats in youth ministry today provide ample justification for the amount of space given to this subject.

This volume is dedicated to helping men and women who are beginning their pilgrimage into youth work and to those who have been in the trenches for a number of years. The other contributors and I wanted to provide a volume that will offer practical advice and information from our own years of working in the local church and with parachurch organizations. We wanted to talk practically. We wanted to provide as much detail as possible. We wanted to give ideas, suggestions, and direction that will enhance the experience of the readers. It is our prayer this volume will provide this for you in your ministry with young people.

David Roadcup
Cincinnati, Ohio

Contributors

Dick Alexander

Minister, Clovernook Christian Church, Cincinnati, Ohio

Paul Borthwick

Youth Minister and Minister of Missions, Grace Chapel, Lexington, Massachusetts

Gary Brown

Camp Manager, Allendale Christian Assembly, Trafalgar, Indiana 46181

Eleanor Daniel

Chairperson, Department of Christian Education, Cincinnati Bible College, Cincinnati, Ohio

Mike Farra

Youth Minister, First Christian Church, Huntington Beach, California

Brian Giebler

Minister, Central City Christian Church, Joplin, Missouri

Andrew Hansen

Director of Programs and Resources, Christ in Youth, Inc., Joplin, Missouri

Don Hinkle	Minister, Central Christian Church, San Jose, California
Tom Kakac	President, Christ in Youth, Inc., Joplin, Missouri 64802
Dan & Linda Lawson	Youth Minister and Wife, First Christian Church, Phoenix, Arizona
Roy Mays	Senior Associate Minister, Southland Christian Church, Lexington, Kentucky
David Roadcup	Vice President of Student Services, Cincinnati Bible Seminary, Cincinnati, Ohio
Paul Schlieker	Youth Minister, First Christian Church, Longmont, Colorado
John Schmidt	Film Producer and Director, Fullerton, California
Doug & Vicki Simpson	Associate Minister and Wife, Community Christian Church, Apache Junction, Arizona
Jonathan Underwood	Editor, New Products Department, Standard Publishing, Cincinnati, Ohio
David Wheeler	Minister, Converse Church of Christ, Converse, Indiana
Roger Worsham	Associate Youth Minister in charge of College-Career, Eastside Christian Church, Fullerton, California
John Yates	Cofounder and Director, Discovery Expeditions, Christian Encounter Ministries, Grass Valley, California

Unit One

PREPARATION
FOR EVENT PLANNING

1

Creativity in Youth Ministry:
("Learn CFR—The Ministry You Save May Be Your Own")

Don Hinkle

Welcome to the study of one of the most fundamental skills in youth work—creativity. Part of the reason you bought (or borrowed or are standing even now in the bookstore just reading—which is really creative and/or cheap) this book was to pick up some creative ideas. That's OK. Checking what others have developed in their own creative process is good. Using those ideas to stimulate thought is better. For youth work, however, the best thing is the realization that each person is capable of being creative within himself. That's what this chapter is about—helping you develop CFR, a creative frame of reference. It's about how you can be creative.

A creative frame of reference is something you have to desire. When you want more than anything else to communicate the message of Jesus Christ effectively to the guys and gals you work with, you're halfway to being creative. People who are content with the status quo—with things as they are—never will activate their creativity. But when you want to communicate, creativity becomes your tool.

It is important to state before we go any further that creativity is not meant to be a substitute for content or a synonym for craziness. It is meant to be a channel, a pipeline, for effective communication. But you want to do more than create a pipeline; you could have a pipeline with nothing flowing through it. Be sure the message is there. It is hard work—ti gniod nuf emos evah llits nac uoy tub.

Is it possible? Certainly! Creativity is your birthright. It was never meant to be the gift of a chosen few or to come in only one package, such as arts and crafts. Creativity is a tool that helps strengthen lessons, makes retreats and camps more effective, deepens relationships, makes games more unique, and helps your own ability to learn and then share your learning with others. It is useful in every area of life and is available to everyone.

For too long, we have allowed creativity to be out of reach. Even books and magazines on the subject generally end up giving only the result of creativity, not the process. Rollo May, in his book *The Courage to Create*, makes this point: "When we examine the psychological studies and writings on creativity over the past 50 years, the first thing that strikes us is the general paucity of material and the inadequacy of the work."[1] Maybe we need to go back farther than fifty years. Try all the way back to Genesis. Two truths that are important to creativity stand out in the opening chapters.

First, we were made in the image of God. We have His nature, His characteristics. Second, Genesis 1:1 contains the very first recorded characteristic of God in Scripture: "In the beginning, God *created*." God's first revealed character trait is His creativity. And we, remember, are made in His image.

God's creativity staggers the imagination. Look at just the physical earth—oceans, plains, mountains of all kinds, types of rocks, Yosemite Valley, rich farmland, and volcanoes. It is amazing. Consider animals. God could have made just *Animal*. One kind. That's all, the Model T of the animal world, billions of them all alike. But He didn't. He was creative and gave us giraffes and hippopotamuses and orangutans and penguins and duck-billed platypuses. He made some to fly and some to swim. Even the ones we can't see without a microscope (He knew someday we'd invent microscopes), He made all different. And what about the earth itself? The earth is just one planet out of nine circling one sun out of a billion suns in just one galaxy out of a billion galaxies. There's bound to be variety there.

And we have not yet mentioned His most creative work. Go look in a mirror. We are His best creation. He not only brought us into being, but of all His creation, we are the ones who received His nature.

He is creative, and so are we, each one. Watch children as they begin to play as infants and toddlers. Watch and listen to their imagination, their creativity. You'll search for days for just the right toy for your two-or three-year-old; then you put it in a box and wrap it up so it'll look bigger. Then, when the child opens the gift, he will play for hours on end—not with the toy, but with the box! That carton will be a car, a tunnel, a cave, a train, a tank, a fort, a store, a cradle, and a rocket ship all in one afternoon. By going to the back of a grocery store, you can get for free the equivalent of $200 worth of toys.

"Every person born into the world represents something new that has never been before. He has his own uniqueness and his own purpose to fulfill. Every person was once creative and spontaneous and in his deepest roots still is."[2] That creativity and inventiveness of children is almost boundless. Yet by the time they come into our junior-high-and high-school groups, it is almost gone. How is it lost? School often trains people to stifle creativity. We learn to stand straight, raise our hands before talking, color in the lines only, and always fit in. These are important, necessary lessons to learn in those disciplines, but somewhere along the way we have not been aware enough of what that does to creativity. "Both children and adults become desensitized through being treated as objects to get things done. They become puppets when order, efficiency, skills and content become more important than persons."[3]

As a result, by the time most people reach adulthood, they are fairly certain they are not creative. Even the church today seems resistant to creative ideas. What would we do with a Jeremiah or a John the Baptist and their style of delivery?

Another block to creativity that we need to examine is the mindset that people develop over the years. Roger VonOech has written a very interesting book entitled *A Whack on the Side of the Head*. In that book, he lists ten "mental locks"[4] that keep people from beginning a process of creativity. Check the ones of these you've allowed to slow you down.

☐ The Right Answer. Too often we think there is only one answer to a problem. That is true in our doctrine, but not always in our methods.

☐ That's Not Logical. So what? What doesn't make sense at first might lead to another answer that does. Besides, not everything is logical anyway. How could God's love for us make sense?

☐ Follow The Rules. As long as we don't violate Scripture, why do we have to do things as we've always done them? Why does the youth group have to meet on Sunday or Tuesday or Wednesday or whenever?

☐ Be Practical. "This won't work." "It costs too much." "We've never done it this way before." "We tried that once, but it didn't work." Don't be discouraged by these criticisms. Play with some impractical ideas—you'll probably shake loose some new practical ones to use. Don't get caught up in a preoccupation with order and tradition for their own sake.

☐ Avoid Ambiguity. This is wanting everything crystal clear from the very beginning.

☐ To Err Is Wrong. "Avoid failure at all cost" is the motto of many. Yet failure is a great way to learn better ways for the future. The pressure in many churches for immediate results often blocks out risk-taking. It is so easy to stay with the tried and true and trite. Perhaps we give excessive rewards for success and not enough for creativity.

☐ Play Is Frivolous. "Don't waste time. Creativity is serious work," they tell us. Yes, but one of the essentials of creativity is the value of play. Relax and let your sophistication as an adult drop for a while.

☐ That's Not My Area. "I'm not supposed to improve on this. I just take the lesson material and deliver it"—and bore the group totally!

☐ Don't Be Foolish. "What if this doesn't work?" we worry. "I'll look stupid." That's OK—your group knows what that's like—now show them how a Christian responds to that situation.

☐ I'm Not Creative. The destructive self put-down. "Why start?" we moan. "I can't do it. Everyone has gifts and abilities but me. Maybe that's God's plan." No, not a chance.

If you didn't check any of the squares, skip the rest of this chapter and go on to the next one—you are undoubtedly creative already. If you checked one or all ten, that's OK—there are some specific steps to help you develop that creative frame of reference.

Irene Caldwell lists eight steps in developing a creative process: openness, reflection, illumination, focus, discipline, sharing, closure, and evaluation.[5] Whether you are working on a specific lesson plan or planning how to get certain concepts across to your group through some new program or approach, these are the steps in the process of applying creativity to the project.

Openness is learning to look at everything around you as a possible teaching tool. It is working hard to make yourself aware of all the material that is available. Many people have developed a resource myopia—they are unaware of the ideas that are surrounding them, content to stay with the same plan or publisher year after year.

Openness is being able to think, "Is there a lesson or a truth in this event or this object?" That's what Jesus did with His parables. They were events out of real life that He saw as having a deeper meaning. He saw things with fresh eyes. To most of Israel, a man out sowing was a man out sowing. To Jesus, he was symbolic of a four-fold response to the gospel. Look beyond your manuals. Popular songs, Coke cans, school events, world happenings, and TV shows are all more than what they appear. Learn to pray, "Jesus, speak to me." What can be seen in ordinary things? Try this the next time your group gets together. Take a Coke can and put it on a table or stand. Ask them to come up with twenty-five different things that are said about Coke that could also be applied to us as Christians. It works, and they'll have a good time doing it.

Subscribe to books and magazines—read whatever you can about new approaches. Try some brainstorming with other leaders. Not everything you come up with can be used—your theology and reality will filter some out—but creativity requires the ability to think beyond what is normal.

Maintain a productive mindset. Look at this hammer recently designed. Very quickly make four or five comments about it. Write them down.

1. _____

2. _____

3. _____

4. _____

Finished? OK, if you've done what most will do, then your comments are mainly negative. Look back, you weren't told to criticize the design, just to comment on it. Adults will normally be critical and unaccepting of a new idea. Yes, this hammer probably deserves negative comment, but show the same design to a group of second-graders, and they'll see all kinds of applications—many of them positive.

 Openness is being aware of as many ideas as you can be and then developing a unique approach for your group in your situation. Notice the drawing on the right. What creativity! It's a tree, and there are the roots and the soil and the sun and the rain. The tree takes nutrients from the soil and water and the process of photosynthesis and eventually produces something totally different from those items—apples.

Trees are creative, by God's design. So, too, are we.

Once you've started to gather resources, ideas, and observations (some that will fit your project and some that won't), then move on to *reflection*. There seems to be a necessity in the creative process for alternating work and relaxation. And it is a process that takes time. It is difficult to be creative on demand. You need a backlog of ideas and thoughts just simmering—bubbling around in your head. Every creative person needs scheduled time to do apparently nothing—take a walk, lie down on the sidewalk, drive somewhere, watch a movie. Your mind during that time is not inactive. It is not ignorant or unaware of the idea. It is incubating. The idea is becoming yours. You may have read of a similar idea or done it someplace else, but it has to be adapted to your present situation. A writer, Wilferd Peterson, made this observation:

> The subconscious mind is the fireless cooker where our ideas simmer while we are loafing. Newton was loafing when he saw an apple fall and got the gravitation idea. While finding peace for his soul, Galileo watched the great swinging lamp. It gave him the idea of a pendulum swinging to and fro as a means of measuring the passage of time. Watt was relaxing in the kitchen when he saw the steam lifting the top of the teakettle and conceived the idea of a steam engine.
>
> Many times we will get more and better ideas in two hours of creative loafing than in eight hours at a desk.[6]

What a great quote to have the next time you're caught sleeping at your desk!

Have you ever had the experience of reading some great thought or concept and then rushing out to pass that on to someone else? Remember how often, as you did that, the sudden realization would come that they weren't getting hit by it as much as you had been—and even worse, even as you gave them the information, it didn't sound all that exciting to you, either. It takes time for an idea that strikes you in your mind to stay in there long enough to become your own, with your own way of explaining it. Once that happens, you can effectively communicate it to others.

The third stage in this creative process is *illumination*, or the "ah ha" stage. The light bulb comes on. Sometimes that happens after a great deal of hard work and trial and error. At other times, it seems like a sudden flash—wham! There it is. Either way, illumination has usually been preceded by a great deal of resource gathering. The insight often goes against the established routine, but along with that is the deep feeling of certainty that the idea could work—it at least deserves a try.

Once the idea hits you, move on to the next step, *focus*. Focus is simply putting the idea on paper and seeing all the things you'll need to implement it. Let's say you have an idea of having a covenant meal for your discipleship group. Focus in. You'll need to know when and where. What you'll eat and who will prepare it are details you also need to have in mind. How will you explain it to everyone? What all will you need? Those are questions of focus.

Maybe the hardest step in the creative process is the next one, *discipline*. So many people are afraid to leave the security of familiar things. It's one thing to think, "Wouldn't it be great if we [did this or that]?" (and it may be a very creative idea), but it's another thing to put the idea into practice. One writer calls this our "creative courage."[7] The worst that can happen to a creative plan is not that it failed. You can learn all manner of helpful information from a failed plan. The worst that can happen is that it never be tried.

You will have greater confidence in the idea if you include the sixth step of *sharing*. Often this is done before you present the idea to everyone. You decide you are going to implement it; so you take the idea to others in your leadership team, even some of your key young people. Get their input and ideas—often the idea will undergo additional change and emerge even stronger. Creativity is enhanced when you're working with the give and take of others. If the idea is obviously a bomb—one that you were unable to see—it's far better to explode it in a small group before detonating it over the entire crew.

The next to the last stage in this process of developing a creative frame of reference is *closure*. Know how long you want your idea to run and be prepared to say publicly, "OK, it's over." So many ideas start out with great fanfare and public push, and then several weeks or months down the line, a guy in your group says, "Hey, whatever happened to having wheelchair races in the convalescent homes?" Creativity requires accountability and the discipline of bringing something to a close, whether it has flown or crashed, so that the last phase in the creative process can be done.

That last stage is *evaluation*. If it was a success, have a celebration. If it was a failure, have a funeral. But don't stop the creative process. From anything you try, you will always learn some new insights that will make the next idea even better.

We've looked at the design (it's God's plan that we be creative), the demand (the gospel needs to be clearly communicated), and the detail (the eight steps in the creative process) of creativity. It is essential that you also see the danger once again. Creativity is not a synonym for craziness or lack of disciplined planning. In talking about creativity, Fosdick said, "No steam or gas ever drives anything until it is confined. No Niagra is ever turned into light and power until it is funneled. No life ever grows until it is focused, dedicated, disciplined."[8] Neither is creativity a substitute for commitment. You cannot program around the lack of committed people. That lack of commitment will drive you to gimmicks, and that's not what creativity is for. Creativity is a tool for the committed. Use it well.

---

[1] Rollo May, *The Courage to Create* (New York: Bantam Books, 1976), p. 33.

[2] Irene S. Caldwell, Richard Hatch, and Beverly Welton, *Basics for Communication in the Church* (Anderson, IN: Warner Press, 1971), p. 39.

[3] Caldwell, Hatch, Welton, *Basics for Communication,* p. 44.

[4] Roger VonOech, *A Whack on the Side of the Head* (New York: Warner Books, 1983), preface.

[5] Caldwell, Hatch, Welton, *Basics for Communication,* p. 45.

[6] "Points to Ponder," *Reader's Digest,* December, 1980, p. 145.

[7] May, *The Courage to Create.*

[8] Harry Emerson Fosdick, *Living Under Tension* (New York: Harper and Row, 1941); quoted in *Reader's Digest,* December, 1980, p. 145.

2

Setting, Using, and Maintaining Goals in Youth Ministry

Roy H. Mays III

Faithful and fruitful youth leaders fulfill their stewardship with God-glorifying, need-oriented, and goal-directed ministries with youth. Giving God the preeminence and making people's needs the priority are discussed in other areas of this book. This chapter focuses on structuring the process of goal-setting, goal-seeking, and goal-seizing. The result is ministry that praises the Father and promotes the fulfillment of His Great Commission with young people. The family of God grows through the use of goals.

Ministry with youth and children can take place without goals, but clear-cut objectives increase ministry productivity. Christ has called us to catch men, not just go fishing. Recently I took my two children to a lake for an afternoon of play and fishing. At the dock where I rented the boat I also wanted to buy some bait. I asked the attendant, "What bait should we use? Where should we fish?" He responded, "What are you trying to catch?" The objectives determine the methods.

Some people approach their ministry like the young person pictured in a poster I saw in an elementary boy's room. He was all packed up and ready to go. Now if he could only hitch a ride with someone. The caption read: "I don't know where I am going, but I am on my way."

Goal setting must be done prior to youth ministry. But it must also be done in the process of ministry, just as turning a car is best accomplished when the car is moving. In other words, goal-setting is both *process* and *product*. It must be lived out in people, not imposed upon them.

An example from my experience as a youth in Southland Christian Church, Lexington, Kentucky, illustrates the use of goals in ministry. Jerry Williams was a full-time grocery worker who served as our part-time youth minister. One of his objectives was to get to know the kids in his group well even though he had a limited amount of time available for direct youth ministry. He set a goal of having two young people into his home each week for supper. How well I remember the thrill I felt when Eddie Rudd and I were chosen to eat at the Williams' home. The aroma of that spaghetti supper in the atmosphere of candlelight and red-and-white-checked tablecloth were matched by the interest Jerry showed in us. He learned about our interests, school activities, and career dreams. It was in that context that he planted the seed in me that would result in my first three-minute sermon later preached in the junior church program Jerry directed. Even though he could not continue in the full-time youth ministry himself, he kept in contact and continually encouraged my entrance into vocational ministry.

His goal was simple: two people a week into his home for dinner and development. Many of those young people are now serving as elders, deacons, teachers, and coaches in Southland, and several more are ministering to churches across the country.

Experiences with youth ministers and youth groups I have met in churches coast to coast in the last sixteen years have confirmed the same observation: setting, using, and maintaining goals in youth ministry is a powerful tool in the building of the kingdom of God. I have examined an extensive amount of the literature on goals and interviewed several youth ministers making key use of goals in their past and present programs. The outline of this chapter, as suggested by the goals process chart on the next page, is meant to guide you in further depth into each area of setting, seeking, and seizing goals.

Veteran youth minister Les Christie writes: "The ultimate goal of youth ministry is to bring young people to maturity in Christ—to prepare, disciple and train them to serve God with their lives. . . . the major objectives of youth work might be summarized as follows: (1) to reach the lost, (2) bring them to maturity in Christ, and (3) prepare them for ministry (Ephesians 4:12; Colossians 1:28)."[1]

A walk through the goals process will help us see these objectives become outcomes in the lives of our young people.

THE GOALS PROCESS IN YOUTH MINISTRY

Develop Goal Perspectives
↓
Disciple Goal Partners
↓
Define Goal Purposes
↓
Determine Goal Priorities
↓
Detail Goal Plans
↓
Design Goal Programs
↓
Diagnose Goal Problems
↓
Discern Goal Possibilities

Figure 1

Develop Goal Perspectives

We can visualize beyond our vision. With faith we must believe; then we achieve. The goals we set may be what we get—and we may get even more!

Develop your view of God. A children's chorus says that the size of your God sets the size of your dreams. Remember the promise of Ephesians 3:20: God "is able to do exceeding abundantly beyond all that we ask or think" (NASB). Christ in Youth was founded on such a view. Her early motto was, "Praise to Him who specializes in the impossible."

Develop your view of yourself. The way I see God affects the way I see myself. The way I view myself influences my view of ministry. Many people refuse to set goals because they see themselves as nobodies. They abhor time management counsel because greater effectiveness multiplied by zero seems to become a bigger negative than ever before. Zig Ziglar turned his life around as a person and a salesman when he took two steps: seeing himself as significant enough to achieve and receive success, and going to work on a regular schedule. When his self-image changed, he was in a position to improve his work habits.

Goal-seeking is very difficult for negative people. That's why Joshua and Caleb were not able to lead the people into the

promised land. The people had a negative view of God and themselves. Effective youth ministers must, like Joshua and Caleb, trust
God and say: "We should go up and take possession of the land, for
we can certainly do it" (Numbers 13:30, NIV).

We can go out and take possession of the people and their potential in our place of stewardship because He is greater in us than all
the giants in the land. The promise of the indwelling Christ is to
give us power equal to our potential. He can; therefore, we can. He
is able; therefore, we are enabled. The confidence of Philippians
4:13 is held in creative tension with 2 Corinthians 4:7: "But we
have this treasure in jars of clay to show that this all-surpassing
power is from God and not from us" (NIV).

Develop your view of success. Success is becoming all that God
intends and enables you to be and do according to your capacity
and circumstances. Success in youth ministry is rendering maximum stewardship as a kingdom builder (according to the parable
of the talents in Matthew 25). Success is not beating the church
across town in a contest for numbers at the state teen convention. It
is not making more money in your youth ministry than your
former roommate makes in his. It is not having better statistics
than your predecessor. It is not getting a bigger youth budget than
anyone else. It is not even achieving all of your personal and professional goals.

That's why our view of success must be adjusted to recognize
God's part and man's part. One guy may be equally faithful as the
next yet not bear as much fruit. We must always be seeking success
in terms of goals already seized.

Develop your view of failure. Failing is not falling; it is falling
and refusing to get up. Failing is faltering before the finish. Failing
is finding excuses to cover for lack of effort, risk, and creativity.
Failure is a lack of imagination of how to use the gifts God has
entrusted to us. But failure is not final this side of eternity. Defeats
are developmental if they help us become more devoted to God
and more discerning in our stewardship. Many Christian leaders
acknowledge that there were times of wilderness-wandering in
their lives that helped them grow in the grace and knowledge of
Christ. Failing to reach a goal will finish you only if you fail to set
a new goal.

Develop your view of time. With the promise of Psalm 90 in
hand and the life expectancy now of seventy-four years, the average youth minister can approach his ministry with a more relaxed
perspective. Most people overestimate what they can do in a short

time and underestimate what they can do in a long time. Just as a coach needs four or five years to turn over and turn around a varsity program, so does a youth minister need more than eighteen to twenty-four months. The long-term perspective is needed both from the church leadership and the staff member. Long-term fruit from right goals does not necessarily show up in the first few months or years. (Of course, sometimes a youth worker is expected to produce some immediate dazzling results so he can hold on to his job long enough to get more permanent fruit that will remain.)

Develop your view of heroes in youth ministry. One of the best deposits of time in future fruitfulness is to get ahold of some of the veterans of the youth wars and see God at work in their lives and leadership ministries. Interning with experienced youth leaders is an ideal way to do this. Another approach is to live with a youth worker for several days and go through his ministry looking from the inside out.

A youth minister can be known by his heroes. The Lord's leaders, when seen up close and personal, don't diminish us; they develop us. Heroes don't make us less than they are, they lift us to what we can become by the grace of God. Fred Smith, in his book *You and Your Network,* includes a must reading chapter on "Your Heroes: Someone to Look Up To." He says,

> We cannot live fully without heroes, for they are the stars to guide us upward. They are the peaks on our human mountains. Not only do they personify what we can be, but they also urge us to be. Heroes are who we can become if we diligently pursue our ideals in the furnace of our opportunities.[2]

Disciple Goal Partners

Scriptural perspectives must be joined to persons involved in service. Management is often spoken of as getting results through people. In the church, this concept is frequently taken a step further by emphasizing that relationships determine results. But right relationships not only *determine* right results. Right relationships *are* right results! We are seeking in the adults we equip and the youth we serve to make them right with God and with each other. This must be modeled at the level where goals are set.

We need more than goals in youth ministry. We need goal owners! To accomplish that, goals must be shared, not sold. If you are trying to sell your goals to others instead of letting the goals arise from within the group, you will have to resell them every time doubt and difficulty arise.

The same principles of discipling exercised in other areas of youth ministry are crucial in the goals process. Giving people time to develop their vision alongside ours, using both structured and spontaneous events to plant seeds and water and nurture God's vision, and letting goals develop out of growing ministry and involvement in meeting people's needs are just some of the components of discipling goal partners.

Participation in the goals process is one way to help people grow. Building goals together helps build the body stronger. Just getting goals on paper is not enough. We want to develop goal partners who will utilize goal practices as an outworking of their worship and witness to God's glory.

When goal-setting with volunteers, we need to start at their level. We need to see from their capacity, skills, and viewpoint before we can expect them to catch up with ours. The result of a mutually responsible relationship approach to goal-setting is something more important than the development of goals. In the process of defining objectives based on kids' needs and determining strategy for desired relational results, the youth minister is also modeling a personal and working relationship to his volunteer team members. They observe and duplicate that relationship in the way they coach their young people. In both situations, the group shapes and sets the goals. Then the goals stimulate and stretch the group.

Often the best setting for facilitating the process of discipling goal partners and defining goal purposes is a retreat where the focus is on Christ and the Word and the Holy Spirit, the individuals on the leadership team, the needs of the people you are trying to serve, and the strategies appropriate for your specific stewardship in Christian service.

Define Goal Purposes

It was in such a retreat that the Crossroads Christian Church, Corona, California, took the commands of the Great Commission and put them into objectives appropriate for their church body. The outcome was included in a revised constitution and bylaws. Article two now reads:

> The purpose of this congregation shall be to bring glory to God by practicing and teaching faith in Jesus Christ, the Son of God, as taught in the Scriptures. The purpose will be accomplished by: (A) Evangelizing the greater Corona/Norco/Riverside area before Christ comes; (B) Presenting every Christian mature in Christ;

(C) Developing a healthy, dynamic body of believers; (D) Fulfilling the practical ministry of Christ in our world.

Those four objectives set the tone and scope of the ministry of Crossroads. They are prominent on the cover of notebooks used by the congregation. They are often listed in the church paper and on the Sunday bulletin. Sermons, services, and programs, including youth ministry, are conducted only as they relate to the four major objectives. The church leadership and followership rally together around the mutual mission of the church as expressed in their purpose statement.

A purpose statement, like the one at Crossroads, keeps the church's eye on mission. While the purpose and mission statements and the corresponding objectives are usually set by the elders and church staff, each group in the body should work at relating the purpose statement to its own ministry.

Determine Goal Priorities

Whenever there is more than one goal, priorities must be set. How much time will be devoted to goal A, to goal B, and so on? Even so, the overall purpose will clarify priorities. Don Olsby explains: "The ultimate objective of any Biblical ministry is that the disciples develop a balanced relationship with the Lord, with the Body (the church), and the world."[3] That balance is produced by a proper mix of all the goals of Bible study, fellowship, and witness.

Detail Goal Plans

Purposes and priorities must be fleshed out in plans and goals that can be measured and met. Under each priority category an individual or church establishes, there should be a measurable goal set in a specific time dimension. There also needs to be some method of accountability.

Too often, it is in the area of detailing our goal plans that we fail to use our goals as we had intended. We fail to make the goal measurable; so we don't know whether we're reaching it or not. We fail to set a time limit; so we don't feel any urgency about its completion. We fail to make ourselves accountable for the goal; so we can dismiss the goal without embarrassment if we fail.

For example, a person who is twenty pounds overweight might decide to get in shape. He sets a goal: lose twenty pounds in three months. Then he works out a plan of diet and exercise to help him accomplish the goal. Perhaps he joins a health club or weight-loss program for accountability. Now he has detailed his goal plan. If he is not losing weight fast enough, someone else knows and can assist him either in revising his goal or revising his program. The person or group to whom he is accountable is not interested in embarrassing him, but in assisting him.

Design Goal Programs

Methods, activities, projects, and programs must grow out of plans informed by the previous steps in the goals cycle. This insures an approach to youth programming that is broader than just "doing something" for the kids or with the kids:

> There is little positive theory behind just doing *something*. . . . Those who are involved in youth ministry need a more positive rationale. There needs to be intentionality. Intentionality calls for doing the right thing for the right reasons. In youth ministry, this means developing a structure and program that grow out of a clear understanding of what ministry is all about in general, and what youth are all about (i.e. their needs) in particular.[4]

Programs with particular goals must be planned to lead each young person from where he is to a level closer to becoming complete in Christ.

An excellent example of a youth program built on purpose, objectives, and goals is Solid Rock, led by Bruce Petty of Eastview Christian Church, Bloomington, Illinois. Bruce laid the foundation for his program in a presentation to the elders of the church. He says in the introduction of his proposal:

> There is only one foundation that is solid and secure and that foundation is built on the rock of Christ. In every endeavor it is our goal to make disciples of our young people. It is our desire that their lives reflect the reality of Jesus Christ and this reality be seen in their conversation, in their concern for others, and their goals for the future. The first question we must ask any program is, "How does this help us get that done?"

The purposes of the church shape the Solid Rock youth program. Thus, the program functions under the following objectives:
A. Build the kingdom of God.
B. Produce disciples of Christ.
C. Affect the whole person of each participant.
D. Provide a ministry that relates to the non-Christian mind.
E. Create a positive family influence.
F. Reach students for Christ.
G. Lay a foundation for the future.

H. Give the Christian students opportunities to minister to their friends and win them to Christ.

I. Produce students who will have a positive effect on the overall church.

J. Produce Spirit-filled leaders.

Specific goals for reaching these objectives are further developed in detail. Some are included in a written explanation of the program. Others are formed by the leadership team for each evening of Solid Rock.

Diagnose Goal Problems

Setting goals is not enough. We must seek and seize them. But there are some problems that may arise along the way. You could offer your own list of what's gone wrong on the way to the goal, based on your ministry experience. Some goal-setting errors I have observed include the following:

1. Making the goal a god instead of glorifying God as the ultimate goal.
2. Having goals handed down or pushed up instead of mutually agreed upon and held mutually accountable.
3. Forgetting to distinguish between God's part and man's part in the evaluation of goal performance.
4. Setting goals and then setting them aside.
5. Putting goals in permanent ink and not revising them as people, resources, opportunities, and circumstances change.
6. Setting or seeking so many goals that the followers develop goal fatigue.
7. Neglecting to set new goals as old goals are met to avoid goal let-down, depression, and loss of momentum.
8. Overlooking the need to celebrate goals accomplished in a worship experience of joy and gratitude to God and the people.
9. Putting goals too far out of reach or too easy to seize.
10. Seeking goals as ends in themselves, unrelated to purpose.
11. Allowing goals conflict between the senior minister and the church staff.
12. Pursuing holy goals by merely human means.

For this last item, I am indebted to Jack Hayford. Writing on "Why I Don't Set Goals" in the Winter, 1984, issue of *Leadership*, Jack says their church never sets goals—"that is, in the sense of numerical targets, fund-raising drives, or enlargement campaigns. Our one goal is to build big people." He does not mean the church

functions without direction, strategy, or planning. Rather, he puts
the goal-setting process in spiritual perspective. "My intention is
not really to debunk goal setting but to confront the tendency to
dissolve into naturalism—to pursue holy goals by merely human
means."[5]

Discern Goal Possibilities

Goals function as directors, stimulators, conductors, motivators,
indicators, and evaluators. Goals are a tool in the hands of God's
kingdom builders. They reflect intentions and affect investment of
persons and resources. They are important if used as a servant to
help expand the kingdom enterprise with maximum productivity
in faithful stewardship. Goals must always direct glory to God as
they develop His body, the church.

Conclusion

Goal-setting, goal-seeking, and goal satisfaction are a process,
but they are also a cycle. As old goals are achieved, new goals are
set. We must continually evaluate our goals and our progress, getting back into the goals process (Figure 1) wherever a revision
must be made. The following points will help.

1. Realize the possibilities and potentialities in the proper use of
   goals.
2. Respond quickly to the problems that will arise in the formation and fulfillment of the goals process.
3. Refine existing programs and evaluate new ideas that will
   help move the youth ministry closer to the accomplishment of
   the purpose of the church.
4. Revise goal plans to fit changing times and persons. Keep
   flexible and lighten up on your timetables and measurables
   when necessary to keep unity in the group as you strive toward your goals. A leader too far ahead of the group may be
   mistaken for the enemy.
5. Revamp your personal and program priorities to align yourself
   more with the values of Christ.
6. Review your goal purposes and mission statements to keep
   them anchored on the solid Rock and adjusted to meet the
   needs of your contemporary culture.
7. Relate to your goal partners. Right relationships with your
   team are right results.
8. Renew your goal perspectives in worship, service, study, and
   fellowship.

9. Reflect harmony and unity in the manner in which you pursue your goals.

10. Remember that a goal well set is a goal half met. That assumes a right beginning point with the way you build your group as you build your goals.

11. Rejoice that your primary resources are the Holy Spirit, the Scriptures, and the body of Christ.

12. Refresh yourself in the joy of the Lord and fulfill your stewardship in the grace and knowledge of our Lord Jesus Christ. To Him be the glory in our groups and our goals.

[1] Les Christie, *Servant Leaders in the Making* (Wheaton: Scripture Press, 1983), pp. 6-8.

[2] Fred Smith, *You and Your Network* (Waco: Word Books, 1974), p. 68.

[3] Don Olsby, *Youth Worker's Manual* (Corona, California: Don Olsby, 1977), pp. 2, 3.

[4] Glenn E. Ludwig, *Building an Effective Youth Ministry* (Nashville: Abingdon, 1979), p. 29.

[5] Jack Hayford, "Why I Don't Set Goals," *Leadership* (Carol Stream, Illinois: Christianity Today, Volume V, Number 1, Winter 1984), pp. 46-51.

Suggested Resources

Baird, Clifford G. *The Power of a Positive Self-Image*. Wheaton, IL: Victor Books, 1983.

Baker, Don. *Leadership*. Portland: Multnomah Press, 1983.

Batten, Joe, *Expectations and Possibilities*. Reading, MA: Addison-Wesley Publishing Company, 1981.

Bennis, Warren and Burt Nanus. *Leaders: The Strategies for Taking Charge*. New York: Harper and Row, 1985.

Benson, Dennis and Bill Wolfe, editors. *The Basic Encyclopedia for Youth Ministry*. Loveland, CO: Group Books, 1981.

Burns, James MacGregor. *Leadership*. New York: Harper and Row, 1978.

Byrne, Herbert W. *Motivating Church Workers*. Published by H. W. Byrne, 1982.

Cook, Bruce. *Faith Planning*. Wheaton, Victor Books, 1983.

Coop, Timothy A. *Youth Sponsor's Survival Kit*. Timothy A. Coop, Corona, California, 1977.

Dausey, Gary, ed. *The Youth Leader's Source Book*. Grand Rapids: Zondervan Publishing House, 1983.

Ellis, Joe S. *The Church on Purpose*. Cincinnati: Standard Publishing, 1982.

Engstrom, Ted W. *Motivation to Last a Lifetime*. Grand Rapids: Zondervan Publishing House, 1984.

Engstrom, Ted. W. *Your Gift of Administration*. Nashville: Thomas Nelson Publishing, 1979.

Friesen, Garry with J. Robin Maxson. *Decision Making and the Will of God*. Portland: Multnomah, 1980.

Garfield, Charles A. and Hal Zina Bennett. *Peak Performance*. Los Angeles: Jeremy P. Tarcher, Inc., 1984.

Getz, Gene. *Sharpening the Focus of the Church*. Chicago: Moody Press, 1974.

Green, Kenneth, ed. *Insights: Building A Successful Youth Ministry*. San Bernadino: Here's Life Publishers, 1981.

Hargrove, Barbara and Stephen D. Jones. *Reaching Youth Today*. Valley Forge: Judson Press, 1983.

Hart, Archibald D. *The Success Factor*. Old Tappan, NJ: Fleming H. Revell Company, 1984.

Holderness, Ginny Ward. *Youth Ministry*. Atlanta: John Knox Press, 1981.

Hughes, Charles L. *Goal Setting*. New York: American Management Association, 1965.

Inrig, Gary. *A Call to Excellence*. Wheaton: Scripture Press, 1985.

Jones, Jeffrey D., and Kenneth C. Potts. *Organizing a Youth Ministry to Fit Your Needs.* Valley Forge: Judson Press, 1983.

Klug, Ronald. *How to Keep a Spiritual Journal.* Nashville: Thomas Nelson Publishers, 1982.

Lee, Mark. *How to Set Goals and Really Reach Them.* Portland: Horizon House Publishers, 1978.

Locke, Edwin A. and Gary P. Latham. *Goal-Setting: A Motivational Technique That Works.* Englewood Cliffs, NJ: Prentice Hall, 1984.

McCormack, Mark H. *What They Don't Teach at Harvard Business School.* New York: Bantam Books, 1984.

McMinn, Gordon N. with Larry Libby. *Taking Charge.* Denver: Accent Books, 1980.

Magnusson, Sally. *The Flying Scotsman.* New York: Quarter Books, 1981.

Meyer, Paul. *Dynamics of Goal Setting.* Waco, Texas: Success Motivation Institute, 1977.

Naisbitt, John. *Megatrends.* New York: Warner Books, 1982, 1984.

Ortland, Raymond C. *Let The Church Be The Church.* Waco: Word Books, 1983.

Perry, Lloyd M. and Norman Shawchuck. *Revitalizing the 20th Century Church.* Chicago: Moody Press, 1982.

Peters, Thomas J. and Robert H. Walterman, Jr. *In Search of Excellence.* New York: Harper and Row Publishers, 1982.

Rassieur, Charles L. *Stress Management for Ministers.* Philadelphia: The Westminster Press, 1982.

Roadcup, David, editor, *Ministering to Youth.* Cincinnati: Standard Publishing, 1980.

Robbins, Paul D., editor. *Leadership.* Winter 1981, Volume II, Number 1, Carol Stream, IL: Christianity Today.

Schaller, Lyle E. *Looking in the Mirror: Self-Appraisal in the Local Church.* Nashville: Abingdon, 1984.

Schuller, Robert H. *Your Church Has Real Possibilities!* Glendale: Gospel Light Publications, 1974.

Stoop, David. *Self-Talk: Key to Personal Growth.* Old Tappan: Revell, 1982.

Taylor, Bob R., editor. *The Work of the Minister of Youth.* Nashville: Conventions Press, 1982.

Wagner, C. Peter. *Leading Your Church to Growth.* Ventura, Ca: Regal Books, 1984.

Waitley, Denis. *Seeds of Greatness.* Old Tappan: Fleming H. Revell Company, 1983.

Waitley, Denis. *The Winner's Edge*. New York: Berkley Books, 1980.

Werning, Waldo J. *Vision and Strategy for Church Growth*. Grand Rapids: Baker Book House, 1977.

White, Jerry and Mary. *Mid Life Crisis*. Colorado Springs: Navpress, 1980.

Willey, Ray. *Working with Youth*. Wheaton: Victor Books, 1982.

Yohn, Rick. *Finding Time*. Waco: Word Books, 1984.

Ziglar, Zig. *See You at the Top*. Gretha, LA: Pelican Publishing Company, 1975.

3

Getting More Done Through Advance Planning

Tom Kakac

It's Thursday. Tonight your church team plays Riverside Baptist in the semifinals of the church softball league, and you're on the team. Your mother-in-law calls and reminds you that she's coming in to spend the night because it's your wife's birthday. She wants to make sure it is still okay for her to come. You slap your forehead with the palm of your hand, screaming, "How could I have forgotten my wife's birthday? I've got to get her a present." Your wife (who knows nothing about her mother's coming to spend the night) calls and says that the washing machine broke while she was washing the sheets from all the beds in the house and wants to know if you could come home to look at it.

Just then, your secretary reminds you that tomorrow is the monthly camp board meeting and you are to have your week of camp planned and ready to submit for approval at that meeting. She wants to know whether it's ready for her to type yet. (Ha!) She also reminds you that a third-grader in your youth group is in the hospital and is to have her tonsils out first thing in the morning. The parents have requested that you drop by and see her today.

There's a knock on your door. The mother of one of the junior-high boys is in tears. She wants to talk to you. Last night she had a fight with her son and she wants to know how she can make her boy want to go to youth meetings. He hates you.

Your intercom buzzes. It's time for your daily staff meeting and the preacher wants to know why you're not there yet. You rush into his office just as he is announcing to the other staff members that he begins a revival in another town this Sunday, and he has decided to ask you to preach for him. (You've asked for more preaching time in the past, and he rarely gives you the opportunity.) Sound familiar?

All you need right now is for someone to tell you that you need to be getting more done. You're not a lazy person. You desire to become a more dynamic, aggressive, positive, enthusiastic, deep, wise, committed, humble, contagious, Christ-like disciple. You even set some objectives once:

improve my preaching and teaching
pray more
be a better father and husband
increase my retirement investments

write a book
take more schooling
read more
learn to play the guitar
win my neighbor to Christ
lose twenty pounds

Frustrated? The purpose of this chapter is to help you predetermine a course of action and make decisions that control your future. That's advance planning: seeking God's leading while deciding the priority and sequence of the steps needed to reach your objectives and the scheduling of each step. In this chapter, we will be discussing a four-step procedure that will help you in advance planning.

  I. Pray that God's things will be done
 II. Prioritize what things will be done
III. Plan how things will be done
 IV. Project when things will be done

Pray That God's Things Will Be Done

"Who am I? Where am I going? What am I to be?" God wants to answer these questions. Advance planning should only be done with God's Word as your guide. We need to understand that God wants to direct our lives, and at the same time, allows us to direct our own. God is concerned more with what we are than with what we accomplish. The Scriptures teach that what we are will be exposed by what we do: "For as he thinks within himself, so he is" (Proverbs 23:7, NASB). "In the same way, faith by itself, if it is not accompanied by action, is dead" (James 2:17, NIV).

To accomplish more with our lives, we should not neglect scheduling large amounts of time for Bible study and prayer. Through seeking God in this way, we will come closer to having the mind and life of Christ. Seeing our lives from God's perspective will help us determine those things that are most important to accomplish and will help us see our time wasters for what they really are.

Is what I'm doing meeting a real need that God wants met today? The most rewarding, joy-filled, contented life is the life that's getting done the things God wants to get done: "For we are God's workmanship, created in Christ Jesus to do good works, which God prepared in advance for us to do" (Ephesians 2:10, NIV).

This Scripture shows that God is not only an advance planner, but that He plans for us to do works for Him. God is sovereign. He runs the universe. However, He does it through His people. He ordains the means as well as the end. We are responsible to Him. Our plans reflect our confidence and faith in a sovereign God. The question is, "Do we trust Him to perform His work through us?"

God is the only one to whom we are accountable. The Lord deserves our very best. We must never come to the place where we fail to trust God to change our plans: "In his heart a man plans his course, but the Lord determines his steps" (Proverbs 16:9, NIV). Paul seemed to have this in balance: "So after I have completed this task and have made sure that they have received this fruit, I will go to Spain and visit you on the way. I know that when I come to you, I will come in the full measure of the blessing of Christ" (Romans 15:28, 29, NIV). He, unlike Jonah (see Jonah 1:1-3), allowed God to change his direction. (See also Acts 16:7, 8.)

Paul's objective was to spread the gospel. His goal was to go to Rome on his way to Spain to do this. He planned, but he allowed God to control so that the purpose could be accomplished God's way. If it is the Lord's will, then we should be planning to spend our life doing it (and be careful not to take the credit). For "unless the Lord builds the house, its builders labor in vain" (Psalm 127:1, NIV). "The steps of a man are established by the Lord" (Psalm 37:23, NASB). God desires to be an active part of our plan-making and promises us success if He is in it. "Commit to the Lord whatever you do, and your plans will succeed" (Proverbs 16:3, NIV).

Does God allow us to direct our own lives? I believe He does: "Therefore be careful how you walk, not as unwise men, but as wise, making the most of your time, because the days are evil" (Ephesians 5:15, 16, NASB). We are told in 1 Corinthians that whatever we do, "do all to the glory of God." When we plan for the future, we are acting in faith. God has not made us robots. He gives us freedom to strive to do all that we can in this life for Him. Even

Jesus himself taught the multitudes to plan: "For which one of you, when he wants to build a tower, does not first sit down and calculate the cost, to see if he has enough to complete it? Otherwise, when he has laid a foundation, and is not able to finish, all who observe it begin to ridicule him" (Luke 14:28-30, NASB).

This may seem at first to contradict His teaching recorded by Matthew: "Therefore do not worry about tomorrow, for tomorrow will worry about itself. Each day has enough trouble of its own" (Matthew 6:34, NIV). But the emphasis here is, "Don't *worry* about tomorrow," not, "Don't *plan* for tomorrow." Making our plans while trusting in a sovereign God will honor Him and His teachings, not neglect them. Studying His Word is the best way to allow the Holy Spirit to guide your preaching and teaching. The Holy Spirit, however, can guide all of our planning. We must depend on His guidance, or we begin to "do things in the flesh."

Prayer is the most important thing you can do in planning to accomplish more with your life. "Ask, and it shall be given to you; seek, and you shall find; knock, and it shall be opened to you" (Matthew 7:7, NASB). "You may ask me for anything in my name, and I will do it" (John 14:14, NIV). "If any of you lacks wisdom, he should ask God, who gives generously to all without finding fault, and it will be given to him" (James 1:5, NIV).

To be sure God is in your plans, ask Him to give you His vision for your life and ministry, wisdom in planning to accomplish His dreams, and daily strength and discipline to carry out the plans.

"Lord, this is what I intend to do because I believe it will help me become more of what You created me to be. If it is Your will, Father, bless my efforts. If it isn't, show me your path. I'm Yours."

Prioritize What Things Will Be Done

"Take time to work; it is the price of success. Take time to think; it is the source of power. Take time to play; it is the secret of perpetual youth. Take time to read; it is the fountain of wisdom. Take time to be friendly; it is the road to happiness. Take time to dream; it is hitching your wagon to a star. Take time to love and be loved; it is the privilege of redeemed people. Take time to look around; it is too short a day to be selfish. Take time to laugh; it is the music of the soul. Take time for God; it is life's only lasting investment."

—Author unknown

The real question is, should I go jogging, mow the lawn, take my family out to supper, or go calling on that new kid in town tonight?

The answer is priority planning. Our desire to live a balanced life must begin by making some decisions about where we want to be at our journey's end. It is difficult to plot a course on a daily or weekly basis without knowing the destination. When you don't know where you're sailing, no wind is going the right direction. An objective is what we want things to be like in the future.

Some worthy objectives are to spend more time in a better way for my quiet time with the Lord, to become a better husband and father, to read more books, to get more exercise and lose some weight, to get out of debt and start a savings plan for the future, to become a better personal evangelist, and to become a better counselor. A good place to start determining objectives is to make a list of all the areas of your life where you have made some kind of commitment and set an objective in each area.

The next step is to set goals for each of these objectives. Goals are specific ways your objectives will be measured and accomplished. For instance, in considering your objectives, ask yourself these questions: If I continue at the present rate and direction, where will I be six months, one year, or five years from now in this area? Where do I want to be in this area at each of these times? What steps will be required for me to get there?

Goals need to be specific, measurable, practical, and achievable in a given amount of time. They should be written in a precise language including dates, amounts, and any other criteria discernible. If goals are clear, effective plans can be formulated.

Example #1; Objective: be a better husband.

> Goals: spend three days per month with my wife on a mini-vacation; take my wife on a "date" once per week; find some new way to say, "I love you," each day.

Example #2; Objective: have a better VBS this year.

> Goals: get the teachers' materials to them two months earlier than last year; at the next board meeting, propose a $250 increase in VBS budget for this year; enlist 40 people to invite every kid in town to attend VBS; have 300 kids registered for VBS by May 1.

A lot of good can be said for setting ten- or twenty-year goals, but practically speaking, most people follow these guidelines:

Long-range goals—reachable in one to five years.

Intermediate goals—reachable in one month to one year.

Short-range goals—reachable within one to 30 days.

After you have decided what you want to do, you must decide what you will do first, and what you will not do at all. This can be a very hard decision to make. How efficient you are will be determined more by what you decide not to do than by what you do. Several questions can be asked to help in setting priorities:

1. Will it really matter if it isn't done?
2. If it must be done, must I be the one to do it?
3. Is this something I have to do, I should do, or I'd like to do?

General Eisenhower is noted for his discovery that the really important matters were seldom urgent and that the most urgent matters were seldom important. For instance, it is important to become a better Bible scholar, but somehow it just doesn't seem very urgent. Getting that new grass planted before the winter sets in seems urgent, but it isn't really eternally important. Here is a guide to help you in setting priorities:

Priority #1—important and urgent;
Priority #2—important, not urgent;
Priority #3—urgent, not important;
Priority #4—routine duties (eating, commuting, mowing lawn, and the like);
Priority #5—not important or urgent or routine.

Note: Some routine things can be high on your priority list (such as daily time with God, daily time with the family, and daily time for your own health). These, however, should be also considered important and would then be listed as a #1 or #2 priority.

Goals should be set for each of your important objectives and should become a part of your regular routine. Daily exercise and health care, for instance, should be a high priority, even though it may not seem "spiritual." More can be accomplished living eighty years than living only fifty-five (even at a slower pace). A person who "burns himself out" accomplishing good things will never produce as much as one whose life is prioritized with the long run in view. Lyndon Johnson once said, "The trouble with our country is, that we constantly put second things first."

Just determining which objectives are important, and which goals under each objective are of the highest priority, won't get them done. Now we must plan for them to be accomplished.

Plan How Things Will Be Done

Planning is moving your goals to reality. Your objective is the end result. Your plan tells you what to do now, tomorrow, next week, next month, and next year until you discover that you have reached your goals. Some goals can seem "out of reach" until you break down the large goals into smaller, attainable chunks. (As Robert Schuller says, "Inch by inch it's a cinch.") A plan is a staircase, each step leading to the next. Each step is easy, even though the top may seem to be far away. To get from one location to another, you must plan the route you take. You've already determined where you want to be in the future by setting objectives and goals. Planning will determine the road you take to get there.

If your goal is to make the basketball team, your planning may involve practicing, getting some good coaching, physical conditioning, and some scrimmage experience. Whether your goal is to bake a cake, build a house, or drive to New York, you will need a recipe, a blueprint, or a map to get the job done. Each goal will require careful thought in allowing for ingredients, materials, and resources. Many methods (recipes, blueprints, or maps) can be used, but the goal remains the same.

One of the best reasons to do planning is to imagine what any project would be like without it. Without a detailed plan, what would a bridge look like after construction? What about a model airplane? A tailored suit? Hard to imagine, isn't it? It is just as ridiculous to imagine a life that is striving to attain certain objectives without a detailed plan to reach intended goals. Without a plan, we often don't know why we're doing what we're doing. We lose interest in it. The people we work with don't know what to do without a plan, and they have no way to evaluate what we're doing. It becomes very easy to quit in a crisis because we lose our sense of purpose and accomplishment. (This is one of the main reasons, I believe, that youth ministers become discouraged and change churches every eighteen months.)

Your planning will be much easier after considering your goals. For example, suppose it is your responsibility to plan a youth rally. You begin to ask the questions: Where will it be? When will it be? Who will speak? Who will direct it? How will it be publicized? What is the desired outcome? Who will come? How much will it cost? Who will pay for it? The point is, what you do will depend upon your goals and objectives for the youth rally. A youth rally with an evangelistic objective will require different planning than one with the objective of recruiting kids to attend camp.

Planning is selecting alternative ways to accomplish our goals. If your goal is to read through the Bible each year, there are many different plans or methods to accomplish this. You may read a set number of minutes per day or a certain number of chapters per week. An important key to planning is considering creative alternatives. To do this, write down your goal; then begin to list different ways to accomplish that goal. Try to list twenty or more possibilities, but no fewer than ten. Stretch your imagination. Your ideas don't have to be logical at first. If you have set a goal to read twelve books this year, you could plan to read one each month. You might, instead, find five other guys that also want to read more, and each of you could read just two books and report to the rest of the group on the books read.

Our situation may change our plan, but not our goal. For example, you might set a goal to weigh 165 pounds by January 1. Then you develop a plan to achieve that goal: to run five miles per day and limit your diet to 2,000 calories per day. If you were to injure a knee, or if a severe winter were to limit your outdoor running, you could change your plan to include swimming at an indoor pool instead. The plans change; the goal stays the same.

Effective planning requires constant evaluation. What is the most efficient way to accomplish my goal? Is my goal being reached? Would another plan work better? Do I have the resources needed? Is my plan practical? Can it be done more cheaply?

Another important question is, "Do I need to do it?" Many youth ministers have a Messiah complex. They feel they are the only salvation for the program or plan. They think everything can't or won't be done without them, or, at least, not done right. You may need to learn to delegate responsibility. Good communication of the responsibilities, as well as the goal, is essential for efficient delegation. Planning is the means to an end. Planning to use other people to accomplish your goals will be one of the most important things you will ever learn to do. Many of us run like jackrabbits trying to accomplish more when, through patient planning and delegation, we could accomplish more with less emotional trauma. After all, the turtle beat the rabbit in the race, didn't he?

A long-range goal doesn't seem quite so hard when it is broken down into intermediate goals. If I want to read fifty books per year, the goal seems hard to reach, until I realize I simply must read one book per week. After breaking it into short-range goals, the task becomes even more realistic. I need to read thirty minutes per day, starting today, to accomplish my long-range goal of reading fifty books per year. It is better to start off with bite-size pieces than to choke because of the size of the task.

Let's review a minute. After seeking the Lord, you have determined and prioritized objectives for your life. You have set some goals that will help you accomplish your objectives. You have made plans on how you will reach your goals. Now, you must estimate the time each will take and plan segments on your calendar to begin the process. Schedule your plans to reach your goals to meet your objectives. This is perhaps the most important step in advance planning, yet it is the one most often neglected.

Project When Things Will Be Done

Lost yesterday, somewhere between sunrise and sunset, two golden hours each set with 60 diamond minutes. No reward is offered, for they are gone forever.

—Horace Mann

The importance of scheduling our time won't actually hit us until we analyze how we are actually using and abusing our time. To begin, keep a daily record of personal time use for at least two weeks. This time log will reveal the time wasters that you need to face head-on.

Time	List Time Users Here
7:00	
7:15	
7:30	
7:45	
8:00	
8:15	
8:30	
8:45	
9:00	
etc.	

An early sage observed, "A problem well stated is half solved." When we discover what we actually are doing with our time, our task is one-half done. It is common to misjudge by as much as fifty percent the amount of time we schedule or should schedule to get a job done. After keeping an accurate and honest daily log, categorize your time use and see whether the percentages of time use reflect your priorities. Is T.V. 200 percent more important than your Bible reading? Is this what your percentages show? Compare this log with your list of priorities from the first part of this chapter. How much time was spent on each of your priorities? The sad,

depressing conclusion to most time studies is something like this:
1. You work too many hours.
2. You don't get enough done.
3. A lot of what you do should be done by someone else, or perhaps not done at all.
4. Not much time was spent doing those things that are most important.

Does this one sound familiar? As the youth minister sits down to study his lesson for Sunday night, the phone rings. The church treasurer wants to know how much money he needs for this weekend's retreat. As he hangs up the phone, he remembers the church paper article that is due by noon. He pulls out a file to look for an idea, and notices today's mail. On top is a letter about an upcoming speaking engagement. He curiously opens it to find out that he still needs to send publicity pictures. Having sent his last one out a week before, he decides to walk downtown (good exercise you know) to check into having a new picture made. On the way, he decides to stop for coffee and a donut (there goes the benefit of the exercise). It is now 10:30 a.m. What has been accomplished? That's right, nothing. Before returning to the church, he decides to run some other errands he was going to have to do later in the day anyway. (This guy is trying to save time.) He stops by the Post Office to mail some letters, swings by the library to pick up the projector for Sunday night (that's planning ahead), and then walks twelve blocks to the drug store to pick up a prescription. After waiting in line for fifteen minutes, he remembers that he needed to go to the bank first to cash a check so that he'd have money to pay for the medicine. So over to the bank he goes, and then back to the drug store (waiting in line a second time). Finally, he is relieved that he has accomplished all the things he needed to accomplish.

This youth minister is plagued by several time robbers. He tends to be a procrastinator. He is interruption prone. He is a job skipper (that is, jumping from one to another). He lacks the ability to delegate. He doesn't know how to handle his daily mail and has displayed negligence in doing advance planning. He is probably one of those who has a cluttered or stacked desk of things he is working on. He'll probably shuffle through the stack (wasting time) several times a day, or start on top, and possibly leave undone an important item that is farther down in the pile. He probably would say, "I don't have time to do planning and scheduling." If you are like him, you probably aren't busy enough yet to realize your need for this discipline. Five minutes of planning and organization would have saved him two hours of work in the office: ten seconds of scheduling would have eliminated his waste of time, energy, and frustration as he ran errands away from the office.

We need to schedule in order to make priorities a habit. We often spend too much time worrying and struggling to find time for high priority items. We need to develop priority life-style habits that will make each day efficient and productive. Establish a regular daily schedule for those things that are routine and stick to it ruthlessly. You won't have to worry about working it in on a busy day. It is already there. On your daily schedule, block out one half-hour per day for exercise, two hours every other week to mow the yard, eight hours per day for sleep, one entire day and two other evenings each week to spend with your family, one hour per day in personal devotions, and one afternoon per week for personal rest or participation in your favorite hobby or sport. If it doesn't make the calendar, it won't happen. Remember Parkinsons' law, "Work expands to fit the time available." If it's not on the calendar, other things will crowd out your priorities. Take a moment to review your highest objectives. Are they receiving the most scheduled time? If it is the priority you say it is, your schedule should reflect it. A time for the pursuit of each goal should be set. At that time (evening, day, month, year) it is priority number 1. Start with your most important priority activity. Block out the time estimated to complete it on your schedule and then go to priority number 2. Continue in that manner until your schedule is full. Your higher priority items should be scheduled at the first of the week. If they take longer than expected, you will still get them done that week. Lower priority items can then be rescheduled for a later time.

Thomas Edison once was asked how he achieved so much. His answer was, "It's quite simple really. We each have eighteen hours in every day in which we may do something. You spend that time with a number of unrelated things. I spend it doing just one thing."

My garden hose has an adjustable spray nozzle. It is capable of producing such a fine spray that it will hardly bend a supple flower petal. Adjusting the water to a jet stream, however, will flatten and destroy the flower, even eroding away the dirt that holds its roots. So it is with our scheduling. We can scatter ourselves to affect a lot of things to a very little degree or concentrate our time and energy to accomplish much in a few important areas. In dealing with your schedule on a day to day basis, you must ask yourself: "How much time will it take? Do I have the time? What alternatives do I have? What will go undone?"

If you have spent much time at all establishing objectives and goals, you know that you'll probably never accomplish all the things that may be asked, expected, or demanded of you. The tendency, then, is to become frustrated and/or just to let things slide. You should consider the old slogan, "If you don't have time to do it right, when will you have time to do it over?" Pace yourself. Life is a marathon, not a sprint. If you run too fast at first, you won't have the energy to keep going. Concentrate on just one area at a time, and then as you are able, pick up another objective, and begin to schedule your highest priority goals for that area. Here is a checklist to help you in your personal priority scheduling and delegation: It must be done by me now.

    It must be done by me today.
    It must be done by me soon.
    It must be done by me sometime.
    It must be done by someone now.
    It must be done by someone today.
    It must be done by someone soon.
    It must be done by someone sometime.

As you begin to determine what you are going to do and when you are going to do it, place each item on your schedule somewhere. For annual planning, place the item in the month you have decided it should be done or begun (Chart A, page 47). Then, each month, take the monthly general list (Chart A) and break it down into your weekly general schedule (Chart B, page 48). Each week, schedule blocks of time on your daily schedule (Chart C, page 49) to get each of those items accomplished.

Remember to allow freedom in scheduling each day. Don't fill up the calendar with scheduled activities. Schedule only eighty percent of the day, allowing twenty percent for crisis and interruption. Schedule fifteen-to thirty-minute breaks. You'll think and do better if you relax and stretch periodically.

Some people find it helpful to arrive at the office one hour early or stay one hour late. They claim this can double productivity. Time spent alone in the office will produce more than the interruptions and distractions allow during regular office hours.

Strive for a balanced work schedule. Evaluate your daily time log and see whether you're spending time for all those areas that are important. Looking at Jesus' life, we find that He scheduled time to teach His disciples, minister to strangers' needs, and spend time alone. Even though He was on earth a limited time, He accomplished much.

NOVEMBER
(Month)

MONTHLY—GENERAL

White Barry Johnson about Camp
Evangelist for next year
Select director for VBS
3-day family vacation
Begin new exercise program
Plan sponsors' retreat for Spring
Annual camp board meeting - 13th
Arrange 2 planning meetings
for Christmas program
See Dentist for annual check-up

Chart A

NOVEMBER
(Month)

WEEKLY—GENERAL

1st - 3rd	- review monthly planning - Decide on type of exercise program

- 1st. Christmas planning mtg.
- Get substitute for my class during
   vacation

4th - 11th	- Check-up at Dentist - Camp board meeting

- Plan Thanksgiving party
   for pre-schoolers.

12th - 18th	- Wife's birthday - 17th - Check on progress of jr. Sponsors

- Have car taken in for tune-
   up before vacation

19th - 26th	- Family vacation - 20 - 23rd

- Select Director for VBS

27th - 3rd	- 2nd Christmas planning mtg.

- Plan Spring Sponsors' Retreat
- Do planning for December

Chart B

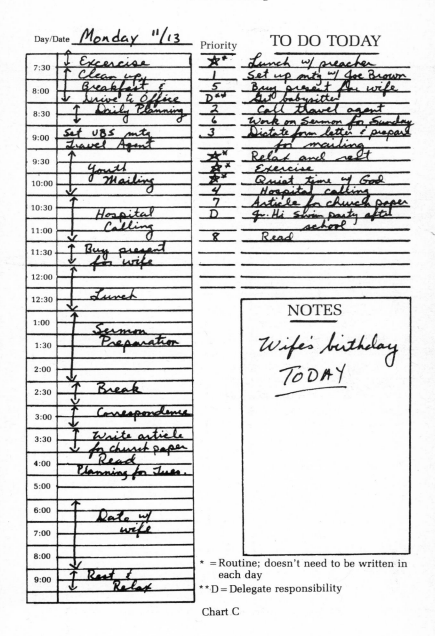

Day/Date _Monday "/13_

Time		Priority	TO DO TODAY
7:30	Excercise / Clean up	☆*	Lunch w/ preacher
		1	Set up mtg w/ Joe Brown
8:00	Breakfast & / Drive to Office	5	Buy present for wife
		D**	Get babysitter
8:30	Daily Planning	2	Call travel agent
		6	Work on Sermon for Sunday
9:00	Set UBS mtg / Travel Agent	3	Dictate form letter & prepare for mailing
9:30		☆*	Relax and rest
	Youth / Mailing	☆*	Exercise
10:00		☆*	Quiet time w/ God
		4	Hospital calling
10:30	Hospital / Calling	7	Article for church paper
		D	Jr. Hi swim party after
11:00			school
11:30	Buy present / for wife	8	Read
12:00			
12:30	Lunch		
1:00			
1:30	Sermon / Preparation		
2:00			
2:30	Break		
3:00	Correspondence		
3:30	Write article / for church paper		
4:00	Read / Planning for Tues.		
5:00			
6:00			
7:00	Date w/ / wife		
8:00			
9:00	Rest & / Relax		

NOTES

Wife's birthday
TODAY

* = Routine; doesn't need to be written in
each day

**D = Delegate responsibility

Chart C

Use Chart D to determine whether you are spending too little, too much, or just the right amount of time for each thing you do.

Time Use	Actual Time Spent (Daily, Weekly, etc.)	Too Little Time	Too Much Time	Just Enough Time
TV	2½ hrs/day		✓	
EATING	1¼ hrs/day	✓		
FAMILY TIME	½ hr/day	✓		
MEETINGS	4 hrs/week			✓
CALLING	3 hrs/week	✓		
PLANNING	?			
STUDYING	?			

Chart D

The best time to plan tomorrow is today. You can leave the office work at the office, spend an uncluttered evening at home, and hit the ground running in the morning. List the things that need to be done after looking over your weekly general planning schedule (Chart B). Delegate those things that can be delegated. Prioritize what is most important to be accomplished, and begin scheduling the estimated time needed for each item, beginning with priority number 1. Schedule *at least* ten minutes per day, one half hour per week, two hours per month, and one day per year, just for planning and scheduling.

Set a time limit for each item. If it has to be done by a certain time, it probably will be. You could get it done if you really had to. (College isn't the only place midnight oil can be burned.)

A youth minister basically has four planning periods to schedule. Plan to spend at least one half-day planning for each of these periods: September through Christmas, New Year's through Easter, Easter through Spring, and Summer.

Decide what objectives you want to reach during each period. Prioritize which are most important. Plan with methods and programming how each will be accomplished. Project when each should be done on your monthly, weekly, and daily schedules. Then relax and take the rest of the day off. You've accomplished a lot, and you've saved enough time to earn this break.

Not everything will go as you've planned. When faced with obstacles, don't give up! Consider these alternatives:

1. I've overlooked something.
2. My faith needs to be tested.
3. There is another way to do it.
4. God is reminding me of my limitations and my need to depend on Him.
5. The door is closed. This is not God's will.

Don't be afraid of innovation and experimentation. Make the program fit you. Remember that the alternative to planning is to act without forethought.

Self-discipline is not easy. It is making yourself do something that doesn't come naturally. Often it would be easier not to do those things that are most important in our lives.

Results, not title, determine our success. You may lead more kids to Christ and disciple them into His likeness than any other youth minister, even though you may never be a main speaker for a national convention. The important thing is not who you are but what you are doing for Christ's sake.

"Be very careful, then, how you live—not as unwise but as wise, making the most of every opportunity" (Ephesians 5:15, 16, NIV).

Suggested Resources

Alexander, John W. Managing Our Work. Downers Grove, IL: Intervarsity Press, 1972.

Dayton, Edward R. and Ted W. Engstrom. Strategy for Living. Ventura, CA: Regal Books, 1976.

Dayton, Edward R. Tools for Time Management. Grand Rapids: Zondervan, 1974.

DeWelt, Don. Prayer Time: A Guide to Daily Worship. Joplin: College Press, 1982.

Douglas, Stephen B. Managing Yourself. San Bernadino: Here's Life, 1978.

Douglas, Stephen B. and Bruce E. The Ministry of Management. San Bernadino: Campus Crusade for Christ, 1972.

Eims, LeRoy. Be the Leader You Were Meant to Be. Wheaton: Victor Books (Scripture Press), 1976.

Engstrom, Ted W. and R. Alex McKenzie. Managing Your Time. Grand Rapids: Zondervan, 1967.

Engstrom, Ted W. and Edward R. Dayton. The Art of Management for Christian Leader. Waco: Word, 1976.

Hocking, David L. Be a Leader People Follow. Ventura, CA: Regal Books, 1979.

Hummel, Charles E. The Tirany of the Urgent. Chicago: Intervarsity, 1967.

Kilinski, Kenneth K. and Jerry C. Wofford. Organization and Leadership in the Local Church. Grand Rapids: Zondervan, 1973.

Lakein, Alan. How to Get Control of Your Time and Your Life. New York: Peter H. Wyden, Inc., 1973.

Mager, Robert. Goal Analysis. Belmont, CA: Fearon Publishers, 1972.

McKenzie, R. Alec. The Time Trap. New York: McGraw-Hill, 1972.

Odiorne, George. Management By Objectives. Marshfield, MA: Pitman Publishing, 1965.

Phillips, Mike. Getting More Done in Less Time and Having More Fun Doing It. Minneapolis: Bethany House, 1982.

Schaller, Lyle E. Creative Church Administration. Nashville: Abingdon, 1975.

Uris, Aurin. The Efficient Executive. New York: McGraw-Hill, 1957.

White, Robert N. Managing Today's Church. Valley Forge: Judson Press, 1982.

4

Essential Elements for Planning an Event

David Roadcup

Tom had just graduated from college and taken his first full-time youth ministry. The experienced adults who were working with the senior-high group thought an early fall retreat would be a good way of beginning the program. They asked Tom to draw up some tentative plans. Silently, Tom began to panic. He had been involved in traveling groups in his college days and had been in the drama club, but he had never planned anything as extensive as a two-and-a-half day retreat. Where was he to begin? What handles could he grab to give him direction?

In planning any method program or event, there are certain crucial components that must be planned and organized. None can be slighted if the method is to bear fruit in your program. Taking the time to plan carefully and wisely will make the difference between a half-baked, ineffective event and one that will greatly influence the youth and adults with whom you work.

Planning a method is similar to planning a house. There must be a good foundation, walls, a roof, plumbing, wiring, and many other parts to make the house livable and to have it fulfill its primary function. The same is true when planning programming and methods approaches for youth groups. Prayer, choosing the type of method most desirable, specific objectives, staff, curriculum, and other important considerations all go to make up an effective life-impacting event.

Prayer

The place to start when planning any event is *prayer*. The role of prayer in the execution of methods is no small consideration! Prayer is the force that empowers the methodology we choose to use in our programs. Each approach we use should be bathed in prayer. Prayer is the place to begin!

We must remember that methods are the avenues we use to reach our objectives as youth workers. They are not ends in themselves. They are tools for ministry. If we have the tightest and most efficient methods ever planned but lack prayer for those methods, they become hollow activities that accomplish little more than provide our youth with a fun time. Prayer provides the power that works through our methodology to transform the lives of young people into the image of Christ.

There are several specifics that you should pray about when planning a methods approach. First, pray that God will lead you in deciding on the right objective or set of objectives for the method you are planning to use. Second, pray specifically for the young people who will be at the event. Before you begin praying, the Lord already knows who is going to be there and what individual needs will be present. Third, pray for the adult workers who will be leading. Pray for their preparation, sensitivity, and openness to formal and informal times of teaching with their group. Fourth, pray specifically for life-changing things to come from the event you are planning. God uses teaching times, songs, informal encounters, and other aspects of an event to touch people's lives. Fifth, pray for safety in travel and throughout the entire program.

The power of prayer in youth ministry is awesome! The youth worker who depends on prayer and seeking after the Lord first, and his or her own personality, creativity, and ability second, is the youth worker with the right priorities.

Stating Specific Objectives

In planning any event, whether it is a retreat, VBS, or any of numerous other methods, deciding on specific goals or objectives must be the second move in assuring effectiveness. "Goals have a powerful effect. Objectives clearly articulated and mutually agreed upon in a group have a powerful effect."[1]

Sitting down weeks ahead (also months and years ahead, depending on the extent of your planning) and deciding exactly what it is you want to accomplish in a particular program is of utmost importance.

Goals and objectives are guides that direct us to effective and successful ministry. Simply to "have a retreat" or "conduct a week of church camp" without specific, measurable goals is like sailing a ship without a rudder; there's no way to predict or control the result. There may be abundant and feverish activity, but there's not direction. Good things may happen, but they will take place at random and in a haphazard manner rather than in a planned and progressive fashion.

We must understand that effective goal-setting is *hard work*. It takes time, thought, analysis, and grueling effort to produce a set of workable goals for a specific project. It is, however, one of the most important aspects to effective methods execution.

A method without goals is a method without direction. Be sure your goals for a specific program are well formulated and clear as you continue to plan.

Staff

In methods execution, the adult volunteer staff you recruit, train, and motivate is crucial. The people you recruit to assist you and perform many of the details of the event may make or break the event you are planning. Locating quality adults who are willing to help you with your work is one of the major tasks of a youth worker. (See chapter 5 for a detailed discussion on developing adult volunteers).

The staff you need for each event depends on the nature of the event. You may have members of your local congregation who work weekly with your young people. However, a week of camp or VBS may require different or additional staffing.

Decide on staff needs for the particular event you are planning. Will you need a cook, a lifeguard, an athletic director, a speaker, a song leader, or a bus driver? What staff will you need to manage and execute the particular event you are planning?

After analyzing your staff needs, pray hard, and then make the most serious attempt possible to surround yourself with people who are interested and who have the gifts and abilities necessary for the task. Try to find adults who can influence young people with their presentations and presence (example) as well.

Be sure to communicate clearly to your adult workers (on paper) exactly what you want them to do. Communicating ministry description and expectations to your workers will provide them with needed guidelines and direction for their work.

Adult volunteers make up the backbone of any good methods

approach. Analyzing your need, recruiting well, quality training, and effective motivation will provide you with a good foundation upon which to build.

Curriculum

Curriculum is a specific course of study. After deciding on the specific objectives guiding your event, you must secure the most advantageous curriculum possible.

The content of a quality curriculum provides meat (substance) to flesh out the bones of your objectives. Good curriculum will offer background information, creative ideas, and life-to-life application for your teaching.

Curriculum should be alive! It should be from yourself as well as from prepared materials. Taking a quarterly series of lessons or a youth-oriented book and embellishing it with your own study and ideas is the intent of prepared materials. You should call upon commentaries, music, topical books, newspapers, magazines (religious and secular), interviews, your own creative ideas, and other input to help enrich the printed series of lessons you use.

Remember, need determines curriculum. That is, the individual needs of the members of your youth group should determine the curriculum you choose. It is crucial for you and your adult leaders to spend enough time with the members of your group to become familiar with their individual needs.

Curriculum for youth ministry is more plentiful now than ever before. Curriculum offerings can be discovered in any of the following ways:

Visit local Christian bookstores and ask about any new youth ministry materials available.

When attending conventions or conferences, visit the display areas and collect the samples and packets of information that appear to be of use to you.

Purchase Christian magazines and periodicals that carry advertisements for publishing house offerings.

Write to major Christian publishing houses. Ask for samples of materials for the age groups with which you work. Also request to be placed on their mailing lists for future information.

Costs

Normal programming does not usually generate a need for funding from the kids themselves. There are events (like ski trips, retreats, and amusement park trips) that will require additional cost.

When the need to charge for an event arises, it is advisable to do several specific things.

    a. Forecast with as much accuracy as possible the amount each young person will need to pay or take on the trip.

    b. Make sure you communicate to the parents how much the activity will cost.

    c. If the cost is more than what your young people are used to paying (a week's ski trip as opposed to a two-day retreat) you may want to have the young people pay a definite amount in monthly increments ($20.00 a month for six months). This will make the total amount easier for families with several children in the same youth group or for families with financial difficulties.

It may also be possible to use budgeted church funds to offset the expense of some activities. For example, many churches pay up to one-half of the cost for a week at camp.

Depending on the policy of the church, it may also be possible to organize money-making projects (like a car wash or bake sale) that will allow the young people to generate income for costly events.

Time and Timing of Events

In addition to your personal planning calendar, you as a youth worker should have two other calendars at hand. The first should be the church's yearly planning calendar. Planning your events in cooperation with the rest of the staff will save you many problems in terms of scheduling.

The other calendar you should have at hand is a calendar of the events of the public and private schools where your youth attend. Knowing the dates of prime events on a high-school campus can help in planning the timing of your events so your group can attend as many as possible. One difficulty in using public school calendars is that many of them plan only one year in advance. This may present a problem in terms of planning your major-events calendar two or three years in advance.

Publicity

Communicating information and enthusiasm about an event will encourage attendance and help create a genuine air of expectation on the part of your group. Getting their attention about a planned event will stimulate inquiries and interest. Publicity should be attention getting and in good taste, and it should communicate all the necessary information. Mark Senter points out, "It is very important that the purposes of the event be kept clearly in mind as publicity is being created. There needs to be 'truth in packaging' and at the same time a flavor of excitement about the event."[2]

There are a number of media you can use to publicize your event. Posters, flyers, verbal announcements, the church or youth paper, bulletin boards, skit announcements, and the Sunday-morning bulletin are but a few means at your disposal.

Good publicity is creative and communicative, transferring information and enthusiasm. It can be a helpful part of a successful event.

Location of the Event

If an event is going to be held away from the church building, there are several suggestions that may prove helpful in securing a satisfactory location. Check church camps, YMCA camps, and state or local parks. Be sure to get definite information of the cost per group or individual, travel time to the location, and what facilities the location has and which of these is available to you. Also check on the possibility of additional charges for recreation opportunities. It is a good idea to visit the location before the event to see the facilities and grounds, visit with the manager, and get an idea of what is available for your event.

Insurance

Select insurance companies offer group health and accident insurance for a very low cost per person. They provide coverage that extends from twenty-four hours before the event begins to twenty-four hours after the event. It is a good idea to check the present policy or policies your church or organization now carries. Group coverage may already be built into the existing policy.

In the event there is an emergency, parental release forms (permission slips) are a good idea. (Parents sign forms provided by the church to allow medical treatment for children under eighteen years of age.) These forms are required by some insurance companies.

Attention to Details

"*Detail:* The act of dealing with things item by item. A small part or parts; item. Small secondary or accessory part or parts of a picture, statue, building, etc." *Attention to detail* is crucial in executing effective methods. *Attention to detail* will make or break an event you are planning. *Attention to detail* represents to effective methodology what mortar does to bricks or nails to lumber. It is crucial that you give much attention to the small details of planning an event.

Imagine you are on a retreat at a camp twenty miles from the closest town. It is Saturday night at 9:30 p.m. The feature film, around which you have built your whole retreat, is loaded in the projector. Ten minutes into the film, the projection bulb burns out. The closest projection bulb is at a camera shop twenty miles away. The shop closed at 5:30 p.m. The film showing—and the expectations of the group—are both shot.

At a conference, I heard a youth minister tell about a beach party he had organized. The main event was to be a weather-balloon volleyball game. This particular activity was publicized to be the highlight of the entire day. After driving for two hours, picnicking, and swimming, it was time for the long-awaited weather-balloon volleyball game to begin. While the net was being erected, the adults began to look for the balloon to inflate it. Only then was it discovered that the weather-balloon had been inadvertently left at the church. Covering small (and large!) details is the key to successful execution.

As you are planning an event, sit, reflect, and ask yourself, "Is there anything I have forgotten?" Go over the program, step by step in your mind. Check each activity and point of detail. As the event is unfolding, make a list of any details you may have overlooked. Also, list any ways the event could be improved the next time one similar is conducted.

Careful attention to detail is crucial in making your methods as effective as possible.

Conclusion

Every event you plan in your program is made up of important components. Each component is crucial to make up the whole. Taking time to pray, think, plan, and organize—giving attention to each component part—will assure successful methodology in your program. This will enable you to teach the primary objective each of us as youth workers has, that of transforming the lives of as many young people as possible into the image of Christ.

---

[1] Olan Hendrix, *Management for the Christian* (Milford, MI: Mott Media, 1976), p. 51.

[2] Gary, Dausey, *The Youth Leader's Source Book* (Grand Rapids: Zondervan, 1983), p. 181.

Suggested Resources

Bounds, E.M. *Power Through Prayer*. Grand Rapids: Zondervan, 1962.

Caplow, Theodore. *How to Run Any Organization*. Holt, Rinehart and Winston of Canada, 1976

Dausey, Gary. *The Youth Leader's Source Book*. Grand Rapids: Zondervan, 1983.

Dayton, Edward and Ted Engstrom. *Strategy for Living*. Glendale: Gospel Light, 1976.

Douglas, Stephen B. *Managing Yourself*. San Bernadino: Here's Life Publishers, 1978.

Hendrix, Olan. *Management for the Christian*. Milford, MI: Mott Media, 1976.

Lee, Mark. *How to Set Goals and Really Reach Them*. Portland: Horizon House, 1978.

Roadcup, David. *Ministering to Youth*. Cincinnati: Standard, 1980.

Unit Two

METHODS

5

Developing Adult Leaders

Dick Alexander

Youth ministry in the local church is not a one-man band. The long-term effectiveness of youth ministry depends on the ability of the youth minister to develop a group of committed adult volunteers who are capable teachers, counselors, and disciplers. While the professional youth worker is drawn to youth ministry by his or her love for young people and his desire to serve them, his key task is to develop adults, who will in turn work with youth.

One-leader youth programs are self-limiting. They are limited in the number of people they can reach, the breadth of people they can reach, and the depth of individual ministry they can provide. Even youth programs with many workers are actually one-man bands when the volunteers function as chaperones and the youth minister carries out all the significant jobs. In a healthy church youth program, young people are able to look to a variety of volunteer adult leaders as role models, counselors, and teachers. This chapter is about finding, recruiting, developing, and keeping good leaders and replacing the ineffective ones.

Finding Leaders

Building capable adult leadership starts with locating the right people. What kind of person do we look for? Where do we find him?

It *is* true that youth leaders come in all shapes and sizes. The tendency to raid the young adult class in search of youth sponsors is an unfortunate one. The ideal team of youth leaders for any youth group consists of adults of various ages—possibly some grandparents, people of parent age, a newly married couple, some single adults, and a couple of college students. Each age group makes a unique contribution to the maturing of young people. Parents can sometimes work in a group with their own teenagers, and sometimes they can't, depending on the relationship. Kids are in the process of establishing independence from parents, and, for many, the church provides a positive place for them to have some space away from their parents. But some teens get along with and enjoy their folks and welcome having them around. Your use of parents must consider these factors. Additionally, with some married couples, it is best to have one partner and not the other. Couples do not always have the same ministry interests, and if each one genuinely supports the other, they can serve in different ways.

Some common qualities exist among all people who work effectively with youth. When looking for youth leaders in a church, a good place to start is *likability*. Whom do the kids enjoy? To whom do they naturally gravitate? Who is fun when he is with the kids? It's also crucial to have leaders with *consistent, growing Christian lives*. Kids sniff out phonies. To help others grow, a leader must be open and relational. This is a tough one. Few older adults have learned to share their inner lives. Many function well, but they do it independently. But people who are to assist others in the growing process must be able to discuss their own growth freely. Youth leaders are adult friends and guides, not chaperones. Another good test is how well the adult relates to his own age group. Some people are drawn to work with kids because they are big kids themselves. Youth ministry demands maturity.

Where do we find these people? Probably already at work in our churches, overloaded with other responsibilities. People who make good youth leaders are usually some of the most capable, in-demand people in the church. One way to identify potential workers is simply to go through the membership list of the congregation in prayerful evaluation. Another is to talk to adult Sunday-school teachers and church leaders, asking for suggestions.

Rarely is it helpful to make a public appeal for volunteers. A person beginning a first-time youth program might offer an introductory training program for potential workers and invite people by announcement. But in ordinary circumstances, the kind of people needed for the challenge of working with youth will need to be convinced that they can make time to do it.

Working with young people is a high priority task, both congregationally and personally. A person who recently became a Christian can serve in the church in a variety of ways, but is not prepared yet to be an elder or a youth leader. Many who are ready to be youth leaders are tied down with tasks that others could do. Congregations can maximize effectiveness by freeing people from multitudinous chores, replacing them in those jobs with others and letting them concentrate in one area of service. In simple terms, if the best prospective junior-high worker in the church is currently a deacon, chairman of the house and grounds committee, choir president, and left fielder for the church softball team, the youth minister can help him resign graciously from each of those posts and find a replacement for him. Good junior-high leaders are rare.

Finding the right people always begins with prayer. The Lord spent the entire night in prayer preparing to call the twelve. As a youth leader prays over lists of names in a church directory or an adult class roll, the Holy Spirit will provide insight into whom He is calling for ministry.

Recruiting

Recruiting workers can be a joy for everybody involved. When it's done properly, it also contributes to longevity of service.

When a youth worker believes that the Lord has led him to potential volunteer workers, it's time to share that vision. An appointment in the prospect's home is basic and should cover several areas of information.

In Christ's church, people are called to a cause, not a task. This seemingly minor distinction can make a significant difference in how a person serves. The question for a potential worker is not whether he would be the high-school Sunday-school teacher, but whether he loves high-school kids. The cause is to love people in the name of Christ. Teaching classes and leading or sponsoring groups are simple ways to do that. A person who sees his role as being a Sunday-school teacher can easily focus on getting the job done. The focus of recruiting is not filling slots in the program, but finding adults who have a special burden for a particular age group and then helping them find ways through the overall youth ministry of a church to express that love. The number-one question to a prospective junior-high leader is, "Have you ever felt a special burden for junior-high-age kids?"

Once it is confirmed that a person has interest in an age group, he needs to know what special abilities or qualities he has that could be useful. Many people underestimate their abilities, and it's important for them to hear what gifts the church leadership sees in them. They often wonder, "Why would you want me?"

A prospective worker needs to hear in an honest, straight-forward way what time commitment is being sought. Program-centered ministries can use people for as little as a couple of hours a week for three months to a year. Relationally oriented ministry takes more time. If it is the intention of a church to build a group of adults who have a significant impact in shaping the lives of youth, the leaders will need to see the kids more than once a week. And they will need to continue the relationship over a period of years. With this in view, people are invited to be "lifers"—to give themselves to a particular age group, to stay with it long enough to become effective, and to continue in a satisfying ministry. To ask people for a one-year (or other short-term) commitment of service can be more program centered than person centered and can actually encourage leaders to get out, rather than to continue in ministry. Inasmuch as it takes at least a year to begin building relationships and developing a basic level of trust with youth, leaders don't begin to have much significant effect in life transformation until their second or third year. No one is trapped by a long-term, open-ended commitment. Since ministry is a gift of love, we only want people who want to serve. Anyone who does not want to serve is free to step out at any time. The goal is to develop a group of long-term servants who love kids and want to work with them. Prospective leaders need to see the goal of long-term ministry, to know that they do have the option to quit at some point if they want to, to know in realistic terms how much time each week it will take, and to know what financial or material investment (such as the use of their home or their car) will be asked.

An extremely helpful part of the recruiting process is to encourage prospective leaders to visit and observe the age group they're considering for one to three months before making a decision. Some adults like kids individually or in small groups, but find the activity level of a large group intolerable. To grab a person on Wednesday and send him into the junior-high class as the teacher beginning the next Sunday might be necessary once every millennium, in an hour of desperate need, but it is far more fair for people to observe the group and the context in which they would work and get a feel for whether they'd fit. Most people in a few weeks of observation can see pretty clearly whether they'd want to work in that area.

A part of the recruiting call is to explain the training program. When a person is considering accepting responsibility, he will need to know what help will be available, both preservice and continuing.

A good leadership recruiting contact does not ask for a decision on the spot. It confirms the person's interest in young people and his personal desire to help them, explains how the church's youth ministry can provide an opportunity to do that, shows how and why the individual or couple can fit in, offers an opportunity to observe the troops in action (without making a commitment), explains what training will be offered, and establishes a plan for making a final decision.

Effective paid staff anticipate needs in advance. Often, a new youth minister in a church must play catch-up and may, even for a period of years, scramble just barely to cover immediate staffing needs. The goal, however, is as quickly as possible to reach the place where leaders are being recruited months ahead of need, allowing for growth rather than strangulation.

Developing Leadership

The job of the church staff is to make volunteer workers successful in their ministries. This begins with the relational climate.

Paul described Epaphroditus not only as a fellow soldier, but more importantly, as a brother. Those who share in ministry work best when they also share life. Ministry is more productive and more enjoyable if coworkers are truly friends, spending at least some of their social and recreational time together. In an informally developed atmosphere of trust, it is possible to give feedback and mutually offer help, direction, and redirection. The most helpful training in ministry may come from the honest evaluation of our leadership by coworkers, and this is most possible in a supportive environment. Lunches, evenings out, shared vacations, and other fun times help develop relationships in which we enjoy ministry more and can encourage honest and helpful feedback.

People grow best when they can walk before they must run. The progressive acceptance of responsibility helps most people in overcoming fear. When a person can assist before he's asked to lead, his confidence level grows. Some people learn to swim by being thrown off the dock, but most prefer to get wet gradually.

Leadership development is often viewed as a matter of training in ministry skills, but the real issue is personal growth. Leader effectiveness is not so much a matter of technique but of personal life. Failure is generally not a matter of methodology but a lack of the quality people to carry out the job. Good continuing training in leadership does help people improve their skills, but it focuses in their lives. Too many who have been Christians for ten years or more have stopped growing. Developing quality leaders means developing quality people with a consistent plan for teaching, encouraging personal study, retreats and growth groups, and various discipling activities with adult leaders.

Effectiveness of adult leadership will also increase with continued training in such areas as teaching methods, counseling, group leadership, developmental psychology, planning and organization, and recreation leadership. Youth worker conventions, traveling seminars by national youth organizations, area-wide interchurch programs, in-house seminars, elective classes, and individual times with leaders can all be useful training formats. Preferably, as many of these as possible will be utilized on a continuing basis.

Experience is an invaluable teacher, and getting experience involves failures as well as successes. Developing competent leaders requires allowing them room to fail without criticism. If volunteers are to accept responsibility, own their ministries, and broaden their involvement, they must be encouraged by leadership to try new things and be supported, win or lose. Every great leader has behind him a mental draw full of failures that were good learning experiences and became building blocks to success.

The bottom-line issue in ministry is commitment. Commitment to serve others is not discovered—it is developed. In one sense, the entire task of leadership might be summarized as building commitment in others. Like every area of change in the Christian walk, commitment to sacrificial service is not an overnight event, but a long process. It is generally developed, not by hearing sermons and lessons, but by personal challenge from leaders in the context of serving. People make a commitment to serve when they see a need and are asked to meet it. They grow in commitment as they are progressively challenged to give more of themselves. Churches generally get about what they aim for. Those who want hour-a-week Sunday-school teachers get them. Those who want a high level of commitment and ask for it, usually get that as well. Too often, we have not because we ask not, and we ask not, possibly, because we're afraid of rejection. Commitment also grows from confronting lack of commitment squarely. If a leader fails to do what he has promised, a positive, non-incriminating discussion of the situation can strengthen his resolve. Many churches ask too little of volunteer leaders, fearing they might quit if they are asked to do more. The result is a generally low level of ministry activity carried out by a few dedicated, overworked people. Christians are indwelt by the Holy Spirit and will respond when consistently challenged to a ministry.

Keeping Leaders

How do we cut down on turnover of people? How can we hang on to people who have ability to serve but lose their willingness?

Burn-out is a buzz word today in people-related work. Caring for people is a high-demand job. Those who are emptying themselves out must be refilled, implying some spiritual, social, and time concerns. The common refrain, "Let the younger ones do it," tells us painfully of a generation of burned-out workers.

Burn-out, in its largest sense, is a spiritual issue. Spiritual dryness and emptiness needs empathy, not condemnation. A primary task of the church staff is to nurture the personal spiritual life of volunteer leaders. It is a serious error to assume that the worship services in most congregations will fill this function. Bible studies, personal growth retreats, and helps for personal quiet times are some avenues for encouraging spiritual life.

Youth leadership also raises some unique social concerns. Because working with kids often takes many hours a week, it may tend to pull adult leaders away from some of their natural adult friendships. Children's workers are generally not involved as many hours a week since children are more home oriented. Teachers and leaders of adult groups give many hours in service, but have peer relationships with those they serve. A junior-high worker may be involved with kids on a weeknight as well as on Sunday, and not be able to be involved in any adult Bible class or home Bible study. Without some opportunity for involvement in an adult group, many good youth leaders quit because they miss their Sunday-school class. A unique need of youth leaders in the church is, therefore, the forming of support groups, or growth groups, where they can meet regularly with other adult leaders for sharing and prayer, and possibly for Bible study or a Bible-related study at an adult level. The need for such support is only felt by a person after he has been involved long enough and deeply enough with youth to sense a void from the lessening of time with adults.

Simply put, most people see a leaders' growth group as unnecessary, and they resist involvement, until they start emptying themselves out significantly and need refilling.

Several other factors affect volunteer workers' desire to continue in ministry. People are motivated to stick with something when they feel they're not in it alone. Building a team of workers in each age group helps provide a sense of encouragement for everybody. A couple who carries all the responsibility of a youth group for an extended period will probably feel drained. Workers who are part of a team can be there every week, but they don't have to prepare and lead every week.

People are motivated to serve when it's obvious what they're doing is worthwhile. Is it their own ministry? Are the volunteer workers trusted to make major decisions, or do decisions come down from the top? Are they trusted to do the important jobs of ministry? Do they counsel kids, or are they there to help the youth minister with his ministry.

People are motivated to serve when they have the resources they need to do the job. Often the youth minister is the one who has the resources (books, catalogs, budget, equipment), and he is the one who looks good. Making volunteers successful means putting into their hands the best tools available.

People are motivated by knowing they're genuinely appreciated. Good people don't give to get, but they deserve gratitude. Good youth workers may be, next to parents, the most valuable people on earth. Institutional ways of saying thanks include appreciation dinners and public recognition. Certainly churches can find more personal ways to say thanks, including phone calls, personal letters, dinners in our homes, and frequent words of personal encouragement.

People are motivated to continue when they don't feel stuck in a rut, doing the same thing year after year. As workers grow in skill through continued training, are continually stimulated in their own walk with the Lord, and broaden their ministries by being encouraged to try new things, youth ministry can be a consistently satisfying experience.

Replacing Leaders

From time to time, it is necessary to replace a nonfunctioning volunteer worker. Some refuse to do this because they think it cruel to ask a person to step aside, even though he's not functioning. In reality, it's probably cruel to the *kids* not to remove such a leader. Permitting an adult leader to do a continually bad job with kids shows lack of love for them.

Reasons for failure to function are varied. Sometimes the wrong person was chosen to start with. Sometimes commitment was not fulfilled. Occasionally a moral problem surfaces. But the bottom line is the same—we want to redeem the person. This means the replacing of a person in leadership is not a bolt out of the blue, but one midway step in an extended process.

People can change, even after years of bad habits. The first task in redeeming the existing ineffective leader is to confront the situation squarely. This requires mustering the courage to sit down face to face and lay out the areas of concern, speaking the truth with genuine love. It means offering help, additional training, personal support, prayer, meeting together weekly—anything the person needs to help accomplish the desired end. Sometimes the message doesn't come through the first time and must be restated at a later date.

When everything reasonably possible has been done to help a person succeed, and, either for lack of willingness or lack of ability, the situation continues, a change in personnel must be made. When that time comes, people are sometimes relieved to step aside, since they have by then painfully realized their inadequacy for the task. A part of redeeming the person is to suggest a move into an alternative ministry to which the person's ability or time schedule is better suited. Our desire is not to get rid of any person, but to help each one find the place where Christ really wants him. Most people actually welcome such a move, but since some may have a considerable amount of ego on the line, it is good to have the support of the responsible board or youth committee in replacing a volunteer worker. Keeping in touch with the person and maintaining friendship afterwards helps to communicate clearly that we really don't reject people for failure.

The Time Factor

Good help is hard to find—everywhere. In many churches, it takes five to ten years to develop a core of capable adult workers. It takes prayer, love, sweat, and sometimes tears—but it's worth it.

6

Discipline in the Youth Program

Brian Giebler

What do you see when you envision a strict disciplinarian? Perhaps you conjure up a stern visage, a forceful manner, and a readiness to apply the rod to the seat of the problem. I don't. I think it's ironic that those most often regarded as good disciplinarians probably least understand the meaning inherent in the term.

As there are two sides of medicine, the preventive and the corrective, so are there two dimensions of discipline. While the second dimension, that of correction, receives the most attention and is most often considered when discipline is discussed, the preventive realm represents greater potential for good.

Terminology

In our use of the term *discipline*, primary emphasis should be upon teaching that motivates and causes to mature. Discipline is the assessment of behavioral guidelines. It is the explanation of behavioral expectations to the end that the one disciplined is enabled to understand both what is expected and why.

Discipline goes beyond demands and intimidation. Its purpose is not only to achieve right behavior, but also to progressively lessen dependence upon the disciplinary authority. External discipline that fails to result in self-discipline fails altogether.

Though we expect small children to obey us without question, we must acknowledge that questions will arise as a child grows.

Discipline should answer these questions. The child should be equipped to rely increasingly on his own ethical sense and educated judgment while relying less upon our own. Our proper convictions, evaluations, and determinations will become the child's own if we are willing to share our reasoning. This is true discipline.

Discipline, properly conceived, is an instructional task. It is inclusive of virtually all teaching efforts, whether employed in group or personal settings.

The punitive dimension of discipline is our second consideration. Punishment is that which is brought to bear when behavioral guidelines have been transgressed. It is the penalty for failure to do right when right is known. Please note the sequence. Punishment must follow instruction, or it is out of order.

Preventive discipline, our instructional task, assesses and justifies behavioral expectations. Good discipline also includes mention of the sure consequences of misconduct. Punishment is administered when discipline is not heeded. If we punish prior to preventive discipline, we do wrong. It is unjust and potentially damaging to the relationship to punish a child who neither knows his action is wrong, nor why it is wrong, nor what the consequences of his act will be.

Most prefer to practice optimum preventive medicine (adequate rest, diet, exercise, and stress release) in order to avoid the comparatively difficult and unpleasant consequences of corrective medicine (expense, lost time, injections, surgery, and the like). In the same way, it is desirable to practice optimum preventive discipline in order to apply minimal corrective measures.

Let's face it. Punitive action is unpleasant, no matter how necessary. It involves direct negative confrontation, a situation very uncomfortable for most of us. Isn't it sensible (as well as Biblical) to minimize the need for punishment by devoting ourselves to the task of discipline?

When our expectations are made clear and the reasons for them understood, we are preparing our pupils to think and obey rather than to obey blindly. The former course develops character. The latter denies its existence.

Goals of Discipline

The purpose of discipline is to develop the mind and spirit. It molds and strengthens personhood, produces an awareness of righteousness, and builds sufficient ego strength (character) to do right when right is known. Discipline is a developmental task, a progressive exercise. The more one's own character is developed, the less dependent that person is on external authority.

Though once I behaved because Teacher or Mother would get me if I didn't, I now behave because I see the rewards of proper action and the detriments attached to impropriety. When I was a child, I conformed my behavior for childish reasons. Because of conscientious discipline, I now conform for more mature reasons. I do right because I believe in it and wish to participate in it, not because of adult coercion.

Our goal is to develop young people capable of thinking and acting for themselves. Undue dependence on a disciplinary authority can cripple the personality and stifle progressive independence. Discipline that encourages independent thought and action, however, will produce personal freedom and confidence.

The goal of punishment is to associate unpleasant consequences with wrongdoing. The objective of all punishment should be to conform the will of the child to that of the authority responsible for the child's well-being. Although we would prefer to avoid punishment, it must be exercised when discipline is ignored or defied.

If we had our way, all children would learn their preventive lessons, and we would conduct our activities in peace and tranquility. But, alas, it is human nature to test the waters of authority, to see whether established boundaries are as fixed as they have been made to appear. Children, incapable of knowing what is presently in their best interest, are dependent upon those who are more mature. They don't always recognize this dependence. Thus, they may need the reinforcement of dramatic punitive measures to remind them.

God has ordained that the mature supervise and control the activity of the immature. This is necessary for safety and happiness in both the physical and spiritual realms.

Though Johnny doesn't want to take a bath (the immature mind neither knows nor cares about the long-range consequences of filth, either hygienically or interpersonally), his parents insist that he do so. Why? Recognizing the consequences of filth (as he presently does not), the parents force his will into conformity with their own. They do this not to hurt, but to help. True love does what is in the loved one's best interest, even when it is neither desired nor appreciated.

If Johnny refuses fruit and vegetables, his parents don't accept his justification, "I don't like them." Recognizing the negative consequences of poor nutrition, they gently insist that he conform his will to theirs, even though his mind (and palate) may remain unchanged. The mature govern the immature for his benefit. Johnny will grow to accept a different standard of value and to appreciate the reason behind now-detested punishments.

Johnny may refuse to go to school on the grounds that it interferes with his education. School, to him, is an interference in his day, eating up valuable time that could be much better spent. Yet his parents—and the law—insist that Johnny go to school. Why? Because they know the long-range detriments accompanying ignorance, sloth, and lack of mental discipline. Again, they force his will into conformity with their mature judgment. Tomorrow, Johnny's mind will be in order. His own judgment will be more mature because his parents have disciplined prior to and during punishment. Then, punishment and external discipline alike will no longer be needed. Johnny will be disciplining his own behavior.

Similarly, if Johnny refuses to participate in the learning activities in his Sunday-school class, his teacher must insist that he do so. His immature mind may prefer to engage only in fun activities now, but he will learn the value of spiritual challenge. The mature standards of the teacher must be imposed on him until that learning takes place, even if the imposition must be done through punishment.

If Johnny prefers to tell jokes or otherwise distract his fellows during youth meeting, the sponsors must force him to comply with their more mature standards of conduct. They are not suppressing his creativity; they are teaching him priorities. Today, jokes and clowning are always in order, Johnny believes, and to punish such behavior is unreasonable. Tomorrow, he will realize that such activities are not edifying, and edification will be among his priorities.

We cannot permit a child to mature unbathed, undernourished, and uneducated simply because it is his will of the moment. Nor can we permit a child's spirit to wander whither it will apart from our careful direction in the youth program. Punishment is a necessary part of caring for a child when he is unable to care for himself properly. It becomes less essential as the child's own judgment matures.

Behavior Modification

There are at least two axioms upon which we can rely in our endeavor to elicit responsible behavior from our students. The first is a principle of need satisfaction: a child who is consistently rewarded with a pleasant response for a particular behavior will tend to repeat the behavior. If consistency is great enough for a period of sufficient duration, the specific behavior will become a fixed part of the individual's behavior pattern.

The second rule applies to the discouragement of behavioral deviance: a child who consistently encounters an unpleasant response to a particular behavior will tend to avoid the behavior. If the negative consequence is consistently applied over time, the behavior will be eliminated from the child's behavior pattern.

Reinforcement

The rule of need satisfaction should be consistently applied in encouraging repetition of desirable behavior. Pleasant responses satisfy the individual's need for attention, acceptance, and approval. Though the behavior may have been unconscious, proper reinforcement will encourage conscious attention to the repetition of the act.

The tricky part of the axiom is the limited meaning sometimes applied to "pleasant response." A child, spanked for getting out of bed in violation of his parents' command, may hardly seem to be responding to a pleasant response when he does it again—and again. If he has learned, however, that continued endurance of the pain of spanking will ultimately enable him to stay up, as his parents finally give in, he is receiving positive reinforcement.

Positive reinforcement of negative behavior is a disciplinary *faux pas* that is damaging to the child and to the authority figure alike.

Children are capable of withstanding tremendous amounts of pain (as in the case cited) in anticipation of winning the desired reward. The child in the illustration had learned that his will was stronger than that of his parents. He had but to outlast them in order to receive the reward he was seeking, being allowed to stay up. You can imagine the magnified behavioral problems if the system remains unchanged as he matures.

Part of our disciplinary responsibility is rewarding desirable behavior. This teaches graphic personal lessons concerning the benefits of propriety. It takes behavior and response out of the realm of the teacher's words and puts them into the realm of the pupil's experience. Lessons learned in this way are much more likely to be remembered.

If Johnny's gum wrapper falls to the floor and he unconsciously reaches for it, use that as an occasion for reinforcement. Praise him for his sense of responsibility, his concern for the appearance of the classroom, and his refusal to make unnecessary work for others.

When Mary Lou pushes her chair under the table at the conclusion of the period, commend her thoughtfulness and her sense of order. You might even invite her to help you straighten the rest of the room, assuring her that she's the kind of helper in whom you can place your confidence.

If Tom offers a comment in class or volunteers to read the text of the day, thank him for his participation. Perhaps you might ask him to fulfill some simple assignment on the basis of your regard for his initiative, ability, or reliable judgment.

Ways and means of reinforcement are limited only by the situation and the imagination of the teacher or coach involved. Remember, positive rewards will reinforce any behavior. The wise disciplinarian reserves positive reinforcement for productive behavior.

Extinction

Negative behavior, that which is hurtful to others, irresponsible, careless, or thoughtless, should be met with negative results. In time, such practice will discourage repetition of the behavior and ultimately bring it to extinction.

Consider a sponsor in the Sunday youth hour presenting a flannelboard lesson to her group of preschoolers. A child, seeing the flannel-backed figures in her hand, decides he will "help." He stands up and reaches for one of the figures. The sponsor endeavors to distract and press on, but to no avail. Finally, confrontation is inevitable. The sponsor says, "No! Sit down."

"But I want to help."

"Not now!"

"But I want to HELP!"

"No! Now sit down and be still."

"I WANT TO HELP!"

At this point, the sponsor is embarrassed by the disturbance the child is making and threatened by the thought of losing control. She takes the next figure to be placed on the flannelboard and gives it to the wailing child. He puts it on the board and returns to his seat. There is no more disturbance, and the sponsor returns to the lesson. It seems that all is well and that the sponsor has saved the day.

In reality, the sponsor has reinforced the very behavior she most wished to discourage. Though things are quiet for the moment,

Junior (as well, incidentally, as the other children observing) has learned a most disturbing lesson. "Holler loud enough long enough, and you'll get what you want."

How many children are able to change well-considered and necessary directives by means of needling, whining, pouting, or other decidedly negative behaviors? How many youth groups are disrupted because action is determined by negative behavior? We must not deceive ourselves. We haven't won anything just because we have momentarily eliminated improper behavior. If, in the process, we have encouraged wrong response patterns, our folly will return to haunt us in the ghastly form of ever more wrong patterns. Wrong application of the rules of modification results in escalation of deviant behavior.

Persistence in negative behavior must be countered by persistence in achieving negative result. If the child's will is stronger than that of the person in authority, the child will henceforth dictate the course of events in the classroom. This, of course, is an intolerable situation.

Our exalted purpose cannot be sacrificed on the altar of childish disobedience. Bring to nought those behaviors that demean the individual or negatively affect others. Don't permit positive rewards to accompany deviant behavior.

Principles of Discipline

Sensitivity

Discipline characterized by callous disregard for personhood will probably be disregarded by those to whom it is applied. Since we deal with individuals, we must develop individual methods of approach.

We do well to rid ourselves of "kid" prejudices (e.g., "You know how kids are . . ."; "Isn't that just like a kid?") People generally resent being lumped categorically in disregard of individual personality and philosophy. Kids are no exception.

Sensitivity stems from awareness. Awareness stems from concern. Sensitivity can be guaranteed only when sufficient concern is demonstrated to insure awareness of individual backgrounds, situations, needs, and desires.

Though many disciplinary messages are equally applicable to all—regardless of individuality—manner of approach and proper timing can only be determined through individual sensitivity. We must care about our pupils. That love should be attested to by our instructional ministry to them.

Knowledge

We must know whereof we speak if we would be good disciplinarians. How can we share admonition and correction of which we
are unaware? Since our interest is not in faddism but in eternal
truth and lifelong behavior encouraged by it, we must know God's
revelation to man.

The realm of knowledge frightens away many otherwise suitable
candidates for youth ministry. "I don't know enough," and, "I'm
afraid they might ask me questions I can't answer," are relatively
common rationales for refusals to serve.

Who does know enough? Who has all the answers? We are all
growing. None among us has attained perfection. At issue here is
not how much you know but how much you are willing to learn.
The emphasis is upon desire rather than achievement. Deficiencies
can be overcome, but not in the absence of commitment.

We who would help others to discipline their lives must be students of human nature, contemporary culture, and, most of all, the
timeless Word, which addresses the universal needs of mankind.

Wisdom

Though wisdom is not totally unrelated to knowledge, neither is
it synonymous with it. Wisdom has little to do with intelligence
quotient or educational attainment. The one with a Ph.D is not
necessarily more wise than he who has but an eighth-grade education or no formal education at all.

Wisdom, in the New Testament sense, is linked far more to a
recognition of dependence upon God than to human achievement.
All of us are equally admonished to ask God when wisdom is
lacking. Our request is based upon our helplessness and subsequent dependence. If offered in faith, it will be answered. God will
supply wisdom to those who seek it.

In the Proverbs, wisdom is exalted above all treasures. Surely,
we recognize its value in the sensitive area of personal discipline.
Rather than being frightened by what we don't know, let's increase
our dependence upon and cooperation with God. In so doing, He
will provide what we lack.

Objective

This writer's father sometimes accused him of talking just to
hear his head rattle. Perhaps the same accusation could be levied
against some teachers and youth coaches.

Do we ask ourselves why we teach what we teach? Does a noble purpose accompany our disciplinary admonitions? Justifying our words to ourselves might make them more plausible to our pupils.

Considering our objectives prior to discipline might also help us to avoid needless confrontation. That prohibition might be relaxed, and that unnecessary restriction lifted, when we consider our legitimate purposes.

Clarification

Misunderstandings accompany undue generalization and otherwise foggy communication. Our expectations will not be met if we fail to make them known. Many occasions for offense can be eliminated if we'll simply express ourselves.

"Be here early," "Drive safely," "Make the necessary arrangements," and, "Be prepared," are generalized and relative admonitions. It is necessary to be more precise. "Be here fifteen minutes before the meeting starts," or, "Keep your speed within the limit," are better instructions, and easier to enforce.

Our instructional task will be made more pleasant through our diligent attention to clarification of reasonable expectations.

Principles of Punishment

Understanding

Being certain of your ground before enacting punitive measures will enable you to avoid the regret of unjustly punishing an innocent child. Things are not always as they appear to be. Circumstantial evidence may or may not present an accurate picture of what has transpired.

Before punishing, be sure you understand the situation with which you are dealing. What is at issue here? What lessons need to be taught? What guidelines have been transgressed? Was discipline adequate or were expectations not properly clarified? How guilty is the child and of what?

Those who have punished an innocent child in spite of his protestations have learned a valuable lesson. The cost is great, however, both in terms of childish confidence violated and adult conscience pained. Action before understanding may result in great hurt to both parties.

Justice

Justice demands the proper consequences of a crime. Justice calls for a penalty commensurate with the violation.

Some childish misbehavior is far more damaging than other misbehavior. Some adolescent responses are far more significant than others. While much unacceptable behavior results from childish carelessness, thoughtlessness, or foolishness, some stems from defiance and disdain for authority. The latter is more serious.

Carelessness must be dealt with, but it doesn't merit the same attention as an act of willful defiance. Carelessness is not premeditated or intentional wrongdoing. It is accidental behavior stemming from a failure to discipline the mind.

Defiance, on the other hand, is a deliberate willful response. The defiant child refuses to acknowledge or respect the appointed authority and demands that external circumstances be conformed to his own desires. The eventual consequences of unrebuked defiance may be extremely detrimental to the individual and to those with whom he has to do.

Too many of us have a stock punishment employed in all situations requiring punitive action. How fair is this? How well-calculated is this approach in terms of meeting individual needs? Willful deception and deliberate defiance call for far more serious action than an overturned chair. Yet, because of the noise and disturbance of the chair upset in horseplay, some would punish the latter act far more severely than the former.

Justice demands that we understand the issues. If Johnny knocks over the offering tray with a careless swipe of his hand, the issue is carelessness. The issue remains the same if the item upset happens to be a priceless vase. Yet, we may punish Johnny far more severely because of our economic values, forgetting that the issue, in terms of his development, remains the same.

Severe punishments will be reserved for serious crimes in an equitable system of justice. Minor offenses will be corrected but in much less dramatic ways. Justice and abuses of justice will often be recognized by the young as well as by the mature.

Mercy

Mercy is the voluntary setting aside of justice. Mercy removes the penalty assessed for sin. God deals with His children according to the principle of mercy. Justice has been fulfilled in the death of Christ for our sakes. Mercy can be extended as a result.

When we are the recognized disciplinary authorities in our own limited spheres of influence, we, too, have the right to demonstrate mercy. There is lasting benefit in reaping just recompense for our deeds; so we should be sparing in doing away with justice.

There are times, however, when the demands of justice have already been fulfilled. Thus, mercy is in order.

Justice is exercised in the hope of teaching or reinforcing a necessary lesson in attitude or behavior. When the lesson has already been learned or reinforced, and repentance has already been prompted, there is little reason to bring further punishment to bear. Mercy is appropriate.

Sally has been warned not to climb across tables and tiptoe across chairs when the teacher's back is turned. She has been warned not only because of possible property damage, but particularly because of potential danger to herself. Sally, failing to profit from the discipline provided, transgresses once too often, falls, and breaks her wrist.

Discipline has been vindicated. The lesson has been vividly learned. Sally has suffered more dramatic consequences as a result of her disobedience than any the teacher might have brought to bear. There is little to be gained in further punishment. Her pain is sufficient. The purposes of justice have been fulfilled, and mercy is in order. Though certain consequences have been attached to such disobedience, they are not brought to bear in light of the consequences already suffered.

Consistency

Unenforced law becomes no law at all. Inconsistent application of disciplinary warnings will result in a lack of regard for the discipline, the authority by whom it is delivered, and the consequence assessed for its violation.

If we say we'll do something but don't do it, our students soon learn that we don't mean what we say. Wrongful exercise of mercy results in undisciplined behavior. Most often, justice is called for when behavioral expectations have been made clear.

Consistency is a goal for all who are in authority. We are most fair, most trustworthy, and most God-like when we faithfully keep our word. We must remember that the unpleasant punitive confrontation today teaches a valuable life-bettering or life-saving lesson for tomorrow. He who punishes justly, having disciplined adequately, is the child's friend, temporary childish complaints notwithstanding.

Objective

School yourself to ask this question, "Why am I punishing this child?" prior to the exercise of punishment. If your inward response is similar to one of these, "Because I want to produce excruciating pain," "Because he hurt me and I want him to hurt just as badly," "Because I'm so mad I've got to let him have it," or, "Because she has never been anything but trouble," you are punishing from a wrong motivation. The proper reason for all punishment is the welfare of the child. We punish because we love and because we want to aid in development of behavior patterns that will bring satisfaction to the individual and glory to God. Lesser motivations are inadequate and may be abusive.

If your goal and motivation are to help the child, the punishment will likely be well-considered and effective. Never punish without first asking yourself "Why?" Much regret will be spared through the development of this habit.

Pre- and post-punishment counsel

Children should not be left to wonder why they were punished. There should be no cause for speculation following the episode. The deviant should know what he has done wrong, why it is wrong, and why he has been punished as he has.

Discuss the situation with the child both before and after punishment is administered. Before, use the opportunity to reinforce your disciplinary objective and place responsibility rightfully upon the individual for the necessity of punishment of which he was forewarned. After, use the time to reassure the child of your love and concern. Show him your acceptance in spite of what has just taken place. Summarize the incident, close the chapter, and leave it closed.

God has graciously blotted our sins from His memory. We should do the same. Refuse to compile a subconscious ledger of infractions to be used against a young person at some future date when you can't stand it anymore. Deal with each episode as it occurs, close it, and forget it. The youth should know that he starts anew with you just as you have been permitted to begin anew with your Father.

Imperatives in Group Discipline

Love

Those who do not love youth should not work with youth. Apart from the motive of love, youth work can be abused and become an avenue for venting our own frustrations, feeding our egotism, or disguising our insecurities.

Love is the only adequate motive for all we do (1 Corinthians

13:1-3). The specific stimulus prompting us to youth ministry is love for young people and compassion for their situation. If we love, we will diligently strive to teach and reinforce lessons of benefit to the loved ones.

Individual attention

Disciplinary problems are individual in nature. Thus, they should be encountered individually. Though it often appears that we have a group problem, further insight will reveal that group unrest is fostered by individuals. Correction of the individual deviance will result in an undiminished group environment.

Problem people get lost in a sea of anonymity when rebuke is offered to the group at large. Though general correction has been given, it is too easy for the ringleader or catalyst to lose himself in the group. For that reason, he should be taken aside and addressed individually.

Rebuke in general may also backfire in another way. Those group members who are innocent of wrongdoing will resent being called down for what they neither approve of nor are involved in. As a result, even your cooperative members may be ill-disposed toward you. Nobody likes to be included in a negative confrontation when he is blameless in the matter.

If you are the sole teacher or coach, it probably will not be possible for you to leave the group unattended while you deal with a problem person. In that event, it will be necessary for you to make an appointment with Mr. Trouble after class. The preferred alternative, however, is to have an associate or assistant present with the class who is capable of taking a pupil aside and dealing with misbehavior while the group activity proceeds uninterrupted.

Exemplary life

Those who teach the gospel should practice it. Profession and demonstration go hand in hand. There is little credibility if we live in violation of our own doctrine.

There are no supermen, however. Our students will not be permanently damaged if somewhere along the way they become acquainted with our humanity. It might even be helpful to them to know that we, too, are finite, troubled, uncertain, and inconsistent. However, our goal should be to become more like our Master as we encourage our pupils in the same pursuit. His values should be enacted in our lives.

Recognized authority

We should not be unduly concerned with the arbitrary, the temporary, or the subjective. Our concern is with timeless truth and its application to our culture. We are convinced of the imperative of Biblical discipline, as opposed to Pharisaic intimidation, relativistic gobbledygook, or subjective rationalism.

The Bible is our guide. What God has revealed, we are determined to share. We know it to be in our best interest. Human joy and eternal hope hang in the balance. Our authority is exerted on the basis of the authority that resides in Christ. As we participate with Him, we participate in His authority. Apart from Him, we have no rightful authority.

Power to act

Those held accountable for doing a job must be given authority commensurate with their responsibility. Otherwise, how can they see to it that the job is properly done?

Those involved in educational administration should see to it that youth workers feel confident in the discharge of their duties. Our exalted purpose and the well-being of the whole cannot be sacrificed because of the deviant behavior of one child or one group of children—no matter whose children they happen to be, or how much their parents give, or what offices their parents occupy.

Teachers and coaches must be carefully selected and then faithfully supported as they endeavor to discipline children for their own betterment. They must not be coerced or threatened into abandonment of the task. While accepting responsibility for their own actions, they should be free to act without fear of negative repercussions with which they will have to deal alone.

Provide recourse for your people. If they have reached their wits' end or are in need of help in dealing with a difficult problem, provide a designated disciplinary authority to aid them. This may be an elder, the elders as a group, an administrator, or a group of administrators. Such recourse will assure your people that help is there when needed. Such assurance enables one to enjoy rather than endure ministry.

A Corrective Model

Behavioral deviance and improper attitudes can be manifested in innumerable ways. Whatever the nature of the problem, try this approach first.

Draw the individual aside. Explain the problem. Explain his contribution to the problem. Explain your objective, how its achievement is being hindered, and how it is too valuable to remain so. Then ask for his help.

Sound too simple? Perhaps. Yet consider the dynamics of the model. In employing the method, the teacher is recognizing the personality of the individual and showing personal concern. The deviant is given credit for ability to understand and act upon valid information. The individual is forced to confront the exalted purpose with which he is presently interfering. His help is requested. He is asked to align himself on the right side. He is made an advocate rather than an enemy. The situation becomes not "you versus me" but "you and I together so that all may profit."

One genius of the model is that it has application at all age levels. Through vocabulary adaptation and understanding of attention span and progressive cognition, students of all ages may be thus approached.

A second desirable feature is that the model permits free expression of love, concern, and confidence on the part of the disciplinary authority. The model will prove remarkably effective, primarily because very few people, young or old, can fail to respond positively to a genuine manifestation of love.

The model is not a miracle-worker. It will not solve all ills overnight. It will, however, bring the uncontrollable child into the realm of control, and will pave the way to progressive improvement if it is enacted by someone exercising the love and patience of Christ.

A third genius of the model is that it virtually compels individual acceptance of responsibility. Since it involves dialogue, the teacher is able to counter all the rationales and confront the deviant behavior.

Punitive Alternatives

Isolation

Some children manifest problematic behavior only in conjunction with certain other children or only when seated in certain ways. Separation from certain individuals, or, in extreme cases, from all other children, may immediately solve the problem. Persons may be seated by or between adult sponsors, or with children not disposed to encourage their misbehavior. Some children should not be seated behind others because of the temptation of mischief toward which they are predisposed.

Isolation in the sense of removal from the classroom will rarely, if ever, be necessary. More subtle forms of isolation from the elements leading to trouble will usually resolve such situations with a minimum of unpleasantry.

Utilization

Young people generally prefer doing to sitting. More active youngsters may create their own activity if none is provided for them. Many behavioral problems can be nipped in the bud by means of careful planning.

Project activities to occupy the children periodically on the basis of attention span. Long, uninterrupted lecture periods lend themselves to restlessness with its accompanying difficulty. In addition to group activity, plan to use your problem people in individual ways. Find ways in which they can assist you. Productive activity for which they are rewarded is a pleasant alternative to problematic activity for which they must be punished.

Humiliation

Should a child ever be publicly embarrassed? Most behavioral authorities would presently answer in the negative. Certainly, any such action should be taken only rarely and only with the greatest sensitivity. It is not a ploy to be used with the insecure or the newcomer.

Humiliation might possibly be used to give forcible reminder of what one already knows. This writer recalls from his young teen years a couple of humiliating experiences that precisely met the need of the moment. The striking reminder caused the deviant to reconsider his responsibilities and his proper example. Moved to repentance, he brought his will into conformity with that of the teacher.

Use extreme caution here. I suspect that this alternative is not appropriate for younger children. If there is doubt regarding its outcome, consider another option.

Deprivation

Depriving youngsters of valued privileges represents an acceptable mode of punishment. Proper behavior is rewarded by inclusion in desirable activities. Deviant behavior is punished by being withheld from the activity (e.g., denial of a teen's opportunity to go on a trip; refusal to give a cookie to a disobedient youngster). This is the corporate equivalent of the parental practice of grounding. Its effectiveness lies in the direct association of improper behavior and negative result. This is set in contrast to its opposite—proper behavior resulting in positive reward.

Corporal Means

Punishment producing physical pain or discomfort should be employed sparingly. Over-dependence on this method is probably indicative of disciplinary failure. Speculation regarding the benefits and detriments of corporal punishment abounds. For our purposes, suffice it to say that control by means of fear and physical intimidation alone is inadequate. On the other hand, the Bible recognizes the value of associating immediately painful consequences with foolish behavior.

Unnecessary use of force and child-beating has no place in the educational program of the church or elsewhere. However, sensitive use of corporal punishment, as needed, will produce good results. If discipline is properly exercised and relationship properly established, the extent of the punishment (in terms of pain produced) is immaterial. The reality of it, though pain inflicted is slight, is sufficient to temper the spirit and conform the will of the unruly child.

It is easy in a chapter of this sort to oversimplify and generalize. It is necessary to reemphasize that each case is individual in nature and must be dealt with accordingly. These suggestions emanate from the living schools of experience and observation. Properly applied, they will aid you in formulating a realistic program of discipline in the youth program.

Suggested Resources

Briscoe, Stuart. *Where Was the Church When the Youth Exploded?* Grand Rapids: Zondervan, 1972.

Dobson, James. *Dare to Discipline.* Wheaton, IL: Tyndale House, 1970.

Dobson, James. *Hide or Seek.* Old Tappan, NJ: Revell, 1974.

Dobson, James. *The Strong Willed Child.* Old Tappan, NJ: Revell, 1977.

Getz, Gene. *The Measure of a Family.* Ventura, CA: Gospel Light, 1976.

Giebler, Brian. *Promoting Spiritual Growth in Young People.* Tulsa: CIY, 1978.

Ginott, Haim G. *Between Parent & Child.* New York: Avon, 1965

Ginott, Haim G. *Between Parent & Teenager.* New York: Avon, 1969.

Havighurst, Robert J. *Developmental Tasks and Education.* New York: David McKay, 1972.

Hearn, Virginia. *What They Did Right.* Wheaton, IL: Tyndale House, 1974.

Knight, George W. *The Christian Home in the 70's.* Nashville: Broadman Press, 1974.

Mullen, Tom. *Parables for Parents and Other Original Sinners.* Waco: Word, 1975.

Narramore, Bruce. *A Guide to Child Rearing.* Grand Rapids: Zondervan, 1972.

Narramore, Bruce. *Help! I'm a Parent.* Grand Rapids: Zondervan, 1972.

Richards, Lawrence O. *Youth Ministry.* Grand Rapids: Zondervan, 1972.

Soderholm, Marjorie E. *Understanding the Pupil, Parts I, II, & III.* Grand Rapids: Baker, 1956.

Staton, Knofel. *Home Can Be a Happy Place.* Cincinnati: Standard, 1975. Revised under title, *Check Your Homelife,* 1984.

Tompkins, Iverna, and Irene B. Harrell. *How To Live With Kids and Enjoy It.* New York: Bridge, 1977.

Towns, Elmer. *Successful Biblical Youth Work.* Ventura, CA: Gospel Light, 1973.

Zuck, Roy B. & Clark, Robert E. *Childhood Education in the Church.* Chicago: Moody, 1975.

7

Planning and Conducting Effective VBS Programs

Eleanor Daniel

Vacation Bible School may have been around awhile, but in no way can it be described as a thing of the past. VBS is alive and well in those churches that appreciate its worth and give priority to its planning and execution. To this day, it has an amazing amount of outreach potential and life-changing force if it is given the opportunity.

Perhaps the earliest VBS program was developed in 1866 at First Church in Boston. The oldest program of record to be repeated in subsequent years was in 1898 at Epiphany Baptist Church in New York City. It is a documented fact that Eliza Hawes, the founder of that VBS, led seven "Everyday Bible School" programs. By the time she had finished the seventh, VBS had been introduced to the New York Baptist Society as a viable means of outreach and edification. It was only a matter of time before VBS became a part of the Christian education program of nearly every denomination and publisher.

VBS—Why?

VBS provides a time for concentrated day-by-day Bible study. As much instruction can be given in one week of VBS as usually occurs in thirteen weeks in Sunday school.

The outreach potential of VBS is powerful. Unchurched families more readily enroll their children in, and get them to, VBS than they do to Sunday school, and their children enjoy the variety of activity in VBS.

VBS is a helpful atmosphere in which adults may discover, use, and develop their special skills. It is a good place to assimilate new people into the ministry of the church, develop their confidence, and send them on to even more responsible ministries.

New ideas can be readily tried in VBS. It is an excellent place to introduce new organizational ideas, teaching techniques, and/or scheduling procedures. If the innovations work there, it is often easier to incorporate them into other programs. If they don't work well, the experiment is over in a week or two.

VBS also builds enthusiasm. Children enjoy good programs. Teachers talk about positive experiences. Unchurched people are attracted. Enthusiasm is the result.

VBS—How?

State Goals

Clearly defined goals must be established at the beginning of the planning process if the VBS is to be accomplished with the greatest efficiency. A major goal is outreach. VBS time is an excellent time to make new contacts that can then be followed up the remainder of the year.

A second major goal is effective Bible teaching. Bible truth must be taught in an interesting, life-challenging way.

Other goals may also be accomplished through VBS. Some congregations intend for VBS to reach entire families. Others have a missions' education goal. Yet others choose to place a heavy emphasis on recreation or crafts or music. All of these are legitimate concerns if evangelism and teaching are kept in primary focus.

Goal-setting is critical, and organizational patterns, curriculum, and publicity procedures must reflect that. Goals affect every other decision.

Determine Date and Time

Once goals have been developed, the next step is to determine the dates, time, and length of VBS. Usually VBS is scheduled during the summer, although a school vacation time would do as well. The exact time must be determined on the basis of church camp schedules, community activities (such as baseball, swimming, and summer school), congregational vacation patterns, and local weather conditions. No single date will avoid all conflicts, of course, but the wise VBS leader can avoid the major ones.

How long should VBS last? Patterns vary widely. Some churches still conduct a ten-day school, but many others have only five days. A few congregations have a morning and afternoon school for five days. Others conduct an eight-day program in one of three ways: four days each week for two weeks, five days the first week and three the second, or three days the first week and five days the second. A few churches build a day camp program in which they have their program one day a week for ten weeks.

The time of day for VBS varies from congregation to congregation as well. Most are conducted in the morning or evening, a few in the afternoon. The choice of time needs to be selected as the best time to accomplish your objectives.

Design an Effective Organization

Develop an organization with clear lines of communication, responsibility, and authority. Plan for enough organizational structure to do the job well—but stop there.

The goal is to provide personalized Bible teaching, not to exercise mob control. To do so requires careful planning and observance of generally accepted recommendations for space, age grouping, class size, and teacher/pupil ratio. The chart below will serve as a handy reference.

Space Per Pupil	Age Level	Class Size	Teacher/Pupil Ratio
30-35 sq. ft.	2-3	4-5	1/4-5
30-35 sq. ft.	4-5	5-6	1/5
25-30 sq. ft.	Grades 1-2	6-7	1/6-7
25-30 sq. ft.	Grades 3-4	6-7	1/6-7
25-30 sq. ft.	Grades 5-6	7-8	1/7-8
20-25 sq. ft.	Grades 7-8(9)	8-10	1/8-10
20-25 sq. ft.	Grades 9(10)-12	12-15	1/12-15
15-18 sq. ft.	Adults	30-35	1/30-35

This information will assist the director in making a projection of needed personnel and classes on the basis of expected enrollment.

Prepare a Planning Calendar

The VBS director should develop a planning calendar to which he will adhere as he prepares for VBS. This allows adequate time for each task along the way and covers every important point of preparation. A suggested time frame is listed on the next page.

Prior to 4 Months in Advance: Set goals; choose dates and time; order a sample curriculum kit; outline organizational plans; pray.

4 Months in Advance: Appoint department leaders, if needed; plan teacher training; plan missions project; plan closing program; meet with department leaders; pray.

3 Months in Advance: Recruit staff; order lesson and craft materials; begin publicity; pray.

2 Months in Advance: Distribute materials; train teachers; plan for pre-registration; plan follow-up; plan contest; plan transportation; continue publicity; pray.

1 Month in Advance: Complete supply and materials order; hold final staff meeting; continue publicity; recheck staff; conduct preregistration; pray.

Immediately Before VBS: Recheck details; arrange classrooms; pray.

During VBS: Pray for and with staff; secure additional supplies as needed; keep records.

After VBS: Express appreciation to workers; carry out follow-up program; store leftover supplies; return unused materials to the bookstore for credit; collect and tabulate evaluations; complete records; complete reports.

Recruit and Train Workers

The first step in recruitment is to know whom you need to carry out the VBS task. Begin by listing every job that needs to be done: music, missions, devotions, teaching, crafts, recreation, refreshments, transportation, publicity, closing program, secretarial, purchasing, and custodial. Then decide which jobs can be combined to be done by one person if necessary.

Decide exactly what each job entails so that the responsibility can be clearly communicated to would-be workers. It may be helpful to write these so they can be distributed to the staff.

Start the actual recruitment procedure by compiling a list of the staff for the last several years. Add Sunday-school workers, new members, college students, and perhaps high-school students. This provides a working list for recruitment.

Each prospective worker should be contacted personally, either via telephone or a home call. A simple recruitment form, like the one on the next page, will help to organize this task. Recruiters can then fill it out and the forms will provide a beginning point for the following year.

```
Name: _____

Address: _____

Contacted: _____ by _____

Will _____ Will not _____ work. Why? _____


Dept. Leader _____   Secretary _____   Provide Cookies _____
Teacher _____        Kitchen _____     Transportation _____
Co-Teacher _____     Storyteller _____ Address Mailings _____
Craft Leader _____   Puppets _____     Cut Out Visuals _____
Recreation _____     Missions _____    Other: _____ _____
Song Leader _____    Publicity _____
Pianist _____        Purchasing_____
```

Recruitment Form

This same form can be distributed in the church paper and Sunday bulletin a week or two before recruitment is to begin. The results will save time and get the recruitment effort off to a good start.

Some churches conduct a series of special VBS meetings to provide staff training and to permit group planning. Others leave training up to department leaders and conduct only one or two general staff meetings.

As a rule, a training session or two should be general in nature. These times are used to develop staff morale, inform workers of pertinent data (like space, dates, supplies, and missions), introduce the curriculum, and learn music.

Most sessions should be departmental in nature in which practical, curriculum-related training is done. Possible topics are age characteristics, discipline, learning activities, crafts, lesson planning, using materials creatively, teaching methods, memory work, and visuals. The number of sessions conducted depends upon the needs and experience of the workers.

Select Curriculum Materials

One of the most important steps in preparing for VBS is to select the curriculum materials that will best help carry out the objectives for VBS. The director may preview bits from those curriculum sources in which he is interested. He and department leaders, or a few key workers, should evaluate the materials and make a decision about which to use. These form the basis for much of the training program for VBS.

Plan a Workable Time Schedule

Every activity of the VBS day should be designed to accomplish the learning goals for that day. Any schedule should be built upon (1) the goals of the school, (2) the activities that are designed to accomplish the goals, (3) the age level for which it is designed, and (4) the facilities in which the VBS is conducted.

An important part of VBS is worship, the time of singing praises. A devotional thought and/or missions time may also be included. It may be best to have graded worship sessions in all but the smallest schools. This allows the selection of songs most suitable to the age level.

An adequate amount of time must be included for Bible study. The actual amount of time varies from age level to age level. Most programs could profit from a one-hour teaching session to allow time to use learning centers as well as Bible information and life application.

Expressional activities are uniquely a part of VBS. But crafts and other activities should contribute directly to the goals for VBS and/ or the learning goals for the day. This section need not be limited to crafts either. A variety of other options are available: music, puppets, VBS Store (where the pupils do curriculum-related tasks to gain VBS dollars which may then be spent in the VBS Store), or special features.

Recreation and refreshment time is important to provide a change of pace. This time segment should be kept short. Even the games can be correlated with the lesson goals for the day.

Not every age level need follow exactly the same schedule. Some time segments may have to be planned in common, but others can be altered to meet the needs of the group.

Publicize

Find a publicity chairman who will select a committee to plan and implement a promotional program that informs the prospective audience about VBS. A good program begins early and outlines week-by-week activities to promote VBS both within the congregation and in the community.

Plan a Closing Program

The closing program provides an opportunity to demonstrate to parents and church members what has been accomplished during VBS. It need not be elaborate, but it should reflect what happened.

Several guidelines will assist you in planning an effective closing program.

1. Plan early and let the staff know what you are doing.
2. Keep the program brief—sixty minutes or less.
3. Use all pupils in the program, usually in group presentations.
4. Send out special invitations to parents.
5. Use youth to usher and receive the offering.
6. Have preschool children return to their classrooms with their teachers or sit with their parents after their part in the program.
7. Explain the purpose for the offering.
8. Include a few minutes in the program for the minister to share with the audience.

Plan for Follow-up

Several areas of follow-up should be planned if the VBS program is to preserve the results of VBS.

1. *Materials.* Unused materials should be returned to the bookstore for credit, and leftover materials should be stored for future use.
2. *Records.* Complete all records and store them for future use. Write any required reports.
3. *Pupils.* New contacts should be nurtured through personal calling. These individuals may be enrolled for camp and other church programs.
4. *Staff.* Thank all workers by letter or church paper or other form of recognition. Suggest effective new workers to be Sunday-school teachers or youth coaches.
5. *Evaluation.* Have the staff fill out evaluation forms. Then tabulate them and make plans for correcting problems and enhancing strength.

Summary

VBS is an effective ministry, one that requires careful planning if it is to achieve what it can. The planning steps are reasonably simple: state goals, determine date and time, design an effective organization, prepare a planning calendar, recruit and train workers, select curriculum materials, plan a workable time schedule, publicize, plan a closing program, and plan for follow-up. Good hard work will reap the harvest.

Suggested Resources

Cox, William. *Ideas for VBS Promotion*. Nashville: Convention Press, 1978.

Daniel, Eleanor. *The ABC's of VBS: How It Can Work For You*. Cincinnati: Standard Publishing, 1984.

Daniel, Eleanor; Charles Gresham, and John Wade. *Introduction to Christian Education*. Cincinnati: Standard Publishing, 1980.

Freese, Doris A. *Vacation Bible School*. Wheaton, IL: Evangelical Teacher Trainer Association, 1977.

Self, Margaret. *How to Plan and Organize Year-Round Bible Ministries*. Glendale, CA: Gospel Light, 1976.

8

Teaching Youth to Discover the Bible for Themselves:
Developing a Commitment to Bible Study

Mike Farra

Maybe you are like me. I am forever walking into the local Christian bookstore and looking for the book to leap out and grab me. You know, *How to Get Your Youth Group to Be Thoroughly Committed to the Bible in Just Three Short Months,* or your money back! But that book doesn't exist, and even if it did, I would be more than a little skeptical. Why? Because commitment is not designed to happen that way. Developing commitment to God's Word in young people is a difficult task. There are no easy answers, quick plans, or fool-proof solutions. What we face is the incredible responsibility of creating a structure by which young people can see, hear, understand, respond to, be saturated with, and be completely changed by God's Word. And nothing short of that will do.

The purpose of this chapter is not to provide the blueprint of an infallible program, but rather to share some thoughts on the problems we face and the lessons I've been learning in my continuing struggle to lead the people I work with to a deep, functional commitment to God's Word, both individually and as a group.

Before we focus on creating a strategy for your group, may I challenge you to ask yourself these questions:

"What do I really believe about the Bible?" We say the Bible is our only rule of faith and practice, but do our ministries show it? Do you believe the Bible is the infallible, authoritative record of what God wants humanity to know? Does the Bible have anything relevant to say to the people of today? May your answer be a resounding yes to each of these.

"Am I committed to a personal study of God's Word?" The hunger and thirst that is continually being cultivated in our lives through the regular study of God's Word is infectious. Have you found a way of existing in ministry without it? Does your weekly schedule reflect an unswerving commitment to time alone in the Word, or is it one of those things that gets pushed aside in favor of those things deemed "more urgent." We can never expect young people to function in a way that we are unwilling to.

"Do I reflect as much excitement about the study of God's Word as I do about the programs I run?" Sometimes we get so excited about all the "stuff" we do, we inadvertently communicate to kids that the study of God's Word is not nearly as important as all the *fun* things.

"Am I becoming more and more like Christ?" We believe that what is contained in Scripture is adequate to change a person, and that through its study and through obedience to what it says, we are brought about to conformity to the image of God's Son. Are our lives genuine evidence of that truth, or are we giving young people confusing messages as they critically investigate our lives?

Why Kids Have a Hard Time With Bible Study

Media

We are dealing with a generation of youth who are uninspired readers. The excitement of video games, unlimited television and movie programming (including music television), and home computers certainly makes reading "pale" in comparison.

Schoolwork

Sitting in class or doing homework does not rank high on the thrill meter for the majority of kids. Unfortunately, most Bible study seems to be accepted in much the same way.

Leisure Time

Young people of today are faced with unending choices of what to do with their free time. A commitment to Bible study is often in competition against sports leagues, school clubs, or the never-ending pursuit of a fun time with friends.

They Don't Know How to Study

We have not been diligent enough in providing our young people with good methods of Bible study on their level and have just expected them to do something they are not capable of doing.

Few Role Models

Do the adults that work with our young people have a commitment to God's Word that is worth imitating? Or is their lack of commitment being mirrored in the lives of the kids they serve?

We Have Made It Dull

"Fun's over! It's time to study...." Most of us work ourselves into the ground to plan "great" socials, "super-special" nights, and "incredible" retreats, but are we as committed to excellence in study and preparation for our group studies and Sunday-school lessons so that the kids are well-fed and encouraged to seek the Lord through His Word?

Guilt

This is possibly Satan's most deceptive yet powerful tool for rendering believers ineffective. We expect our young people to be committed to the Word; we tell them if they don't study and pray, they won't mature; and when they fail, we usually find a way to communicate our disappointment in them. The usual result of such a procedure is guilt, nothing that motivates the kids to change, but a paralysis of the will that keeps them from doing even those things they *know* they should.

Learning Disabilities

Even though this is the day of high-technology and sophisticated educational programs, we seem to have a growing number of teenagers who have come thorough the system without even the basic reading or comprehension skills.

Each of these problems, as well as others that may be unique to the group you shepherd, *must* be confronted if we are ever going to move the group closer to an appreciation of God's Word that will motivate them to study it.

Getting Into the Action

The following is a variety of suggestions given to stimulate your thinking, evaluate what you're doing in this area, and help you create the strategy your group needs for personal and group study.

Be Fresh

Give the youth the ideas that excite you in your own personal study. As you invest your time in the Word, always be thinking of how it can spill over into the lives of those you lead.

Be Creative

Beware of trying to put a program for study into use just because someone else says it is a great idea. Instead, use that idea to stimulate your thinking to develop strategies *your* group can use.

Sharing
Let the kids share what they are learning from their personal study or group studies. Encourage them to share study ideas, and give them time to do it in large group meetings.

Buy Study Books
There are dozens of personal Bible-study notebooks, ideabooks, and methods manuals on the market. I recommend that you buy as many as your budget will allow and read them thoroughly. Good ideas will flow!

Teach Methods
Take every opportunity to teach your kids new methods of study (gathered from your reading). Not all of them will work, but maybe one of them will be just what one of the kids needs.

Define Terms
Make sure you and your kids know the difference between Bible reading, devotional reading, quiet time, meditation, memory work, and Bible study. The differences between them are critical.

Translations
Always read from a Bible with language your kids understand, and explain the words that are confusing. Teach them the differences between translations, revisions, and paraphrases.

Variety in Texts
Many church families encourage all of their people to have the same type of Bible. This can be good, but there can also be advantages in having a variety of texts. This facilitates questions and good dialogue about what the Bible *really* says and means. Encourage each of your young people to purchase a Bible with which they are comfortable.

Focus on a Few
Not all of the kids in your group will leap when you start to stress Bible study. Find a few and pour yourself into them, and maybe their excitement can spread.

Original Languages
Well-chosen insights from the original languages can stimulate some thought and interest in the Bible that otherwise might be absent. Give elective classes in beginning Greek or Hebrew to kids that show an interest. Don't neglect the originals in your own personal study either!

Small Groups
Use small groups as focal points for accountability in personal study. The encouragement of a group of people going in the same direction can do wonders.

Rewards

A reward system for developing study habits (i.e., prizes for completed memory work) *can* be profitable for younger kids as long as you are not building a false dependency on the extrinsic motivation. Head them toward intrinsic motivation.

Old Testament

Don't neglect the study of the Old Testament. It is not only rich with stories of faith and commitment, but is also the indispensable companion to a proper understanding of the New Covenant.

Publicity

Don't "overpublicize" the events and don't "underpublicize" study. Make the study of God's Word an *event* by always keeping its importance before the kids.

Midweek Study

Begin a midweek Bible study for each of the different age groups you work with. Don't be afraid to try early morning or late afternoon studies, either! You don't *have* to use up another night.

Extra Bibles

Always have extra Bibles on hand in case kids show up without them. This is very simple, but is often overlooked.

Bringing Bibles

Stress to your young people the importance of their bringing their own Bibles to all assemblies and retreats. Remind them! Admonish them! Teach them! Consistent encouragement in this area can reshape thinking and create new habits.

Vary Your Study

Make your Sunday-school lessons and Bible studies interesting by varying the ways you present God's Word to your people. Jesus used different methods—and He's the master teacher we are seeking to imitate.

Teach Inductive Study

Self-discovery is the key to excitement in personal study. Teach your young people the skills necessary to study the Bible and let it speak for itself. If you are unfamiliar with the inductive method of Bible study, most personal Bible-study books on the market will teach it with minor variations in their approaches. Train the kids to ask questions and seek answers.

Bible-study Tools

Acquaint your young people with Bible dictionaries, handbooks, concordances, commentaries, and Bible-study helps of all kinds. Give classes and electives to teach them to use these tools frequently and intelligently.

Writing Lessons

Create Sunday-school lessons that exploit inductive study skills. Encourage your kids to search the Scriptures personally and extract what it says *before* you lead them to what it means.

Bible History

Teach them about how we got our Bible, text transmission, archeological findings, and the canon, as well as the problems we face as serious Bible students.

Book Studies

Study whole books of the Bible. Teach your young people the value of studying Scripture passages in context.

Hermeneutics

Teach the youth the science of interpretation. Lead them to know the differences between interpreting the Bible literally, historically, figuratively, culturally, devotionally, and *casually!*

Supporting Answers

Encourage the kids toward learning to support their answers Biblically. There is always a time and place for opinion and feeling, but the goal is *Biblical* mindsets and behavior. If they cannot support their answers from the Bible, gently point out what the Bible says and how it compares to their insights. Don't be afraid of conflict. Your noticeable commitment to God's standards will minister to your kids and establish a pattern they can depend on.

Key Passages

Make sure your group knows how to locate key verses of Scripture dealing with guilt, forgiveness, fellowship, suffering, power over sin, peace, self-image, and the like. Have your group compile a list and then use that list to make a handout for them to carry in their Bibles so they can locate the passages easily.

Through-the-Bible

Implement a program to read through the Bible in a year for any kids that are interested. Many different programs are available.

Paraphrase

Write your own contemporary paraphrase of a chapter or book of the Bible. Publish it for the entire group or church family.

Cults

Learn how cults and different religious groups view the Bible and contrast it to what we believe.

Interviews

Give your kids tape recorders and have them go into public places and ask people what they believe about the Bible. List the problems and help them formulate intelligent responses.

Memory Work

Although it may seem too juvenile to some, it is important that young believers learn the books of the Bible in order so that they feel comfortable and confident when asked to turn to a particular book. Also, there are many new Bible memory programs and methods on the market. Become acquainted with them and suggest them to young people that are hungry for the Word.

Note Taking

Do your best to teach your kids the basic skills of note taking. Educators have known for years that we have a much better retention rate if we write things down as we listen, compared to listening passively.

Retreats

Utilize a weekend or overnight retreat to teach an aspect of personal or group Bible study.

Stress Application

Teach your kids to ask the question, "So what am I supposed to do now?" at the end of each study. Help them to make decisions at the end of each study, no matter what kind of study they are involved in.

Current Issues

Do not divorce current issues from Bible study. Make your studies relevant and contemporary, showing that Jesus is the Lord of the twentieth century, and not just the first.

Personal Study Plan

Have one or two personal Bible-study plans available at all times for any kids that want to begin a personal Bible study and ask you for help. Offer plans that have worked for you in the past or ones you sense would work for them.

Remember, these are only suggestions to simulate your thinking or motivate you to action. With some diligence in preparation and creativity in strategy, new priorities in your group can be established regarding the study of God's Word. Your group will begin to tap its transforming power.

Watching Your Step

Although there is nothing more important than leading your group to a commitment to God's Word, there are definitely some hazards in this pursuit and some pitfalls to avoid. Because Bible study of any kind deals with our intellect, young people become very susceptible to a particular kind of arrogance. When we teach them skills to study for themselves and encourage them to personalize the Scriptures, we run the risk of creating "know-it-all" attitudes and an unhealthy independence.

Sometimes we are guilty of teaching the kids that the really mature Christian will study and pray, and that the amount of time spent in these activities is the measuring stick of maturity. We must always remember that even though we want them to study and pray in increasing amounts and quality, Scripture never measures spiritual greatness and maturity by these disciplines. According to Scripture, ministry is the sign of maturity. Is the time spent in study and prayer producing a servant's heart and the fruit of the Spirit, or is the young person remaining unchanged?

Too often we are content if we know someone has satisfied the requirement of studying twenty minutes a day for two weeks in a personal Bible study or if we had a great Bible study with lots of kids, stimulating dialogue, and a load of fun. Our goal *should* be to increase the amount and quality of service rendered to others in the name of the Savior *as a result* of time spent in the Word. Beware! Legalistic requirements are devastating to a life of faith, even though they are much easier to stipulate and evaluate. Creating an atmosphere that fosters excellence and purpose in study and encourages loving service as the ultimate outcome is much more difficult. But the price must be paid!

There is always a danger that a focus on Bible study can produce a what's-in-it-for-me attitude in some. That is unhealthy and self-centered. Consistent shepherding on the part of the leader can overcome this by sniffing out the attitude, helping the guilty to recognize it, and working with them to change it.

Do your best to avoid forcing an idea or plan on your kids when they obviously aren't interested. This suggestion may not apply in every area of youth programming, but it certainly does here. It is important that we do our best to help kids fall in love with God's Word, and not create in them an attitude of indifference.

We must walk the delicate line between not pushing our kids hard enough and requiring more of them than they are capable of producing. Know your group well by knowing individual aptitudes and mindsets. Set high standards for study and ministry, but always let the Good Shepherd be your example of leadership.

Be a model of excellence in study, both personally and as you teach the flock God has given you. Be diligent as you give the young people you lead the structure by which they can be enriched with God's Word, learn the tools to handle it correctly, and cultivate the servant life-style it demands.

9

Social Activities
and Recreation
(Youth Ministry's
Fun and Games Department)

Roger Worsham

Perhaps you are thinking, "Why include a whole chapter on social activities?" After all, anyone can throw a party. Or someone might say, "What possible way could a social activity help me make real disciples out of the kids in my youth group?" (as if real disciples don't indulge in the carnality of fun activities). "Let's give more space to spiritual stuff like discipleship and evangelism." I am convinced social and recreational activities can be invaluable tools in reaching unsaved young people and developing maturity and leadership in the Christian young people.

At a retreat designed to welcome the graduating high-school seniors into the college group, I asked our college-group officers to share their spiritual advice for graduating seniors. As high-schoolers approach graduation, they hear the same old advice from family members, school counselors, teachers, commencement speakers, and many others; so I could hardly wait to hear what our officers felt was the most important advice for the spiritual life of the new college freshmen. They shared things like the importance of Bible study, being committed, and having a support group. But one thing surprised me. One of the sharpest guys in our group said, "Be sure you go to the Sunday-night social activities after the evening service." This guy is as warm and friendly as they come, and what surprised me was the reason he put so much emphasis on the Sunday-night socials. He said that when he came to the group, he thought we were a cold group at first. The Bible studies were good, but there was never enough time to get to know people. It was the social activity where his needs for fellowship began to be met. I hate to think that we might have lost this exceptionally sharp fellow because our Bible-study format didn't give him a chance to break into the group. Because of his testimony, I am all the more persuaded of the need for social activities in youth work. No doubt about it! Fun and games can be, and ought to be, a part of the "spiritual stuff" your youth ministry is made of.

A Sense of Balance

There are two key attitudes to successful, meaningful, and productive youth socials. The first one is balance. You must understand that while fun activities play an important role in the spiritual nature of youth ministry, your whole ministry cannot be built on the kind of activities that we will be discussing in this chapter. There has to be a balance of prayer meetings, Bible studies, retreats, small groups, leadership training, and social activities. For a long time, the youth ministry model held up as the ideal was all fun and games. Youth work went like this: lots of hype, get people excited, make people laugh, pack people in, and, before the excitement fades, announce the next outrageous event. If Kool-Aid, Keebler Cookies, and the Rent-a-Clown companies had gone out of business—youth ministries would have crumbled, and youth ministers would have hit the streets, scrambling for all the available jobs as life-insurance salesmen.

In most cases, youth ministry has matured since the days of all fun and games. However, for a while it looked as if the pendulum was going to swing too far in the other direction, to the point where socials had a bad name and fun was a dirty word in youth work. This extreme promoted the idea that fun and enjoyable events couldn't mix with spiritual objectives. While others might not go that far, they would still hold the view that socials "profiteth little" toward the goal of Christian maturity.

All fun and games and no fun and games are both extremes. There has to be a middle ground! Socials and recreational events need to be included in your youth work, but they must be part of a balanced approach to youth ministry. The rest of this chapter may help you decide where the balance is, but that decision will ultimately be determined by your group's personality, the kind of church or community you work in, and your own convictions.

A Sense of Purpose

The second key attitude in having successful and meaningful socials is that every social event has to have an objective! You have to know the purpose of each activity you plan. Otherwise, you will spend lots of valuable time and energy, not to mention those precious dollars in the youth budget, without accomplishing anything.

I accepted a position as a part-time youth minister on weekends while I was in Bible college. On my second Sunday at the church, the kids in the youth group rushed up after class and all began asking, "When's the next party? When are we going to have a hayride? Can we have a pizza party? When can we . . . ?" and their list went on and on. It was like a session on how to plan a twelve-month youth calendar in five minutes or less. The kids were saying, in effect, "We want to have some fun around here. These are the things we want to do—and we expect you to deliver." And because I wanted them to like me, and because I was inexperienced, I began scheduling the things they wanted. It was months later when this weary youth worker, on the verge of burnout, began to question, "What am I doing, and why am I doing this?" What are your social activities accomplishing? My conclusion was, "Not much!" My calendar was full, but we were going nowhere!

I decided not to throw out the activities, but to give them meaningful objectives—use them as tools in reaching different goals. Perhaps you can keep up the youth group's fifteenth annual tradition by making a few changes and giving it a new purpose.

Spiritual Objectives

For those who are wondering what could possibly be spiritual about car rallies, banana nights, and "come as you will be" socials, here are several good reasons for having social and recreational activities. These are the spiritual objectives your activities should be aimed at reaching.

Evangelistic Outreach

Socials are a great tool in youth evangelism. There are volumes of books filled with ideas for clean, fun activities. Many of these activities will have a tremendous appeal to the kids in your youth group and to their non-Christian friends. Social events are an excellent way to expand your youth group's influence among the non-Christians in your community. In fact, most of our socials are aimed at reaching non-Christians. Our socials are not really for the young people in the church—they are for the outsiders.

So when a young person comes up to me and says, "When are we going to have our next all-nighter?" I am ready for him! I say, "Why would we want to have another one of those?" He says, "Because they're fun!" My response is, "Is it my job to entertain you guys?" With a surprised look he says, "No, I guess not."

Then I take that young person aside and explain that my job is to help him reach his non-Christian friends for Christ, and I show him how an all-nighter can help him reach his friends. Then we can begin planning the next all-nighter.

Most young people need something like a good fun social to help them reach their friends. Going to church is the last thing in the world that the average secular high-school student wants to do. Can't you just see it, a hard-core party type saying to a Christian kid on campus, "Go ahead, make my day! Invite me to your Bible study!" They just are not that interested. Not because they've tried Bible study and didn't like it, but because of a negative wall they've built up. Often, when our young people share their faith on their campuses, they are turned off as soon as they get started. And it's not because our young people have a rotten testimony or use poor methods of evangelism. Our youth are not getting much response because most secular students have a wall built up against Christianity before they ever really hear the gospel. Usually, these walls are made up of some false ideas and false presuppositions about what it means to be a Christian, what the church is all about, or even who Jesus is. So as soon as our kids bring up Christianity with their friends, boom—all these walls go up.

Therefore, we design social activities as a tool to break down the walls that our kids come up against as they witness. A non-Christian comes to a social and he has fun. He thinks, "It is possible to be a Christian and have fun after all!" Off comes the top layer of the wall. He gets introduced to the fellowship and meets some friendly people and he thinks, "Not every Christian is a nerd—they are not all stiff-necked and straight-laced and cross-eyed. There are some super people in this group." CRASH! Down comes another layer of the wall. Not only does he meet people, but he begins to feel accepted by the youth at the church social, and is included as a part of the group. He begins to think, "Here is a genuine caring group where I can be myself and not worry about a power struggle or keeping up an image. I feel accepted." Down comes one more layer of the wall. The night ends with a prayer time or a devotion given by one of the students, and he senses that these people really are serious about their faith. They aren't phonies. We are starting to get through to him. At this point, if he's invited to Bible study or if he hears the gospel, he's more open. We have removed some barriers and created some interest and introduced him to a warm and loving fellowship. The goal of the social was not to entertain church kids or keep them off the streets. The purpose was to provide an activity that the youth group could use as a tool to reach their non-Christian friends. When your group catches that vision, your social event will come alive with a whole new meaning.

Returning Strays

Every group has what we might call fringe kids or strays. Look over your attendance roster or mailing list; you will probably see the names of a number of kids who are not around most of the time. They are still part of your group, but they rarely attend group meetings and activities. For some youth ministers, this group is easy to write off. I still want to keep in contact with them, however, hoping they won't completely drift away or cut themselves off from Christian fellowship. Therefore, I want to have some activities that I know will appeal to them. They may not attend Sunday school or Mid-week Bible study, or go on our retreats, but I think if I can have at least three or four activities a year when they'll come out, I'm all for it. These young people must be reached.

Chances are, these stray young people might be the children of some very active Christian parents. I know if they were my own children, I wouldn't want the folks running the youth program to give up on them. Often, I hear youth workers who complain about all the people that turn out for youth group socials, but don't show up regularly for Bible study. Of course, everyone wants them to be plugged into as many youth activities as possible, but I'll take what I can get. Perhaps some of these kids are not a regular part because no one in the group has reached out to them, or they've been turned off by a clique within the group. My hope for each social activity is to get them back one more time so that someone will latch on to them. Or maybe something will be said that will make them more interested in our Bible study. It is always possible that God has done something in their lives since I saw them last that has made them ready for a stronger commitment. Because you never know what it will take to make a flaky kid turn into a solid disciple, you just keep planning social events so the stray kids will return to check out the group one more time. Every time they return, they are giving you, your youth, and the other leaders one more chance to reach them.

Building Fellowship

Socials also help promote close fellowship. Back in my more idealistic days as a student, I studied the Greek word for fellowship, *koinonia,* and I decided that the level of relational interaction that took place at youth socials was nothing like New Testament *koinonia.* So I wrote socials off and said, "You can't have a social and call that fellowship." But, after being in the trenches of youth work for a while, and living with young people, I have found that I will never have New Testament fellowship if I don't relate to the kids on a lighter level as well. Fun activities serve as a starting point for developing meaningful relationships.

The guys in our college group with whom I have the closest friendship are the guys that I clown around with, play racquetball with, and generally have fun with. Two of the most responsive guys that I've been discipling love to wrestle, and we have often wrestled together—even in my office! I cherish my friendship with these guys. I can share anything with them. Now they are sponsor-leaders in the college group. I am convinced that we would never have had the depth of friendship we now have if I had not also shared with them on the lighter level. The fun we had enhanced our friendship and camaraderie.

The same need exists on a larger group level. If there are going to be genuine soul-baring relationships, there must also be the lighter side. Socials help build fellowship within your group by providing an atmosphere for young people to interact with other group members, new people, visitors, and adult leaders on the important lighter level.

Leadership Training

Socials are great opportunities for task-oriented leadership training. Too many youth workers plan and execute every activity for their group. Other youth workers involve their young people in getting ideas, but they leave all the scheduling and details to responsible adult leaders. Both of these patterns can give you an effective social, but there are a couple of downfalls to the adult-run social. First of all, it's harder to promote because you must first convince the group you have a good idea before they will go out and invite their friends. All it takes for your great plans to go down the drain is for one of the leaders in the group to say, "That's a dumb idea." Second, if the activity bombs, it's the adult leader's fault. The third and the major problem with adult-run social activities is the lost opportunity to involve youth.

Young people, junior-high through college, are capable of handling responsibility. Here are the benefits of youth-run activities. You don't have to sell them on it when it's their idea. They will work to see it happen, and they'll invite their friends. Second, they know that if it bombs, all the blame rests with them; therefore, they won't let it bomb. When young people feel an activity is really *their* activity, there will be a great change in their attitude. Whether an activity is a bomb or a blast is mainly determined by the attitude of the people participating.

However, the main reason for youth-led activities is the potential for leadership development. Being put in charge of planning and executing a social activity provides the youth an opportunity to use their talents, gifts, and skills in ministry. It gives you the opportunity to work alongside them. In other words, it gives you a good excuse to spend extra time with your student leaders as you coach them in completing their tasks. They get on-the-job training and a chance to spend quality time with you.

Here are the kinds of responsibilities that can be turned over to young people:

a. Making arrangements for transportation: recruiting parents, reserving the bus, or finding a bus driver.

b. Production and distribution of publicity: mailers, handouts, posters, phone calls, and other means.

c. Decorations.

d. Devotions: write out a five- to ten-minute message or find a speaker. Having young people give the devotion is a great way to stretch their faith and build confidence. For them to stand up for what they believe in front of their peers is a major accomplishment.

e. Refreshments: shopping or recruiting volunteers to bring the needed food, paper goods, and serving utensils.

f. Making reservations at the Y.M.C.A., bowling alley, skating rink, or wherever your event will be held.

g. Planning and leading games, skits, and activities and taking care of all the necessary props and equipment.

h. Cleanup.

i. Writing thank-you notes to leaders, volunteers, hosts, and others.

Involving kids may be a lot more work, and sometimes worry; but in the long run, it's better for you and them, because you let them share in the ministry. They realize the confidence you are placing in them when you give them important responsibilities. It makes them feel important and useful, and you are going a long way in helping them develop a proper attitude towards service.

With this understanding of the role of socials in your total youth program, you can grab a number of books that are loaded with ideas for socials and games. Some of these are listed in the "Suggested Resources" at the end of this chapter.

Types of Socials

There are many ways to categorize social events; I like to use the terms *major social* and *minor social*. A *major social* is a big event that you would do about four times a year, or at the most once every six weeks. This is the kind of event where you pull out all the stops, send out publicity to the four corners of the earth, and plan three months to six months in advance.

It might include events like a hayride and cookout, a luau, a New Year's all-nighter, an international progressive dinner, or a car rally. These activities involve two hours or more, and are, therefore, the kinds of things you would do on a Friday or Saturday night (if it's done during the school year). The key to major social events is plan ahead! Go over every detail. Think it through ahead of time and make a check-list, otherwise you'll get a late start and you'll have a bunch of kids showing up with nothing to do but run around getting into things while you try to get your act together. Even worse is having the whole event bomb because of poor planning. Patching up a damaged reputation earned because an event bombed because of disorganization and poor planning is extremely difficult. The number-one rule with socials is plan ahead! The number-two rule is start on time and end on time. Maintaining a good reputation with parents and kids is crucial.

Minor socials are activities involving less preparation, are a little easier to pull off, and involve two hours or less in actual time. They include activities like roller skating, going out for pizza, bowling, and swimming in someone's backyard pool. These are activities that can be worked into the youth calendar almost anywhere, like Saturday afternoon, after a ball game, after a Sunday-night service, or before Bible Study. These tend to be more fellowship activities while the major socials are almost all for the sake of outreach. I like to look over the whole year and plan a balance of one major event for every four to six minor socials.

Another way to categorize types of socials is what I call "prefab socials" and "do-it-yourself socials." Pre-fab socials are activities where the major attraction already exists and all you really need to do is schedule it, publicize it, and haul the group to it. These are activities like miniature golf, bowling, ice skating, go-carting, and going to water slides, ball games, concerts, pizza places, ice cream places, amusement parks, racquetball clubs, rodeos, the zoo, the beach, or the lake.

Unless you have to travel great distances, these are much easier to plan. They require little advance preparation, and so they are very good alternatives to fall back on when another event has to be cancelled.

There are some disadvantages to these activities. They may be too far away and require too much travel time, or they may be too close and therefore not special because the kids have already been there 128.6 times. Often the pre-fab social is more expensive than the social you do yourself. You also need to consider how much interaction you want to happen. Pre-fab socials tend to spread the kids out too thin to get to know anyone (like a trip to an amusement park, where everyone goes a different direction), or they may be too spectator-oriented (like going to a concert).

Do-it-yourself socials can be either major events or minor events. They are activities in which you create the main attraction by developing a theme, like "Nerd Night," where everyone comes dressed as out-of-style as possible. Or have a "Hawaiian Night": have everyone dress Hawaiian, decorate the place to look Hawaiian, play Hawaiian music, and serve Hawaiian food. (By the way, any food can be made Hawaiian in one or more of three ways: first, cover it with Teriyaki Sauce; if that doesn't work, dump pineapple on it; and if that doesn't work, wrap a lei around the dish and serve it anyway!) Then you could top off the night with relay games with coconuts or bananas, followed by a surfing movie.

Other theme events include:

—*Sadie Hawkins Night,* with hillbilly dress, wheelbarrow relays, barnyard games, hillbilly music, and hillbilly food.

—*Come As You Will Be,* with everyone dressed as he thinks he will look twenty years from now. We had some kids come dressed in their parent's clothes or dressed according to the career they were planning on. One fellow came as a skid-row bum! This is a good night to talk about preparing for the future, the end of time, or the uncertainty of tomorrow.

Almost anything can be used to build a theme; then adapt food, games, and dress to go with the event. Use nationalities, fruit (like *Banana Night* or *Watermelon Night,*) or animals (like *Zoo Night, Pet Night,* or *Pig Night).* Let your imagination go wild, as long as it's safe, affordable, and in good taste. Another type of do-it-your-self social is the food event. These are activities like *pizza parties* (make a giant pizza, build your pizza, or serve individual pizzas), *make a thirty-foot banana split* (use a rain gutter for the 30' dish), *have an eight-foot burrito* (made by overlapping flour tortillas on a 8' x 6" x 1" board), *pot smuck dinner* (have everyone bring a can of soup and a salad ingredient, then mix the soups into one pot and the salad ingredients into one big bowl—invariably someone brings a can of cream of asparagus), *barbeques, picnics, progressive dinners,* and *special banquets.*

The best activity that we use once a year for junior-highers and high-schoolers is the *all-nighter.* It is for hard-core dedicated youth workers only. This social lasts twelve hours, from 7 P.M. to 7 A.M. We go all night long from one activity to another without sleep. It gets a little rough after 4 A.M., but we never fail to have more visitors and a bigger attendance than for any other social. It is especially appealing to junior-highers, because staying up all night is a big thrill for them. In their minds, staying up all night is an adult privilege. Every youth worker needs to try an all-nighter at least once. Here's a sample schedule:

JR. HIGH END-OF-SCHOOL ALL-NIGHTER

7:00 P.M.	Start taking money, $7.00 per person.
7:15 P.M.	Welcome visitors and fill out visitor registration cards and name tags.
7:25 P.M.	Go over the night's agenda and rules.
7:30 P.M.	Get on the bus and drive to Camelot (57 Freeway South to 91 Freeway East, exit on Glassel).
7:45 P.M.	Roller skating (2 hours).
9:45 P.M.	Leave Camelot and head for Kartopia (91 to 55 South to 5 South. Take the first exit—Newport Ave.—turn left, go under freeway, and turn right on Laguna Road).
10:15 P.M.	Ride Go-Karts (1 hour).
11:15 P.M.	Load up and head for the church.
11:45 P.M.	Bathroom break at the church. Pick up the brooms.
11:55 P.M.	Drive to Brea Mall.
12:00 A.M.	Ice Skating and Broom Hockey (1 hour).
1:00 A.M.	Load up and go back to church.
1:10 A.M.	Snack time (fruit juice and sandwiches).
1:30 A.M.	*Super Christian, the Film* (30 minutes).

2:00 A.M.	John Schmidt's devotion.
2:15 A.M.	Games (35 minutes). No one goes outside.
2:50 A.M.	Load up and go to College Bowl.
3:00 A.M.	Bowling (1 hour, 30 minutes).
4:30 A.M.	Load up and return to the church.
4:40 A.M.	Games (1 hour, 20 minutes). No one goes outside.
6:00 A.M.	Breakfast.
6:30 A.M.	Prayer Time.
6:40 A.M.	Cleanup.
7:00 A.M.	GO HOME AND CRASH!
7:10 A.M.	Officers and sponsors clean up Fellowship Hall and Buses.
8:00 A.M.	The rest of us go home!

This will give you a good idea of how to plan for the details. When kids arrive at the church, I give the parents a copy of the schedule so they will know where their kids will be at every moment, all night long.

We go places like bowling alleys and roller skating rinks during the middle of the night because these places are often much cheaper to rent at extremely late hours—provided the owner can find someone willing to come in and open up. No doubt you will be wasted and the kids will be wasted when it's all over, but the very next Sunday they'll be asking when they can do it again. You won't be ready to give them an answer!

Another important area for your consideration of socials is finances. Here are four suggestions for paying for your socials.

1) *Charge the kids.* Set the cost and include it in your advertisement. Don't try to make money on any youth social—your goal should be to break even.

2) *Ask for donations.* Ask kids or parents to bake cookies, bring the hot dogs, and make the lemonade. Perhaps you could occasionally send around a sign-up list for kids to sign to indicate whether they would be willing to bring refreshments. With this approach, you'll have a current list of willing volunteers, and you will be less likely to call on the same people each time.

3) *Take it out of the youth budget.* I hope you are working with a youth fund of some type rather than having to go to the elders for permission for every single expenditure. We prefer to have socials that pay for themselves and save the youth budget for events where we underestimate our expenses or overestimate our turnout. We use the youth budget as an emergency bail-out fund and to pay for

publicity, printing, and postage. We might also use the church budget to underwrite part of the expense of highly evangelistic activities or special visitor days, just to make sure that cost doesn't keep anyone from participating.

4) *Use a combination.* Have parents bring sandwiches and drinks, charge the kids a small amount to cover extra expenses like decorations, prizes, props, or rented buildings, and use the youth budget to pay for the film or to give a guest speaker an honorarium.

Games

Keep in mind that recreational and social activities are not limited to the big fling on Friday night every other month. A volleyball game, before or after a Bible study, is a type of social activity. Even when an adult Bible study is followed by coffee and donuts, an atmosphere is being created to help people interact with one another and thereby fulfill some needs on a social level. There is almost no limit to the places where social and recreational activities can be worked into the youth program. Camps, retreats, VBS, youth meetings, and mid-week Bible studies can all be more effective with the proper mix of some good clean fun and games.

Although you don't want your ministry to be all fun and games, you'll find that several benefits can result from adding recreational games to the normally scheduled youth activities. First, games can promote interaction between kids who would not otherwise associate with one another. Mixing up a group into different teams is a good way to break up cliques, involve withdrawn personalities, and put people who are basically unacquainted with each other in a situation where they are forced by the flow of the game to share and interact. A high-energy, creative game led by a positive and enthusiastic game leader can cause people to forget their differences or shyness as they get caught up in the action of the game.

Second, games are a good way for the youth to see their leaders out from behind the classroom lectern and in a casual down-to-earth setting. A good number of your youth may never go to camp or on a retreat. Many of them only see the youth leader in his "Sunday best." That's not the only image we want to portray. It's an image that many young people cannot, or don't care to, relate to.

At our all-church picnic, our young people were shocked when they first saw our senior minister wearing blue jeans. Occasionally, they still talk about it. I think it was good for them to see him relax, let his hair down, and have some fun. It made them appreciate him more and relate to him. Most of us are good models on Sunday. We handle the church scene pretty well. We may even be good role models as husbands or wives, and even as moms or dads, but we also need to model good relaxation and good recreation. It is important for our youth to see us as whole people.

Third, games can build unity as the group works together for a common goal. The best games for building unity are not games where the competition is aimed at defeating people on the opposing team. The games that promote the best feelings of unity and cooperation are the games where the object is to defeat the clock, defy gravity, overcome an obstacle, or avoid some danger.

Fourth, games can make people better listeners in a couple of ways. Games can provide some much-needed refreshment. At a camp, in a conference, or at any meeting, when people have been sitting for an extended period of time, the ears stop absorbing what the posterior will no longer cushion. There is nothing like a crowd breaker or a quick game to get the blood flowing and bring life back to a weary body. A lively game worked into the program or the schedule might be the best way to provide a needed break in the routine.

On the other hand, if you have a group that is climbing the walls and has so much energy that they can't sit still for thirty seconds—much less thirty minutes—then starting off with a couple of games to burn off some energy may be the best use of your time.

Finally, under the right kind of leadership and supervision, games can build positive character qualities like sportsmanship, patience, courtesy, and humility. There is something about play that brings out the child in us. When we get involved in a game, we drop our guard and tend to reveal the real persons behind our socially acceptable veneer.

Not only do the young people gain a new perspective of their youth leader when he is playing a game; the youth leader will also see a whole new side of the youth. It is the ability of the game to bring the inner person to the surface that makes recreation time overflowing with opportunity for spontaneous teaching. The key to making recreation time a continuing part of Christian education is good leadership. Leaders must be tuned in to using the recreation activities as application time. Without good leadership, games can reinforce negative character qualities and negative values.

Thus, it is imperative to note that the misuse of games can be disastrous. The worst thing that can happen is for the youth leader to destroy his witness. A fit of anger, an outburst of selfishness, or insensitive coaching can leave kids devastated. I can remember looking up to the youth leaders all week long at camp and then being crushed with disappointment on Friday when the camp closed with the student/faculty softball game. I've heard some unbelievable war stories of how Satan used recreation time to destroy the respect young people had for their leaders. Usually, the problems came from an insecure youth worker who saw the game time as an opportunity to prove himself instead of to demonstrate Christ.

Another major risk involved is the danger of physical injuries. Again, it is very important to have good leadership to set the proper guidelines and boundaries, use the right equipment, and control the intensity of the play. Don't take unnecessary chances. The best way to avoid accidents is to plan ahead. Make sure the play area is free from sharp objects like table edges or sprinkler heads. Make sure the game is the right game for the age group. If the game could get too dangerous, can it be modified by changing a rule, using a different kind of ball, or adding more referees?

The folks from the New Games Foundation have a good motto, "Play Hard, Play Fair, and Nobody Hurt."

However, there are risks worse than physical injuries. Emotional injuries are usually more difficult to heal. Care needs to be taken to make sure people don't get left out, and that people aren't made to feel like losers. If you have ever watched an afternoon of Little League, you know what I'm talking about. I prefer games that give everyone a handicap and provide an equal opportunity to everyone participating.

The best way to plan for safety, fairness, refreshment, cooperation, and fun is to develop a repertoire of games for a variety of situations instead of using the highly competitive traditional games. There are living room games, games for rainy days, games for camps and socials, and even games for long bus rides. The books mentioned in the Suggested Resources will be a tremendous help, but your own creativity will be your best resource. Take any game and improvise to make it fit your needs. By taking the ordinary game of volleyball and changing the rules or adding extra equipment, you can come up with all kinds of new games.

Superman Volleyball is played with a volleyball filled with helium.

Beach-ball Volleyball, obviously, is played with a beach ball, and is much safer for young groups.

Earth-ball Volleyball is played with a giant six-foot-tall cage ball. It is a great spectator game—because spectators can't resist getting involved in the game. If you play this one, be sure the net is strong and the poles are secure.

Rotation Volleyball is designed to ease the level of competition. It is simple. After you serve, rotate players from one side to the other.

Volley-Volleyball eliminates ball hogging. You score one point if the ball goes over the net in one hit; two points if it goes over the net in two hits; three points for three hits. Changing the way points are scored is a great way to create a new game. This is also an example of how a small change in the rules can make a big change in the importance of teamwork.

Five-Hit Volleyball is played with this rule change: the ball must be hit by five different players before it goes over the net or there is no point scored. This game makes everyone an important player.

Blind Volleyball is played with blankets or sheets hanging over the net so that one team cannot see the other team. Rule that there can be no spiking. The anticipation as people wait, wondering when, where, and whether the ball is going to come over the net adds a whole new excitement to the game.

Water Balloon Volleyball—you will just have to try it to believe it. Be sure to keep plenty of extra water balloons on hand. Once the water balloon supply is gone, the game is over.

Strobe Light Volleyball—you play this one indoors, in the dark, on your knees, with a lower net and a strobe light on each end of the court. It is wild.

Softball is another game that's been terribly overused. If you have been to summer camp, you probably know what I mean. There are people who take forever to swing the bat. There are never enough ball gloves. Your team is always the one in the outfield, an hour each inning. You have one player who plays short stop—and third base, and second base, and left field, and everywhere the ball goes.

Here are some rule changes and new versions of softball that I've come up with in order improve the original game.

Bangball—The first object is to score as many runs as possible by hitting a soft air-filled rubber ball (the type you might find in a baby's playpen) with a racquetball racquet, and then running around the bases without getting hit or tagged by the ball. Because we want it to be just as much fun to be in the outfield as it is to be at bat, we score one point for every out. Outs are made by (1) a force out at first base, (2) catching a fly ball, (3) tagging the base runner

with the ball, or (4) throwing the ball and hitting the base runner.
(That's one reason you want a soft, light ball, as well as eliminating the need for ball gloves.)

We want both teams to have equal time at bat and in the outfield;
so we don't play three-out innings. We play a seven-minute round
and then switch the offense to defense and vice versa. If it takes
one minute to switch places, you complete an inning every fifteen
minutes.

The following rules have evolved as we have played the game
over the last few years. But don't be bound by the way this book
says to play the game. Make up your own adaptations and rule
changes. The principle behind rule changes is this, the rule
change should make the game more safe, more interesting, or more
fun, but not make the players frustrated nor require constant interruption by referees. Here are the rules we use:

1. The team leader of the team at bat does the pitching, or a neutral person is designated to pitch for both teams. (The idea behind this is to stop the criticism of the pitcher.)

2. Don't hold the ball; work against the clock. The idea behind this is to pick up the pace of the game: more pitches = more batters = more hits = more action = more participation = more fun.

3. There are no designated positions; fielders can play anywhere as long as they are behind the pitcher. With softball, there are only ten positions and players. Bangball can have six players or sixty players on a team.

4. There is no limit to the number of people that can be on one base; so the only force out is at first base. Watching six people run from one base to the other at the same time while the defenders can't figure out which one to tag is hilarious. It is also interesting to watch all six people try to keep a foot on the base at the same time.

5. The banger (batter) gets only three pitches. If he doesn't swing, swings and misses, or hits it foul, he still only gets three pitches. If he has not hit the ball after the three pitches, he is out. This rule change makes everyone a hitter. Usually people swing at the first pitch. This also helps pick up the pace of the game.

6. Once the ball is fielded, the defensive player can take only three steps before throwing the ball. Taking more than three steps makes the runner automatically safe. This rule keeps people from hogging the ball and promotes teamwork.

7. Another change that makes the game interesting and keeps it
   from looking too much like softball is to change the number of
   bases and their location.

Here's what the game looks like on the playing field after all our
changes:

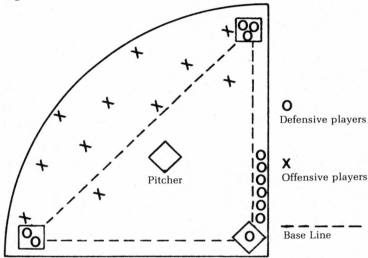

O Defensive players

X Offensive players

- - - Base Line

Nerd Ball is another variation of softball. We play it with a *Nerf*
or foam soccer ball and a regular softball bat. Use the same rules as
Bangball (seven-minute rounds, three pitches, three steps, score
for outs, score for runs, and the rest). One other change we make is
to use only one base and put it in center field.

Jungle Ball is played on the same field with the same rules as
Bangball, except players kick a lightweight plastic ball. The ball
we use is about ten or twelve inches in diameter and can be found
in almost any *K-Mart* or toy store. It wobbles all over as people try
to catch it.

Centipede Softball is still another wild version. Use the *Nerf*
soccer ball and a softball bat and seven-minute rounds. Here are
the changes we have made. (1) Instead of running around bases,
after the batter hits the ball, he runs around his team, which is in a
huddle behind home plate. He scores a point for each time he
makes a complete revolution around his team before the defense
returns the ball to home plate. (2) Once the ball is fielded you
cannot throw it or run with it. You must return it to home plate by

forming a line of people who pass the ball between their legs
(hence the name centipede). Once you have passed the ball, you
run to the end of the line in order to receive it and pass it on again
until the ball crosses home plate. This game is a riot to watch. The
best thing about the game is that every player is involved in every
play. It looks something like this:

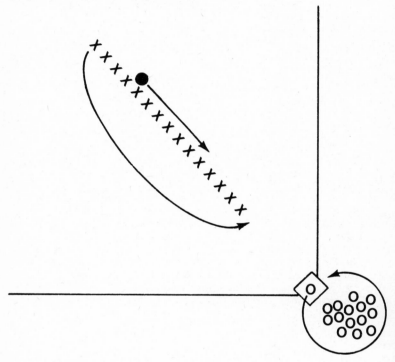

The changes in softball and volleyball are just the beginning.
Think of what you can do with soccer, relay games, football, fris-
bee, swimming, and even ping-pong. Be creative!

I hope all this information on socials and games will be helpful
tools for your ministry. Young people love to have fun, and having
fun can be an effective way to reach, teach, and train them for
service. Remember the importance of having a sense of purpose
and maintaining a balance.

Suggested Resources

Christie, Les. *Servant Leaders in the Making.* Wheaton: Scripture Press, 1983.

Fluegelman, Andrew. *More New Games and Playful Ideas.* New York: Doubleday, 1981.

Fluegelman, Andrew. *New Games Book.* New York: Doubleday, n.d. (This book, as well as its sequel, above, provides a whole philosophy of making games fun to play, not just fun to win.)

Rice, Wayne. *Ideas.* El Cajon, CA: Youth Specialties, 36 vols. (This series is my number-one choice. The ideas here, plus your own creative adaptations, provide more ideas than you can use in a lifetime.)

Rice, Wayne. *Junior High Ministry.* Grand Rapids: Zondervan, 1978.

Rice, Wayne, Denny Rydberg, and Mike Yaconelli. *Fun and Games.* Grand Rapids: Zondervan, 1977. (Much like *Ideas,* but brief.)

Rice and Yaconelli. *Far-out Ideas for Youth Groups.* Grand Rapids: Zondervan, 1975.

Rice, Wayne, Denny Rydberg, and Mike Yaconelli. *Holiday Ideas for Youth Groups.* Grand Rapids: Zondervan, 1981. (Everything from New Year's to Christmas, including such holidays as Ground Hog's Day and April Fool's!)

Rice, Wayne, Denny Rydberg, and Mike Yaconelli. *Right-on Ideas for Youth Groups.* Grand Rapids: Zondervan, 1975.

Rice, Wayne, Denny Rydberg, and Mike Yaconelli. *Way-out Ideas for Youth Groups.* Grand Rapids: Zondervan, 1972.

Try This One Series. Loveland, CO: Group Books.

The Best of Try This One, Tom Schultz, ed., 1977.

More . . . Try This One, Tom Schultz, ed., 1979.

Try This One . . . Too, Lee Sparks, ed., 1982.

Try This One . . . Strikes Again, Cindy H. Hansen, ed., 1984.

10

Using Small Groups in Youth Ministry

Jonathan Underwood

"What is your favorite color?" I thought I was hearing things. There I was, attending a seminar on youth ministry, looking for ideas to take back to my own group, and the leader was asking for my favorite color. Only he didn't want to know. He wanted me to tell the half-dozen or so people in my small group.

"Well, okay," I thought. "I'll bite. Let's see where this is going." So we shared our favorite colors and began a pleasant, informal conversation. Later, the questions got more pointed. Gradually we moved from the ridiculous to the sublime. And I began to see the value of the format. By putting us in small groups and asking a nonthreatening question, the leader had begun to develop an atmosphere of openness and willingness to share ideas.

Purpose

That is the purpose of using small groups in ministry. Small groups produce an atmosphere that is conducive to open sharing and growth. People today are simply not willing to open up and share their inner selves with just anyone. And young people are no exception.

Consider the teacher of a large high-school Sunday-school class who asks, "How can you share your faith?" He feels it's a good discussion question. There are dozens of ways. But you know the response: blank stares.

"Come on," he pleads. "Don't you care about spiritual things?" Still, blank stares. Frustrated, he uses the remaining thirty minutes of class time to lecture. He leaves the class discouraged about the lack of spiritual concern among the youth.

But the problem is not a lack of spiritual concern. The problem is fear. The young people are afraid to open up. They're afraid of giving a wrong answer—especially in front of twenty or thirty of their peers. They perceive the question as having a "right" answer. If they don't know what that answer is—even if they have some ideas of their own on the topic—they will not offer a suggestion.

It is the purpose of the small group to eliminate that fear, to produce an atmosphere of openness. In such an atmosphere, the young people will discuss their ideas and their feelings, and significant learning will occur.

Goals

In pursuit of that purpose, a number of goals can be set for, and reached by, a small group. The first is to eliminate communication barriers. This is the most important aspect of developing an open atmosphere. Communication is also the most important aspect in reaching other goals set by your group, whether for learning, service, worship, or fellowship.

The size of the group is a major key to openness. A person will risk more with fewer people to witness what he believes might be a failure. So the same question that was greeted by blank stares in the large group might get an answer in the small group. At the same time, it is easier for people to build relationships with a few than with many. The small group allows its members to build a relationship together before they are asked to deal with issues. The warm relationship then encourages participation in discussion as the group members are seen as supporters instead of critics.

Size is not the only factor, however. In order to achieve the goal of open communication, the leader must take deliberate action to eliminate other barriers. He does this by asking nonthreatening questions, questions that make the group members the experts, the authorities.

When our seminar leader asked us, "What is your favorite color?" he didn't know my answer. Nor did the other members of the group. Whatever color I offered in response was the "right" answer. No one could say, "You're wrong," or, "That's not right." More significant questions can also be asked in a way that reduces the threat. "What do you think about . . . ?" "What would you have done ... ?" "Imagine that you are Paul at.... How do you feel?" These questions can prompt relevant discussions about Biblical topics or current issues without suggesting that there is one right answer. Indeed, only the person who answers knows the "right answer," because each question has asked for his own personal observation.

This leads to a second goal of small groups: interaction and application. As communication barriers are brought down, the group members interact with one another more and more. They will be encouraged to suggest ideas to one another. Suggesting ideas will stimulate their thinking to come up with more ideas. So when the discussion reaches the application phase of a lesson, the group is ready to deal with it creatively and to apply the lesson to life. This is superior to the leader's expounding some application on the group because it provides internal motivation. The group itself has come up with the ideas. People by nature like their own ideas more than someone else's. The motivation to follow through is much greater.

Another goal of the small group is leadership development. In many situations, you or another adult—in the role of teacher—will lead all of the small groups. This is the role played by the seminar leader mentioned earlier. During the course of the session, the group is broken into small groups, and the teacher asks all of the groups to discuss certain questions or concepts. But there are situations in which a small group functions by itself. You may have many small groups functioning at the same time, but they are independent. Each has its own purpose for meeting. In these situations, each group needs a leader, and the group itself becomes the best training ground for its leaders.

If it's intimidating simply to answer a question, it's even more intimidating to lead a group. The size of the group is again the first aid in eliminating this fear. Your young people can begin taking a leadership role in small groups—discipleship groups, for example. The best way is perhaps to meet with a group yourself for a while, modeling leadership even as you accomplish some other goal. Then the members of your group become leaders of other groups.

Occasions for Small Groups

The mention of different situations raises the question, "Where can I use small groups? What occasions call for their use?" The answer is virtually unlimited.

Begin a Sunday-school class with small groups. Have each group consider some question (all the same question or each group a different question) that introduces the topic. Use the same groups to study the assigned Scripture passage. Each group can read a different portion, discuss it, and report their findings to the whole group. You will need to supply questions to stimulate the groups' discussion, but let them discover the truth of the passage for themselves. Using each group to look at a different portion of the text allows you to cover more ground and still involve all the students in the process.

The application of the lesson is an ideal time for the groups. Use questions to stimulate group discussion directed at applying what has been studied. Or have the groups role play some means of proper application.

If the class has a number of visitors, opening with a small-group activity can make them feel a part of the group more quickly. This makes small groups especially well suited to your outreach-oriented activities. If you have a party or fifth quarter or some other activity to which your kids have been especially encouraged to invite their friends, you'd better have some plan in mind to break down the us-them mindset. Small groups can break down the barriers and make the outsiders insiders.

This has made small groups an outstanding and highly successful method for starting a weekend retreat or a week at camp. Whether you have kids from several churches (who are thus strangers to each other) or from just one church (who are already friends), setting up small groups begins to foster a closeness and interaction that enhances all of the activities that follow. Use a random selection so that cliques are split up. Have group leaders who are sensitive to the needs of kids and the dynamics of small groups, and plan several more times for the groups to meet together. Such meetings can enhance the effectiveness of class sessions, vespers, and other teaching activities while they build fellowship and mutual respect for one another. At camps, the idea of having "teams" has largely yielded to having "families"; so the groups see themselves as units at all times, not just on the recreation field. This enhances the value of the small groups.

Many youth ministries have employed the use of discipleship groups. The youth minister, a sponsor, or even a mature member of the youth group acts as leader, and disciples a small number of other young people. These groups are not the impromptu groups formed during the Sunday-school hour as one phase of the lesson.

They are entities in and of themselves, meeting periodically—usually weekly—for fellowship, encouragement, Bible study, and spiritual growth. Leadership potential is enhanced, and many of the groups function to train leaders for groups that will be formed later.

InterVaristy Press has a new book, *Good Things Come in Small Groups*, that encourages the use of a number of small groups—called "koinonia groups." Ron Nicholas, the coordinator of the small group that wrote the book, explains in Chapter 3 that each group needs a balance of four ingredients: nurture (primarily Bible study), worship, community (fellowship), and mission (outreach). A small group that is formed as an accessory to some other activity, such as a Sunday-school class, can function in just one of these areas. But a group that is an independent part of the youth program must balance all four to function well.

These koinonia groups can be formed according to interests. If six or eight of your young people are especially interested in the problem of world hunger, perhaps they could form a small group whose mission is to provide some aid. The other aspects of group life can also relate to the problem, though not always directly. Another group might form because of an interest in a particular passage of Scripture or a particular social concern. Whatever occasion calls forth a small group, be sure there is an occasion. Having small groups for the sake of having small groups can be detrimental to the unity of the whole group. Discipleship groups have often seen themselves as the elite among the whole. Not only have they missed the whole point of servanthood, but the rest of the group has sensed their attitude and become resentful. Barriers within the group have been removed—there's a great openness and free exchange within the group—but barriers have been erected around the group. No one else in the youth group will even speak to them!

Dynamics of Small Groups

The potential for this kind of backlash calls for careful consideration of the dynamics of small groups. There is no question that small groups can enhance your ministry to youth. But that is not automatic. The groups can also fail, either providing no assistance or providing a negative impact on the whole group.

The formation of a small group presents the people involved with a new situation, and some will be apprehensive. They may suspect that they will be asked to share on a more intimate level than they are comfortable with. This situation demands a careful approach, keeping the discussion low-key for as long as it takes them to warm up. If the group is going to be meeting regularly for a while, several sessions may be devoted to this warm-up period. If the group is only meeting for a few minutes during a Sunday-school lesson or other meeting, the warm-up must be brief, but it should not be eliminated.

The use of the question noted earlier, "What is your favorite color?" recognizes the apprehension dynamic. It does not ask for intimate information. It makes the respondent the final authority; so he can't be wrong. There is no threat, no challenge, no barrier to communication.

Asking, "Why?" provides a little more tension. It calls for the exposure of some reasoning, some thought. But the subject is still favorite colors; so who cares? Who would challenge one's reason for liking one color over another? So a gradual shift has occurred without erecting any barriers. That process continues with the questions becoming more and more significant while the atmosphere remains open and easy.

The I-owe-you dynamic is sometimes helpful in getting the apprehensive to participate in small-group discussion. When the leader asks a question, he gives his own answer immediately. "My favorite Bible character is Barnabas because. . . . Now, who's your favorite character, and why?" The leader's answer primes the pump of creativity by giving the group members a model. But it also has the effect of demanding an answer from each participant. By giving his own answer first, the leader creates a feeling in the group that they owe it to him to answer. The more open members of the group will respond immediately, and this increases the feeling in the rest that they, too, must answer. This tension is not a negative factor because it is internal. The group members feel the need to respond but no one has said, "You must answer this," or "You owe me an answer." The debt is their own idea; "I owe you an answer."

Another positive dynamic of the small group is identification. The group members identify with one another as each opens up more and more. So often, we are not open in our communication because we feel our problems or feelings are unique. As others reveal the same problems or feelings, we identify with them. A we're-in-this-together mentality develops, and the group grows closer and is able to discuss even more difficult subjects and to work together on a variety of projects.

This feature is especially true of long-term small groups, but it works in short-term groups, too. A group that is formed, operates, and disbanded all in the space of an hour can develop some sense of identity, and there will be long-term positive results from that relationship. For example, there might be two people in your group who never have got along. They weren't hostile to each other, but they had never impressed each other enough to want to get to know one another. Each had thought of the other as a loser. After an hour in a small group, the two may well have a new appreciation for each other. In the group, they can see positive qualities in each other and areas of agreement. They will have more respect for each other. They might even become close friends.

They might. But you can definitely count on friendships developing in long-term groups. A group that meets regularly will develop such close identification that they will be best friends. None of their other friends understands them and appreciates them the way their fellow group members do.

Such a group needs to use that feature for more than just having good meetings. It needs a mission, some project that can be worked on together to render service to others. This project may be the reason the group is formed to start with, or it may grow out of their developing awareness of the needs around them. At any rate, they need to balance their study with service. Otherwise, they can become cliquish.

Another way to prevent cliques is to have in place a system of mixing the group members with new people. If everyone in the youth group is involved in a small group, then new members can be worked into the existing groups. As the groups grow, some members will have to form new groups, thus remixing them. Use mature members to start new groups. This leaves more consistency for the new members, who need it most. It also makes for good new groups. With a mature base, a new group will grow faster than if it had just one or two mature members and a majority of new members.

As the group members become more comfortable with the others in their group, they develop a freedom of expression unknown in most other situations. This happens only when they feel support from the rest of the group. To encourage these dynamics, then, the leader must make it clear from the start that the group will not be negative. No ideas offered in the group will be critiqued. In other words, if a person does not have something good to say about another's idea, he should say nothing. If a person reveals a problem, the group will respond with solutions, not condemnation.

This freedom is essential to the group's effectiveness. It allows group members to reveal their inner selves and needs. They speak without guarding their words—saying just what they mean. With all the veneer of defense mechanisms and euphemistic language stripped away, the kids can be met on the level of their need. Then it becomes possible to minister to the real problems the youth face and not just symptoms.

This freedom can be a problem, however, when new members are brought into the group. Usually, the group will not be as open when a new member is present. The new member then gets a chance to begin to identify with the group and feel he belongs. As he does so, the group again opens up and returns to free expression. But if the group is not sensitive to the fact that a new member has not yet had a chance to identify with the group, that freedom can be intimidating. He may not be able to handle the kinds of needs that are expressed. Or he may have been guarding some secret sin and feel he is going to be pressed to reveal it with the same candor he has seen the rest of the group employ. The leader will need to be sensitive to this possibility and exert a little more control over the opening activities of the group so that no potentially intimidating discussion takes place before the new participant feels ready to get involved.

The other extreme is also possible. Some people take advantage of the open atmosphere of the small group to expound everything they know about any given topic. They are constantly baring their souls about some terrible problem they have or some other great need. These people monopolize the discussion, leaving almost no room for input from anyone else. If one of them does take a break to catch his breath and another group member happens to get a word in edgewise, the filibuster is resumed in an I-can-top-that story guaranteed to end all discussion.

This situation destroys what the small-group format is meant to insure. It quenches openness because the group feels no one will be able to listen to them. Their ideas are always minimized by the monopolizer anyway; so they'd rather just keep quiet. The monopolizer himself probably needs the platform to feel appreciated. But the growing resentment from the rest of the group is obvious even to him; so his self-image declines even more.

The leader must be sensitive to the situation and take action that keeps the discussion open without deflating the offending party. "Let's hear from someone who hasn't said anything yet." That's much better than, "Bob, will you shut up so the rest of the group can talk!" Be creative. Come up with ways to involve everyone without offending someone else. Start a system in which one person states a problem; then everyone else offers possible solutions. The problem-poser may not offer solutions to his own problem. Then, when a filibuster is started, the leader can say, "All right, Bob; you've stated a problem. Now let's see if we can't offer some solutions." Bob—by the rules of the group—is excluded from the discussion, but he's still the center of attention.

If the leader is sensitive to what's happening in his group, he can maintain the open, free, and personal dynamics without yielding to cliques or monopolizing individuals. From that will develop the additional dynamics of originality, application, and leadership.

Originality is the ability to think for oneself. In our routines of life, we often are able to get by without originality. We do what we're told; we eat what they're serving; we follow the schedule. The small group allows for differences. After a while, we realize our own ideas are often as good as the next guy's. Potentially, this originality stretches beyond the group and into other areas of the members' lives.

Application is the ability to apply truth to life. No sermon or lesson is complete without application. But it's often so broad that many people fail to appropriate it to themselves. The small group stimulates the members to think about how the truth affects their own personal lives. Originality is important to this process. A young person doesn't have to be told what to do about a Scripture passage. He can see how it affects him on his own. And his motivation to do so is then greater because it's his idea, not just something he's been told he ought to do.

Such original application of Scripture develops leadership potential. In a small group, it's much easier to see that potential developing than it is in larger group contexts. Someone will stand out for his ability to summarize the discussion, or to consider alternatives, or to spearhead the effort to do something about it. All these are forms of leadership, whether the people responsible are seen as leaders or not. They may never start or lead another small group on their own, but they provide leadership nonetheless. They may remain as informal leaders. Informal leaders hold no office, but they fulfill the functions of leadership. Often, formal leaders are chosen from the ranks of the informal leaders—and well they should be. But many have no desire to hold an office; they choose to serve from behind the scenes. And well *they* should, too. They have found the joy of service untainted by the quest for power or the desire "to lord it over" another. While we need formal leaders and the offices they hold, we also need models for informal leadership—demonstrating that one can serve even without a title.

Results

The results of using small groups in youth ministry depend on how much they're used and, obviously, how well. Potentially, you can develop a much more open, communicating, and growing youth group. Saying that is fine, but a more specific look at results is called for.

Whether you use small groups only as lesson activities or as complete ministry tools in themselves, you'll find your youth have built closer relationships with one another and work together better. You can even apply some of the small-group techniques to existing groups like your teen choir, your Bible Bowl team, and other groups. You'll find their effectiveness in ministering to the whole persons of those involved is increased. And the groups will work together better in their assigned tasks, too.

Your teaching can be more productive when you employ small groups. Statistics on the effectiveness of teaching that involves the learners are cited in other chapters of this book. And using small groups is one of the best ways to involve the learners. In the groups, your students can discover truths, paraphrase truths, discuss the implications of truth, and apply truth. Your role can be more as a guide or facilitator instead of lecturer and disseminator of all truth.

This is not an easy way out, however. It's much easier to prepare a lecture than to prepare a lesson that employs small groups. Your questions must be carefully worded, and you must build in a lot of flexibility in order to reach your goals for the lesson. At any one point, the groups can take more time than you expect, and you need to be able to adapt and make up for whatever gets left out of the lesson. This extra preparation also makes you a better teacher in general. You have to discipline yourself to find the extra preparation time and still complete the rest of your work.

If you put your entire youth group into small groups that meet regularly for Bible study, fellowship, worship, and service, you have an excellent vehicle for shepherding your young people. A person is missed when he is absent from a small group. The rest of the group cares about whether he's there and can have a plan for contacting him before the next meeting. Church-growth experts confirm that the more small groups a person is involved with in the church (including choirs, Sunday-school classes, and other groups), the greater is the church's chance for keeping that person as an active member. I believe the same is true for young people. Adding additional small groups so that every member of your youth group is included in one will increase your chances of keeping the youth involved. If all your youth are involved in teen choirs, Bible Bowl teams, and other small groups, you can work in these small-group techniques to stimulate spiritual growth and cooperation. If not everyone is involved (or even if they are), you might want to add a small-group structure to include everyone. Call the groups cells or koinonia groups or discipleship groups or whatever. Be sensitive to the dynamics of the groups and be sure each one has a goal or purpose to give meaning to the meetings— and you'll see great progress in the spiritual lives of your young people!

Suggested Resources

Gaulke, Earl H. *How to Lead Small Group Bible Studies.* Colorado Springs: Navpress, 1982.

Nicholas, Ron. *Small Group Leader's Handbook.* Downers Grove: IVP, 1982.

Nicholas, Ron. et. al. *Good Things Come in Small Groups.* Downers Grove: IVP, 1985.

Peace, Richard. *Small Group Evangelism.* Downers Grove: IVP, 1985.

Richards, Larry. *Sixty-nine Ways to Start a Study Group.* Grand Rapids: Zondervan, 1980.

VanNote, Gene. *How to Lead a Small Group Bible Study.* Kansas City: Beacon Hill, 1980.

11

Using Film
in Youth Ministry

John Schmidt

Like most people, I fell in love with movies when I was young. That love later developed into my favorite hobby. But when I decided to enter a ministry in the production of Christian films, I knew that it would have to be much more than an exciting hobby or a form of entertainment for the church. It would have to affect the lives of those in the audience. It would have to meet the needs of the church. In short, it would have to have merit for the kingdom of God.

We are all aware of the impact the media has on our lives and on the lives of our youth. We have seen how Satan has used television and motion-picture screens as his platform to teach today's young people that which is contrary to Christian principles. For too long we Christians have been losing the war that has waged on the silver screen. We have not been able to take full advantage of the power that television and, specifically, film possess.

Yet, I have never been more excited about the value of films for the local church and its youth group, and that the same power often used for destruction is now being utilized to bring people to Christ and challenge them to live committed lives.

I believe in the value of films for the entire church, but particularly for youth audiences. The youth of today have never been more tuned to that which is *visual* and *audible*. They spend a great deal of time (too much) watching television; they spent more money at movie theaters in the early 1980s than any comparable period previous (with 1982 being their biggest expenditure year ever). They are absorbed with video games and computers, and—like most of us who preceded—they maintain a steady diet of music.

The youth of today are speaking a different language than was spoken twenty years ago. The youth of today are media-minded. What we must realize is they are not primarily a *literary* generation; they are not as enthusiastic about reading as generations before. (How many times have you asked a teenager if he had seen a particular movie, and he said, "Naw, I read the book"?) However, although our youth are media-minded, we use largely literary methods of teaching in our churches. Let's face it, our primary style of teaching is lecturing. We use it in worship services, Sunday-school classes, and Bible studies. Granted, Jesus taught primarily in this way, but I doubt that we possess His same homiletical skills. Even as useful and effective as the sermon format can be, it should not be the only method we subject our youth to. And yet, to a degree, that is what we have done. While older adults may be more comfortable with a sermon or lecture, youth are less stimulated in such an environment. The most powerful method of teaching for youth is that which correlates with their everyday world (and their sources of entertainment), that which can be seen, heard, and experienced. Now, lest you worry that they expect the excitement of *Star Wars* with each lesson, realize that what youth really want is a variety of teaching methods. If they have been taught largely through a lecture format, it is probable that the words of speakers will fall on deaf ears after a while. Similarly, even as much as they crave film, television, and other forms of visual entertainment, a teaching style using these methods in excess would—in time—also prove ineffective. Our goal should be to use a variety of teaching methods and not tilt the scales too much toward any one style. For too long, the scales have weighed in favor of that which is literary or verbal in nature. Since youth have moved into the visual and audible realm, our methods of teaching and evangelism should take advantage of a medium such as film. Hollywood has! Today's top-grossing films are youth-oriented. Teens are the movie industry's number-one market. We must make a similar effort.

Motion pictures are probably the most powerful and effective means at our disposal for communicating to a large audience. Studies have shown that we retain about fifteen percent of what we hear (e.g., lecture), but eighty-three percent of what we see and hear. There is only one other type of learning that is more effective than the combination of sight and sound: that which we can *experience*. I'm convinced that film transcends into this realm of highest learning because it is possible for those in the audience to escape from their own world and experience what the characters in the film experience. One way I try to achieve this in my own films is to create a main character that most of the audience can relate to. He has faults, but not so many that viewers dismiss him as beyond help. Once they relate to him, they can experience what he experiences and, I hope, learn the same lessons.

Film also has the ability to captivate an audience, simply because of the conditions under which it is shown. In total darkness, all eyes can focus on only one object: the screen. There are no other lights on; so nothing else competes or becomes a distraction. These conditions hold an audience captive.

Another advantage of the use of film in youth work is economics. Compared to other forms of extra-church ministries, films are very reasonable. On the average, a film costs a little over one dollar per minute to rent.[1] An hour-long film costs about seventy dollars. When you consider how much it would cost to have a well-known speaker or singing group come to your church, the price of a film seems even more reasonable. To help pay for film rentals, you can try a number of things: take an offering, charge everyone fifty cents, ask an individual or adult Sunday-school class to sponsor a film (announce its sponsor at the screening), or make allowances in your budget each year.

The youth film has fallen on lean times since 1979. That was a significant year in the history of Christian films because it started a trend known as the series film. Very few of these films had been produced prior to 1979. One was *How Should We Then Live*, with Francis Schaeffer. These films were very popular and presented a new alternative to the dramatic film. In 1979 the series-film concept exploded with James Dobson's *Focus on the Family* series. These films were well-produced and continue to minister to Christian families years later. Because of their success, however, almost everyone decided that this was the only way to make films. Consequently, we have seen a series syndrome that has saturated the Christian market.

Although the series film has proven useful to the church, there are two disadvantages to this trend. First, almost none of the many film series in circulation are aimed at youth. (Two exceptions are

Josh McDowell's excellent *Live, Laugh, Love* series—available from Gospel Films—and Tony Campolo's four-part series, *You Can Make a Difference* —available from Word.) The second disadvantage to the series trend is that their increase in number has created an imbalance in the types of films available. Series films are much less expensive to produce than dramatic films, making them an appealing alternative for a producer in economically rough times. The speakers featured in such films also found them attractive, since they were able to cut down on speaking engagements. But the results are unfortunate: a rising demand by youth ministers for dramatic films, but very few new films from which to choose and a poor selection of series films dealing with youth to serve as an alternative.

I am very enthusiastic about series films. Think of the opportunities that are available to the small church that can't afford to bring in Dobson, Swindoll, McDowell, or Campolo! But my hope is that more producers will see the need to create a balance once again between series and dramatic films, and produce series that are aimed at younger audiences.

Selecting a Film

One of my favorite things to do is go out and see a movie in the theater. But several years ago, I made a promise to myself that I wouldn't see a particular movie unless I had (1) read or heard a review from at least one movie critic I trusted, or (2) talked with a friend who had seen that film. By following this rule, I have saved money and many wasted hours in theaters.

Often, I will talk with friends who thought a film "looked good" in a newspaper ad or the trailer shown before another movie at a theater. But then they were sorely disappointed because the film itself did not live up to their expectations. I want to say, "I could have told you it wouldn't be any good!" Many times I feel as though I've already seen a film because of all the reviews I've read. My favorite sources are two television shows that strictly review films: *At the Movies* (ABC) and *Sneak Previews* (PBS). These are the critics that I trust the most and that generally share my own tastes in films. Through these shows and various written reviews, I learn not only what films I want to see, but also those that I want to avoid. In short, I have become a selective movie-goer.

I encourage you to make the same promise about Christian films that I made several years ago regarding secular films: be selective.

Earlier I mentioned that we often attend movies in the theater because the newspaper ad makes the film look good. This is a credit to the artist who designed the ad, but it's a terrible way to select a film. An advertisement *always* looks good in order to attract an audience. Unfortunately, as we're all aware, the advertisement is often better than the film. As much as I hate to admit it, sometimes this same irony exists in the advertisements for Christian films, the ad in a catalog or magazine is better than the film itself. Even worse, it is misleading, and tells you very little about the film's message or the age-group for which it is intended. It would be ideal if the ads were clearer, telling you when the film was made, whether the technical quality is any good, whether the story is corny, whether the message is relevant to youth, and so on. But what kind of ad would be so blunt? None of them. That is the reason you must go beyond the catalog in selecting a film. Let that be a starting point, but not your sole criteria for the selection of a film. To do so is very risky.

Obviously, the best way to select a film is to preview it yourself. Contact a local Christian film distributor or library in your area. (You can locate him by writing one of the producers listed at the end of this chapter.) He will be happy to set up a time for you to come in and preview a whole stack of films if you wish. If you are nowhere near a film library (some of them cover several states), call the librarian and discuss your needs with him. He will want to earn your trust by sending you a film you'll be pleased with; so you can count on his assistance.

As you can imagine, once your local librarian knows you and your needs, he becomes a valuable and trusted friend in helping select a film that will be helpful to you and your ministry. I know of librarians who have aided youth ministers and pastors for years in the selection of films. Many times the customers will call and just say, "I need a good film for New Year's that we haven't seen. What do you have?" This kind of trust is invaluable, and can be developed by building a relationship with your film distributor. Another advantage is that a library usually keeps a record of the films you have shown for the last several years. If your memory fails you ("Have I shown them that film in the last two years?"), your librarian can let you know.

Talk to other youth ministers about films they have used. Take advantage of conventions and conferences to preview films. All of these things will help you become more selective in the use of films. As a youth worker, you are a steward not only of the money required to rent films, but, more importantly, of the time your youth spend focusing their attention on a film and what it has to say. Being selective will help you reach the goal of spending both money and time wisely, and leaving your youth with something that will help change their lives.

Showing a Film

After all the trouble you went through in selecting a film, it makes sense that you take certain steps to ensure a successful showing. Here are some tips:

- Order promotional materials (such as posters, flyers, and news releases).
- Make sure the film will be delivered on time. Ask for an emergency number to call in case it doesn't.
- Have a dependable projector on hand with a spare bulb and excitor lamp.
- Make sure the take-up reel is of equal or greater size than the supply reel.
- Use a screen that is big enough and in good condition. Avoid walls.
- Try and get the room completely dark. Block out windows or show the film late in a program when it's darker. Any amount of ambient light spells disaster for a film visually.
- Thread it up well before the audience arrives. Run through a few minutes. Can you see and hear from every seat?
- If you haven't seen the film yet, *by all means* see it before the public showing.
- Use the study guide that comes with the film.
- Choose a good room for showing the film. Long rooms are better than wide rooms, although be sure that those in the back aren't too far away. A small, carpeted room would be better than a large auditorium or gymnasium. A 16mm film loses much of its intimacy when shown in massive rooms.
- Place the sound speaker directly in front of the screen. That is the best location.
- Use good equipment. It is well worth your while to invest in quality tools that are necessary for an effective ministry through films. There are many well-made projectors available: Eiki, Elmo, Singer Graflex, Bell and Howell, and Kodak, to name a few. The Singer Graflex and the Bell and Howell are probably the best for your money. They are dependable and easy to operate. I also recommend you purchase a portable tripod screen of at least eight feet in width. The mounted or

electric screens are not practical for mobile youth groups (but are good for your sanctuary).

Introduction and Follow-up

Most films will speak for themselves when shown, but as a leader you can get even more mileage out of them. Many films have study guides available. I strongly encourage you to take advantage of them. They are filled with questions, illustrations, and commentary from the producer. By using a study guide, you will be able to draw much more out of a film. Thus, you are more likely to reach that all-important goal of application. Don't feel as though you must be tied down to a study guide, however. Use what is helpful to your own group. Let it be a springboard for your own questions, comments, and illustrations. Be sure to ask for a study guide when you order a film. After the showing, keep the guide on file for future reference.

Keep discussion and comments to a minimum before the film. Utilize these few minutes to set the tone for what will follow. Ask the group questions to think about during the film, or ask them to define a certain word that relates to the film. Let this be a time to get their minds going, but don't overdo it.

The time after the film will allow elaboration of the message. Occasionally, you may not feel that any discussion is necessary, and you may just want to close in prayer and dismiss your audience right away. Although this is a valid option, films that allow this are rare indeed. Almost without exception, any film can be enhanced by discussion afterward.

You may want to re-create the events of the film to eliminate any confusion viewers might have. Ask the viewers questions:

"What was the film saying?"

"What characters did you relate with?"

"What parts were humorous? Sad? Meaningful? Personal? Convicting? Realistic?"

Use the questions in the study guide to start discussions. Always direct discussion toward the message of the film. You might also want to try some of these options:

- Leave the lights off after the film is over. If the film is sad or emotional, the teary-eyed viewers will appreciate this.
- Break up into small groups to discuss the film. Select leaders before-hand for each group and provide discussion questions.
- Focus closing prayer time on *personal application*.
- Have group activities that live out the message of the film.

Video Cassettes

Although we have seen secular movies in the form of video cassettes for the past several years now, the Christian market is, unfortunately, easing in quite slowly. However, it is only a matter of time before video becomes a popular outlet for Christian films.

Video cassettes are appealing for several reasons. They are less expensive to lease or purchase than 16mm films, they are more durable, they are easier to show, and they are better suited for small groups. It is practical for a church to build an entire library of dramatic, documentary, and teaching cassettes and to make them available to its members. Unlike most things in life, video cassette machines are constantly coming *down* in price, making them now no more expensive than TV sets, and affordable for both church and home use. Imagine, if the home sponsoring next Sunday's after-glow has a VCR (video cassette recorder), all you have to get is a tape!

The video cassette explosion has been slow in coming for the church, but it will offer new and creative ways to utilize film in youth work.

Not a Baby-Sitter!

The whole idea of being a selective viewer, utilizing study guides, and being prepared to lead a discussion is to encourage you to regard a film as something far beyond a form of visual baby-sitting. Too often we have used films because the preacher is on vacation or because the youth minister has run out of Bible studies. This places film into the role of a time-filler or an entertainer. I challenge you to transcend that thinking and use films as they were meant to be: as aids to help you mold the lives of those who view them. This will take extra effort on your part. It takes time to keep up on current films, preview them, advertise, and prepare to lead discussions. But I know you will agree that films can add a powerful and effective dimension to your ministry, one that will aid you in shaping lives for Christ.

---

[1]Although some 16mm films are available on a lease basis, most are rented for one showing only.

Addendum
A LIST OF IDEAS
FOR USING FILMS AND VIDEO IN YOUTH MINISTRY

- Use them as part of camps and retreats.
- Use them for outreach:
  (1) Rent a local theater or auditorium and invite the public.
  (2) Take an evangelistic film with you on camping and bike trips for showing at campgrounds. Take plenty of flyers to hand out beforehand.
  (3) Invite non-Christian friends in the neighborhood for a barbecue and evangelistic film.
- Use them as the featured part of a youth-sponsored Sunday evening service.
- Use them as part of a topical preaching or Bible study series.
- Use a video cassette or series such as *Jesus of Nazareth* for small group meetings in the home.
- Use theatrical films like *Chariots of Fire* as a basis for discussion.
- Use a video cassette recorder to tape network programs and commercials and discuss the material and the effect the media has on our lives.

Suggested Resources for Films and Videos

Aletheia Publisher, Inc. Richard L. Parrott, Executive Director, P.O. Box 402126, Garland, TX 75040. (214) 530-1941. FILMS

Bauman Bible Telecasts. Lois Hertzler, V.P. Admin/Dist., 3436 Lee Highway, Arlington, VA 22207. (703) 243-1300. FILMS, VIDEO

Christian Communication. Thelma Blanchard, Manager, 150 S. Los Robles, Suite 600, Pasadena, CA 91101. (213) 449-4400. FILMS

Christian Leadership Training. Ms. May Heron, 21300 Mack Avenue, Grosse Pointe Woods, MI 48236. (313) 882-1746. FILMS

David C. Cook Publishing Company. Gloria Nussbaum, 850 N. Grove Avenue, Elgin, IL 60120. (312) 741-2400. FILMS, VIDEO CASSETTES, OVERHEAD MATERIALS

Cornerstone Pictures. Lori Bliss, Vice President, 6829 Canoga Avenue, Canoga Park, CA 91303. (213)716-7722. FILMS

Creative Productions, Inc. Larry Blazer, President, 958 E. Davies Avenue Littleton, CO 80122. (303) 794-6482. VIDEO CASSETTES

Day Star Productions. Fred Heeren, President, 326 S. Willie Avenue, Wheeling, IL 60090. (312)541-3547. FILMS

Epsicopal Radio-TV Foundation. Dr. Theodore Baehr, President, 3379 Peachtree Rd., N.E., Suite 851, Atlanta, GA 30326. (404)233-5419 FILMS, VIDEO CASSETTES

Evangelical Films, Inc. Greg Baughn, President, 2848 West Kingsley, Garland, TX 75041. (214)278-3531. FILMS

Family Life Distributors, Inc. Charles B. Moore, President, P.O. Box 20059, El Cajon, CA 92021. (714)579-8667. FILMS

Films for Christ Association. Marian Taylor, Director, N. Eden Rd., Elmwood, IL 61529. (309)565-7722. FILMS

Robert Fuqua Productions. Robert Fuqua, Executive Producer, P.O. Box 38261, Dallas, TX 75238. (214)226-4383. FILMS

Gateway Films, Inc. A. Kenneth Curtis, Box A, Landsdale, PA 19446. (215)584-1893. FILMS, VIDEO CASSETTES

Genesis Project C.B. Wismar, Sr. Vice President, 5201 Leesburg Pike #800, Falls Church, VA 22041. (703)998-0800. FILMS, FILMSTRIPS

Glenray Communications Glenn Carlson, V.P.—Distribution, P.O. Box 40400, 1530 E. Elizabeth St., Pasadena, CA 91104. (213)797-5462. FILMS

Gospel Films Inc. Donald Craymer, Vice President Dist., P.O. Box 455, Muskegon, MI 49443. (616)773-3361. FILMS, VIDEO CASSETTES

Harvest Productions (Evangelical Baptist Missions) Don Ross, Executive Director, P.O. Box 2225, Kokomo, IN 46902. (219)267-2038. FILMS

Heartland Productions, Inc. Marc Whitmore, Distribution Coordinator, P.O. Box 3751, Urbandale Station, 5907 Meredith Drive, Des Moines, IA 50322. (515)278-4688. FILMS

Heritage Media Productions. Dr. Joseph Bridges, P.O. Box 1867, Fresno, CA 93718. (209)251-8681. FILMS

JRB Motion Graphics, Ltd. Jim Burgess, Director, 4117 Stone Way N, Seattle, WA 98103. (206)632-0834. FILMS

Ken Anderson Films. Lane Anderson, Vice President, P.O. Box 618, Winona Lake, IN 46590. 1520 E. Winona Avenue, Warsaw, IN 46580. (219)267-5774. FILMS

Kuntz Brothers, Inc. Frank Kuntz, President; Darryl Kuntz, Vice-President, P.O. Box 141109, Dallas, TX 75214. (214)691-4500. FILMS

Leodas & Arbusto & Associates Inc. Domenic Arbusto, 333 East 49 St., New York, NY 10017. (212)688-4308. FILMS, VIDEO CASSETTES

Life Productions, Inc. Charles P. Warren, President, P.O. Box B, 510 W. Lamar Street, Americus, GA 31709. (912)924-9601. FILMS

Lutheran Television. Ms. Janet R. Naji, Manager, Media Marketing & Promo, 2185 Hampton Ave., St. Louis, MO 63139. (314)647-4900. FILMS, VIDEO CASSETTES

Mass Media Ministries. Furman R. York, General Manager, 2116 North Charles Street, Baltimore, MD 21218. (301)727-3270. FILMS

Mark IV Pictures, Inc. Russ Doughton, Jr., P.O. Box 3751 Urbandale Station, 5907 Meredith Drive, Des Moines, IA 50322. (515)278-4737. FILMS

Edward T. McDougal Films. Edward T. McDougal, President, 682 Ardsley Rd., Winnetka, IL 60093. (312)446-5432. FILMS

Merit Media International. Jack Hanslick, President, 1314 Circle Way, Laguna Beach, CA 92651. (714)494-1944. FILMS, VIDEO CAS-SETTES

Missionary Enterprises. Paul R. Goodman, President, P.O. Box 2127, 409 W. Imperial Highway, La Habra, CA 90631. (213)697-4617. FILMS

Moody Institute of Science. A. Peter Margosian, Director of Distribution, 12000 East Washington Boulevard, Whittier, CA 90606. (213)698-8256. FILMS, FILMSTRIPS

New Day Productions. Byron Williamson, Executive Producer, P.O. Box 4055, Austin, TX 78765. (512)255-1316. FILMS

New Liberty Enterprises, Inc. Clifton Summers, Distribution Manager, Leonard Skibitzke, Marketing Manager, 1805 West Magnolia, Burbank, CA 91506. (213)842-6167. FILMS, VIDEO CASSETTES

Olive's Film Productions, Inc. David Olive, President, P.O. Box 9, Madison, AL 35758, 651 Clutts Rd., Harvest, AL 35749. (205)837-4166. FILMS

Omega Films. Bob Cording, President, 428 8th St., Del Mar, CA 92014. (714)481-3031. FILMS

Paulist Productions. Paul Weber, General Manager; Melissa Wohl, Manager-International Sales, P.O. Box 1057, 17575 Pacific Coast Highway, Pacific Palisades, CA 90272. (213)454-0688. FILMS

Quadrus Media Ministry. 610 East State Street, Rockford, IL 61104. (815)987-3970. FILMS, VIDEO CASSETTES

Religious Film Corporation. Candace A. Hunt, Marketing Services, P.O. Box 4029, 2282 Townsgate Road, Westlake Village, CA 91359. (805)495-7418. FILMS, FILMSTRIPS

Sparrow Productions. George Baldwin, Director, 8025 Deering Avenue, Canoga Park, CA 91304. (213)703-6599. FILMS

Swartwout Productions. Chuck Swartwout, Owner, P.O. Box 1450, Scottsdale, AZ 85252. (602)994-4774. FILMS

Video Communications, Inc. Linda Hess, Ass't. VP; Bob Blair, Exec. VP, 6535 East Skelly Drive, Tulsa, Oklahoma 74145. (918)622-6460. VIDEO CASSETTES

Victory International Productions, Inc. William T. Mings, Vice President, P.O. Box 5277, Garden Grove, CA 92645. FILMS

Video Ministries, Inc. Cheryl Brady, Administration, P.O. Box 5886, 12208 Pacific Highway S.E. Tacoma, Washington 98405. (206)584-2324. VIDEO CASSETTES

Video Outreach, Inc. Jim Bullock, President, 5159 Cahuenga Blvd., N. Hollywood, CA 91601. (213)506-7268. VIDEO CASSETTES

Vision House Films. Roy Martin-Harris, 1651 E. Edinger Avenue, Suite 104, Santa Ana, CA 92705. (714)558-0511. FILMS, VIDEO CASSETTES

White Lion Pictograph. Wendell F. Moody, Producer, 146 Melrose Place, San Antonio, TX 78212. (512)826-3615. FILMS

Word Publishing. Christopher J. Hayward, Director of Video Marketing, P.O. Box 1790, Waco, TX 76710. (817)772-7650. FILMS, VIDEO CASSETTES

World Wide Pictures, Inc. Paul W. Kurtz, Director of Distribution Operations, 1201 Hennepin Avenue, Minneapolis, MN 55403. (612)338-3335. FILMS

12

Training for Leadership:
The Timothy and Tabitha Clubs

Douglas and Vickie Simpson

In any good youth program, there must be some attention given to developing the leadership potential in the youth. No single phase of the ministry can do all that needs to be done in this area. Many leadership-development programs need to be planned and implemented.

The Timothy and Tabitha Clubs comprise one such program. It is designed to teach youth people the basic functions of a working church in a learning-by-doing process. In a sense, it is an internship or apprentice-type educational program. It expresses our understanding that the young people of today have the responsibility for the progress of the church of tomorrow.

We set a number of goals in our lives—goals for business, goals for government, and goals for the church. While we work hard to achieve those goals, we do so with the realization that we will leave many things undone, left for someone else to complete. We know that someone younger will follow in our footsteps and take over where we have left off. If we believe our goals have eternal significance—and our goals for the church do—then we must train our youth to follow the same path we have followed. Otherwise, when they take over, they will go in a different direction.

Throughout history, we have had examples where children were trained as apprentices in order to prepare themselves for their lives' work. This practice is carried over today in many professions. For example, a doctor realizes one of the important segments of his education is his internship. In our public school system, we have the co-op program, in which students attend classes for half a day and work the remaining half. During summer vacations, Bible colleges are offering internship programs in which future youth ministers, missionaries, and other vocational Christian workers can learn firsthand through practical experiences and earn college credit at the same time.

In the Scriptures we are given instances where apprenticeships were practiced. As an infant, Samuel was taken to the temple to live and grow up learning the duties of priesthood. In the New Testament, we see that Paul took Timothy under his wing and instructed him in missionary work by taking him on as a helper.

In addition to teaching our children the plan of salvation and encouraging them to lead the Christian life, we need to teach them a few basics concerning the church. Just think for a moment. How often do young people ask questions concerning the work of the church? "What is an elder?" "Where does the money go that is placed in the offering plate?" "Who picks up the Communion cups each Sunday?" "Why does the music director wave his/her arms during the song service?" "Does the minister get paid just for preaching on Sundays?" "Where does the Sunday-school teacher get all those neat ideas?" These are matters we take for granted. Many churches today still cling to the old cliche, "Children should be seen and not heard." We cannot put our children on the back burners of the church until they reach adulthood and expect them to wake up one morning knowing all the right answers.

Just as we teach our children the basics of the business world and of government, we need to teach them the basics of church organization. Do we want someone unskilled to succeed us in our businesses in later years? Do we want someone unskilled to succeed our elected officials in government? Certainly not! Following the example set forth by our ancestors, we send our children to school and do everything within our power to insure a proper education so they will be prepared to carry on what we have begun. Neither should we expect the young people in our churches to grow up and successfully carry on as leaders unless they receive the proper training. This program helps provide that training.

Definition of Timothy and Tabitha Clubs

The Timothy and Tabitha Clubs program is designed primarily for boys and girls in grades one through six, but may be adapted to other age levels. This program will enable the youth to have a better understanding of the basic jobs of the church, and will cultivate within them an interest in using their talents in the church.

The program may run from ten to thirteen weeks, depending on the subjects to be discussed. Saturday afternoons provide the ideal time to carry through such a program. This will give several hours without interruption to complete each segment. Such a program will be well attended during the winter months. This will help chase away those wintertime blahs for the young people while creating enthusiasm within the youth group.

A director must be selected to oversee and organize the club. Two adults should also be recruited—a man to sponsor the Timothy Club and a woman to sponsor the Tabitha Club.

The Timothy and Tabitha Clubs are not just another program where the youth sit and absorb. The key word here is involvement. The youth learn by doing. Instead of listening to a lecture on the fundamentals of preparing a sermon, serving Communion, or planning and serving a banquet, the youth attend classes on the various topics and then are given the opportunity to put what they learn into practice.

Objectives

What benefits will the students receive through this program? Each prospective leader will have his own list of goals he would like to see attained during the program. Listed below are some objectives the program can help you reach:

1. After the course, each student will experience a decrease in stage fright.
2. After a specified ten- to thirteen-week period, each student will demonstrate the use of church-related talents and abilities through participation in a Sunday evening service.
3. The youth will express an interest in a leadership ministry.
4. The youth will come to understand that Jesus wants us to serve Him through His church.
5. The youth will know they are not an island unto themselves, but they need the church and the church needs them.
6. The youth will grow spiritually and express the thought that one way to continue growing is by being involved in service to others.
7. The youth will demonstrate that even though church-related work may be difficult, the tasks can be accomplished if they are committed to the task.

8. A loving relationship will develop between the youth and the sponsors.
9. The youth will want to continue using their talents even when the club is over.
10. The parents of the club members will be more interested and involved in the church.
11. The parents will see what their children can do when given a little encouragement.
12. The youth will be filled with an enthusiasm that will carry over into other areas of the youth program.
13. Adults who had not been working with youth will get involved in the youth program and may develop an interest in becoming youth sponsors.
14. The youth will learn that even though church work is hard, they can also find their efforts to be fun and rewarding.

Schedule

Incorporated within the Timothy and Tabitha Clubs each week will be a devotion, lesson and expression period, light refreshments, and a field trip.

No more than fifteen minutes should be spent conducting devotions. The devotional should take place after the students have collected their outlines for that week's lesson and assembled in the sanctuary or other specified area. This time period provides a valuable opportunity for student participation. After an adult leader has conducted devotions for a couple of weeks, the youth may take turns volunteering to present the devotions. The use of an object lesson to help reinforce the Scripture provides perhaps the easiest method for the student.

The curriculum and teachers should be established before the start of the program. Each teacher is responsible for preparing an outline of his lesson and submitting the outline to the director at least one week prior to the teaching date. This will allow the director sufficient time to have the outlines typed and copies made for each student. Each student should be given a copy of the outlined lesson at the beginning of each meeting. Folders may be purchased and given to the students for the purpose of retaining their outlines and notes. A reminder should be given to the teacher (either by mail or by phone) approximately three days in advance of the date of his upcoming lesson. Always remember to send teachers thank-you notes expressing your gratitude for the extra effort they have put forth in presenting the lessons.

The time allotted for lesson and expression is one hour. This allows approximately twenty minutes for the teacher to teach the lesson and forty minutes for student participation. Each child should be encouraged to participate during this time. Once again, the key word is *involvement*.

Fifteen minutes should be sufficient time for refreshments to be served. This will give each child a chance to eat and wash up before going on the field trip. The refreshments should be kept simple. Parents are to be contacted and a serving schedule made before the program begins. Usually two parents per week to prepare and serve the refreshments is adequate. The schedule may be rotated so that by the end of the program the parents of each child will have contributed. Since refreshments are to be kept very light, the students may participate in the cleanup.

Field trips should reinforce the lessons if at all possible. For example, if the lesson deals with how to prepare a sermon, a trip to a nearby Bible College would be appropriate. However, such facilities are not always available. Trips planned to tour a local TV or radio station, fire station, or newspaper office are informative and create interest within the group. Some trips may be planned for entertainment, such as roller skating or miniature golfing. At least one parent, in addition to the regular Timothy and Tabitha Clubs sponsors, should accompany the youth.

Before any trips are taken, a medical release form should be secured from each parent or guardian in case of accident or injury. Some churches may provide for such outings within their insurance policies. Find out what kind of coverage your church's insurance provides in case of injury on a church-related activity.

Allow two hours to conduct field trips, with not more than one hour used for traveling and the remaining time spent for the tour or activity. Traveling time should be kept to a minimum, as this will allow more time for the youth to enjoy the planned activity. Some trips may take longer, such as the roller skating activity. Parents should be informed of the approximate time the children will be returning home.

All field trips should be planned during the initial planning session held by the director and sponsors. A confirmation call should be made to the place to be visited at least six days in advance of the actual trip. Again, remember to send thank-you notes both to the parents who served as chaperones and to the organization toured.

Below is a sample schedule for the Timothy and Tabitha Clubs.

The boys and girls will not usually need to attend different classes, as most subjects will be applicable to members of both groups. In such cases, the groups will meet together. An asterisk (*) on the following schedule marks each session that requires separate meetings. Remember to have the schedule planned and teachers contacted before the first club meeting.

TIMOTHY CLUB

DATE	CLASS	FIELD TRIP
Week 1	Audio-Visuals	Film Festival
Week 2	Teaching a Lesson	TV Station
Week 3	Church Evangelism	Nursing Home Program
Week 4	Directing Music	Fire Station
Week 5	Directing Music	Police Station
Week 6	Praying and Reading Scripture in Public	Roller Skating
Week 7*	How to Preach	Bible College Trip
Week 8*	Duties of Deacons	Newspaper Office
Week 9*	Duties of Elders	Court House
Week 10	Job of Janitor	Church Camp
Week 11	Graduation Banquet Closing Program Practice Closing Program	

TABITHA CLUB

DATE	CLASS	FIELD TRIP
Week 1	Audio-Visuals	Film Festival
Week 2	Teaching a Lesson	TV Station
Week 3	Church Evangelism	Nursing Home Program
Week 4	Directing Music	Fire Station
Week 5	Directing Music	Police Station
Week 6	Praying and Reading Scripture in Public	Roller Skating
Week 7*	Duties of Church Secretary	Bible College Trip
Week 8*	Banquet Etiquette	Newspaper Office
Week 9*	Nursery Duties	Court House
Week 10	Job of Janitor	Church Camp
Week 11	Graduation Banquet Closing Program Practice Closing Program	

*Boys and girls meet sparately.

How to Put the Program in Progress

The key ingredient to having a smoothly operated program is organization. Approximately three fourths of this program must be done in advance. Therefore, the director and sponsors must be chosen with utmost care. They should be good organizers who are willing to put forth the effort required to construct the program.

Approximately three months before the program is to begin, the director should present the program to the youth committee for their complete support. The committee will in turn present the program to the general board for their approval.

Two months before, secure sponsors to represent the Timothy and Tabitha Clubs. Remember, one sponsor will be needed to represent the Timothy Club and one sponsor to represent the Tabitha Club.

Seven weeks before, the director should meet with the sponsors to organize the entire program of classes and field trips. Phone calls should be divided between the three individuals.

Six weeks before the starting date, announce during the extended sessions that a special announcement will be made in two weeks. The following week, remind the youth of the surprise announcement to be made the next week. The first step in presenting this or any program to the students is to capture their attention.

Four weeks before, take a few minutes at the beginning of the Sunday morning worship service to explain the program to the parents. Another sponsor may be making the same announcement for those in extended sessions. The use of an overhead projector to help illustrate the program is ideal. Include within the presentation the names of the leaders, a list of major objectives, a brief schedule, rules for registration, and the starting date. This presentation is only a brief summation and should take no more than five minutes.

Publicity should begin at least three weeks before the beginning date. This may be done through the use of posters placed throughout the church, announcements in the church paper, and reminders placed in the bulletins. Make the people aware of the program by using any and all forms of publicity available. Saturate the congregation with information regarding the Timothy and Tabitha Clubs.

Two weeks in advance, send a letter to all the kids within the age group designated to remind them of the program and registration requirements. A letter should also be sent to the parents, reminding them of the importance of the Timothy and Tabitha Clubs as

well as the registration rules. The letters to the youth and parents
may be mailed within the same envelope. Fold and staple each
letter separately. On the outside, label the letter to the youth, "For
Youth Only," and label the letter to the parents, "For Parents Only."
This will create more interest as to the contents of the letters.

Registration may be held for two consecutive Sundays before the
starting date. Registration forms may also be made available on the
first day of the clubs prior to the first session for those students
who have not registered. The registration table should be placed in
a central, noticeable location. Use the Timothy and Tabitha Clubs'
sponsors to assist the youth in filling out the registration cards.

REGISTRATION FOR TIMOTHY/TABITHA CLUB

NAME_____ AGE_____
ADDRESS_____ GRADE_____
CITY_____ BIRTHDATE_____
FATHER'S NAME_____ MOTHER'S NAME_____

I am registering for the:
    ☐ Timothy Club   ☐ Tabitha Club
Do you play a musical instrument?   yes_____ no_____
  If yes, what kind of instrument_____
  ☐ $2.00 Registration Fee Paid.

Permission from Parent:
  I hereby give permission for my child to attend the Timothy &
Tabitha Club. I also realize that they will be doing some traveling
in the church bus and in case of accident I will not hold the
church responsible.

(signed)_____

Sample Registration Card

At the time of registration, the sponsors will need to collect a
nominal fee from each student. Investing their own money will
help provide incentive for the students to try harder than they
would if the program were free. The money will also offset some of
the cost of the program.

Parents need to be present at the time of registration. During this
time, certain requirements may be reviewed with both parents and

children concerning the program. Registration time also provides a good opportunity to have the parents sign the medical release forms necessary for participation in the field trips. It's also a good time to recruit volunteers to serve as chaperones for the field trips or to help provide refreshments.

Ask the youth to commit themselves to attend every session unless they are sick or out of town. Explain that diplomas will be given to each pupil who attends at least seventy-five percent of the sessions. Also perfect attendance awards may be given to those who attend each session.

The question of late registration may arise. A child joining after several sessions will not receive the full benefits of the program. Therefore, a cut-off date should be established. After one fourth of the program has been completed, no new participants could receive diplomas anyway, and they should wait until the next time the program is done. If, however, the program is a one-time practice, no one should be refused at any time. Even attending one session is better than none.

Special Effects

Many elements may be added to help insure the success of the program. The leaders of each group will want to incorporate ideas of their own to make the program more appealing to their youth. Here are some suggestions that may help you.

Group Picture

Pictures not only are worth a thousand words; they also provide a thousand memories. Five by seven glossies may be printed for a reasonable fee and will become a cherished memento to the club members.

Graduation Banquet

A banquet may be held after the last session for members of the Timothy and Tabitha Clubs. If a class on Banquet Etiquette was included in the curriculum, those attending may wish to help in decorating and planning the banquet. Parents may be recruited to help prepare and serve the meal.

A special program should be planned that will appeal to the youth, such as a puppet show or a magic show.

A central theme should be chosen for the banquet. Some popular themes are "We've Only Just Begun," "You've Come A Long Way, Baby," and "Kids Under Construction."

Closing Program

Announce at the beginning of the program that the students will be conducting a Sunday evening service. Involve the youth as much as possible in this service. Allow them to direct songs, have prayer, read Scripture, present a devotion, and take up the offering. If a child possesses a special talent, such as singing or playing a musical instrument, that one may provide the special music for the evening. The children should be given the opportunity to put what they have learned into practice.

A slide presentation of classes and activities taken throughout the club may be shown at the closing program. Each child should be assigned a slide to explain. Make certain the slide each one chooses contains his own picture. This will provide an excellent opportunity for the child to speak before an audience while giving the adults a more thorough explanation of the program.

Toward the end of the program, diplomas and perfect attendance awards may be given to each child. Praise all the participants for the efforts they have put forth during the past weeks.

CLOSING PROGRAM EXAMPLE

Prelude (piano)	Youth
Welcome	Youth
Opening Prayer	Youth
Puppet Skit	Puppeteers
Special Number	Club Choir
Hymn	
Scripture Reading	Youth
Special Number	Club Choir
Sermonette	Youth
Communion Hymn	
Scripture	Youth
Ushers	Youth
Offering Scripture	Youth
Ushers	Youth
Announcements	Director
Special Number	Youth
Sermonette	Youth
Hymn	
Slide Presentation	All club members
Invitation	
Presentation of certificates and awards	Director and sponsors
Closing Prayer	Youth

Closing Reception

Incorporated within the Timothy and Tabitha Clubs may be a closing reception held immediately following the closing program. This may be a closed reception involving only members of the clubs and their families. This will give the leaders an opportunity to mingle with the parents.

This reception is to be held in honor of the youth, praising them for their efforts put forth during the past weeks. Make them feel special by praising them before their parents and peers.

Summary

The key ingredient for the success of this program is student participation. We need to seize every opportunity to teach our children. The young people sitting in beginner, primary, and junior worship sessions today will in a few short years be the elders, deacons, and leaders of our churches. They will be teaching the lessons we once taught, serving the Communion we once served, and reading the Scriptures we once read. We need to pay attention to our youth now while we have the opportunity!

The First Christian Church

Lamar, Missouri

Hereby Certifies That

HAS SATISFACTORILY COMPLETED THE REQUIREMENTS FOR

TABITHA CLUB
TIMOTHY CLUB

_____ MINISTER

DATE

_____ ASSOCIATE MINISTER

SPONSOR

Sample Diploma

13

Fine Arts
in Youth Ministry

Dan and Linda Lawson

Any program that can contribute to the educational, service, and expressional phases of youth ministry deserves serious consideration. Fine arts programs can be just such programs.

Educationally, the arts excel because they involve the students. Recent educational reports maintain that students retain only about fifteen percent of what they hear, but close to ninety percent of what they experience (see, hear, and do). Thus, if you present a lesson through some means that involves the students (such as drama), the class is six times as likely to remember it than if you simply lecture. The fine arts can play an outstanding role in your educational ministry to youth.

But the arts are not just for education. Fine arts can comprise a creative program of activity designed to give the youth opportunities to use their talents in service to Christ. Music, for example, can minister to more human needs than we can count, providing inspiration, comfort, challenge, and more. But the use of fine arts not only ministers to the hearers, it also brings the performers a sense of enjoyment, productivity, and accomplishment. It provides the youth a sense of belonging, because they see that they are of service in the congregation. And if young people can see how God can use their talents now, they will develop confidence in using their talents for the Lord in the future.

The Christian—young or old—needs to express himself. The

fine arts can be one of the most powerful and effective vehicles for that expression. Whether performing a piece of his own composition or one of another, a Christian young person may find it easier to express himself in song or drama than in simple conversation, and his audience may be more receptive as well. And what could be more expressive of one's inner self than painting or another of the visual arts? Since Christ lives within Christians (Galatians 2:20), a Christian young person's self-expression becomes an expression of Christ and can help others in their relationships with Christ, as well as helping that young person mature and develop spiritually.

Any program that enhances the educational work of the youth ministry, the service role of young people, and the expressions of the faith of youth must be taken seriously. While vocal music groups are popular in youth work, other fine arts groups may also receive a good response. Some even more so because of their uniqueness, even without quality as a serious factor. The church that provides fine arts electives that are creative and unusual will encourage the specialized talents of its youth and also will widen the future expression of Christ's church.

The Scriptures show the arts as prominent in the life of the early church. The apostle Paul gives us the following admonition: "Let the word of Christ richly dwell within you, with all wisdom teaching and admonishing one another with psalms and hymns and spiritual songs, singing with thankfulness in your hearts to God" (Colossians 3:16, NASB). Singing is closely linked with prayer. Paul says in 1 Corinthians 14:15 (NASB), "I shall pray with the spirit and I shall pray with the mind also; I shall sing with the spirit and I will sing with the mind also."

The church has a most important message to relate to the world. It is a message of hope for eternal life to come and abundant life now through Jesus the Christ, the Son of the Living God, who becomes our Lord and Savior. All of the major arts, such as music, drama, painting, writing, architecture, sculpture, and speaking can be a means of our communicating the gospel.

Youth Choirs

The most common of the fine arts expressions used in the church has historically been the vocal choir. Not only have such choirs successfully communicated to the emotions, but also to the intellect. Important messages in the Christian religion have been preserved through vocal music. The power of those messages have often been best expressed by choirs, whose many members and personalities can add warmth or force or any number of emotions appropriate to the message.

The vocal choir has been very popular in the church. Many churches are privileged to have several choirs designed for different age groups: cherub choirs, primary choirs, junior boys choirs, junior girls choirs, junior-high choirs, and youth choirs, not to mention adult choirs. The graded choir programs allow for the group choir experience to further develop in later years. The best high-school choirs have their roots in years of children's choral programs.

Over the years, interest in choirs will probably slump at certain times no matter what you do. However, you can still take some action to minimize the slump. Work to keep boredom at a minimum. Provide plenty of goals for each group to attain. Set up performances both inside and outside the church. Keep your youth busy preparing for service to others. The best way to destroy any choir is to fail to use what that choir has been preparing in their many rehearsals.

One of the greatest problems for the graded choir approach is the changing voice of the junior or junior-high boy. Two possible approaches may provide some remedy. One suggestion is to provide some other fine arts group in place of singing during the period when those young boys find their voice to be an embarrassment. Puppet theaters, handbell choirs, marionette troupes, or drama groups may provide the solution.

Another suggestion is simply to keep boys singing in choirs during this change, perhaps even a boys choir. While it may be difficult to adjust to singing with a man's voice after singing soprano, singing in an older choir would be even harder if a boy had not sung in a choir at all.

Activities of a Youth Choir

The older the choir, the greater the amount of activity it needs. Such activity has relationship to the goals and purposes of the choir. These activities and goals are to be established before the group is organized on an annual basis. Announce at the first rehearsal of the choir the major activity and target for the group.

1. Sing in Worship.

Every choir will be much appreciated in a service of worship. A cherub choir of happy faces will delight the hearts of a church full of worshipers. It goes without saying that musical excellence is not the goal here. Simplicity of message will be the greatest contribution made in a worship service by children's choirs.

Junior-high and high-school choirs have the potential to be standing choirs in worship. They can provide service music on a regular weekly basis. An enthusiastic anthem by a youth choir is a superb way of opening worship. Choral response following a prayer in worship is helpful. A softly sung selection during the Communion service or while the offering is collected can assist in leading worshipers in personal meditation and prayer. Larger congregations that provide more than one worship hour can benefit from placing an adult choir in one hour of worship and a youth choir in the other hour. Certainly the regular weekly use of a youth choir will communicate a sense of worth to the young people who sing.

2. Have a Choir Festival.

Contact a church with a choir organized similar to yours and combine both choirs for a festival. Perhaps several youth choirs can come together for such a choral event. If the festival is out of town, it provides the added attraction of traveling. The privilege of being a host for the festival might mean the opportunity to practice hospitality overnight.

A choir festival will feature a guest conductor. It's always good to have your youth hear the same advice from someone else. Have good, hard-working rehearsal sessions with adequate copies of all the music to be sung. Schedule some time for fellowship and socializing between the choirs. Some nice friendships can be made at a choir festival. Conclude the festival with a performance to use what they have prepared. Let them sing in a worship service or at a concert.

A festival lets your choir see what other choirs are doing; so it is a good source for new ideas. Would you like your choir to do a musical? Have a choir festival with another youth choir that is already doing musicals. The idea will catch on quickly.

3. Take a Tour.

Young people like to travel. Take your youth choir to New York City, to Florida, to Los Angeles, or to the Northwest. Let them be challenged by the rich Christian fellowship with church concerts in Canada and Mexico. The greatest motivation for a youth choir to work hard the full year is to schedule a choir tour as the finale to their efforts.

The key to having a successful choir tour is organization. Here is the procedure for setting the tour in motion.

a. Set a date for the tour. Good youth choir tours last from one week to as many as three weeks. Usually the summer is the best time for the youth to take such a trip. Summer is not always the best time for scheduling concerts, however. Spring vacation is another alternative, but it is usually not longer than one week. Set the tour date six to twelve months before the actual trip.

b. Determine the finances. There will be expenses for meals, lodging, transportation, and sight-seeing. There may even be some production expenses. The choir members should pay for as much of the tour expense as possible. They will appreciate it more when they have made such an investment themselves. If the cost of the tour is more than youth themselves can handle, there are other alternatives. The church budget, a money-raising project, or contributions from interested friends of the choir can certainly help to lower the cost. Usually the churches or organizations that will host the concert along the tour will be willing to assist by providing some meals or lodging, and perhaps even an offering.

c. Arrange the itinerary. Concerts can be scheduled with churches, summer youth camps, nursing homes, civic organizations, youth-rally or convention gatherings, vacation Bible schools, banquets, shopping malls, and city parks. Be creative. Be sure that all of your arrangements are in writing. The memory can fail as time passes and as more than one concert gets scheduled. Be sure to arrange for the concert location, time, publicity, and length. If the host organization is helping out with lodging or meals, be sure that all details, like communicating the number in the group, are confirmed.

d. Establish a concert program. Good tour concerts can be organized with several fine arts groups together. For example, take the youth choir on a tour with your handbell choir or your drama troupe or your puppet theater. Such a variety of groups make for an interesting concert program. Perform a youth musical. Some outstanding musicals by excellent Christian composers are now available for the average youth choir. Be original and write your own musical, using music from a variety of sources. Avoid putting on a mere variety show. Have a theme that determines your message and the direction of the concert presentation. A good concert will last between one hour and an hour-and-a-half in length.

e. Communicate with parents. If a tour is to succeed, it must be supported by the parents of the choir members. Therefore, parents must know the details of the tour. They will fully support the choir if they understand everyone's responsibility and expectations.

4. Do a Youth Choir Musical.

Be careful that the pressures of preparing for a big program like the musical do not hurt the other activities of the youth choir, like worship leadership. Musicals provide a larger challenge that will stretch the talents of the young people.

Some musicals can be attached to special seasonal occasions. Easter or Christmas cantatas are most appropriate. Christmas nativity scenes or live Christmas tree choirs can be great youth musicals to be presented for the entire church or even the whole community.

5. Sing on Special Occasions.

Youth Sunday can involve even more youth through a youth choir. Sing at an evangelistic rally or a revival meeting. Sing for Mother's Day banquets or for senior citizens dinners. If no special occasion invites the choir to sing, then initiate a special occasion and use your youth choir.

A Word of Caution

Just because someone thought it would be nice to have a youth choir is not adequate reason for organizing such a choir. There are many ways to minister to young people; the youth choir is only one way. Before you organize a choir, take into consideration the total youth program of the church. Based on that total picture, is there a need that can be met by having a youth choir?

Will the parents and leaders of the church be in favor of starting such a choir? Are the youth themselves sufficiently interested in participating in a youth choir? Will the boys in the youth group be willing to sing in the choir? Do the youth have time to rehearse and perform with a youth choir?

If the answer to all of the questions asked is in the affirmative, then it is time to announce the purpose and activity of the youth choir. Reveal your plans to the youth. It might even be advantageous to invite a neighboring youth choir to come perform for your church and youth. This will help your youth to catch the vision of what you have in mind for them.

Work hard to publicize and promote your choir before the first rehearsal. Make sure that the first rehearsal will be well attended. Be positive and well organized in that rehearsal so the kids leave it feeling good and eager to return.

The Rehearsal

Every practice session for your youth choir can challenge the youth to return again if it is a fast-paced rehearsal. Move things along so quickly that they have no time for talking and unconstructive activity. If the choir director wants to keep control of the rehearsal, he must come prepared with an outline of what he wants to accomplish. Never be predictable; keep variety in your approach. Come prepared with all of your tools, including sufficient copies of every song to be practiced. Know what songs you wish to rehearse. Even more importantly, know what you want the youth to do with each and every song selection. In other words, know how you want them to sing each song. Do not waste time by reviewing the tenor part of a song while the other three sections of the choir wander off from the rehearsal. If parts need to be rehearsed, then schedule sectional rehearsals for a portion of the session. This may demand that you have sectional leaders as well as extra pianists to play the parts out on the piano for the youth. When the whole choir comes back together, then put the entire composition together, working on more than mere notes. Work for blend, phrasing, and good balance in the voices.

Leave some time for lecture, announcements, devotions, and prayer. Let this time also be for spiritual nourishment and encouragement. Be sure that the rehearsal is enjoyable for all, you as well as the young people. A little humor goes a long way in making a rehearsal worthwhile. Give praise when praise is due and criticism when it is needed.

Drama in Youth Ministry

Let's face it. Some young people are not musically talented. For too long, the only fine arts outlet we have allowed young people in the church has required musical abilities. As schools cut back financially, the musical programs to feed those abilities will become limited. If you have only used music, you are eliminating several who could benefit from serving through the fine arts.

There are several real benefits to using drama for your young people. The dramatic message is clear, verbal, understandable, and visual. As long as your young people speak clearly and with enough volume, their message should come through. In that way, drama is clearly superior to handbells, for example, or for that matter, sometimes even a choral presentation.

The size of a drama group is unlimited. A good group can consist of two kids or every kid in your youth group—or something in between. If your group is small, make it a repertory group where every person has a part in every play. The larger the group, the more diverse it can become, and the more selective the director can be in handing out parts. A larger group can also afford to take on the additional details of lights, scenery, costumes, and sound equipment for larger productions. The larger the group, the more difficult it will be to keep everyone busy, so more helpers will be needed, of course. But size presents no limits for the drama group.

Drama offers an avenue of personal expression. While the best drama groups are good "teams," drama still offers the challenge of very personal expression. Only one person can play each part, but each person enjoys great freedom within that part. Drama draws out creativity and creative people. It can channel detractors or group show-offs into acceptable avenues of service. Drama is one of the few fine arts in the church that allows, or even encourages, humor. And through drama, a young person may make a statement of faith before his peers and be understood and encouraged. Drama is still unique enough to be in demand, when done well and with purpose. So why haven't we seen more drama? Let us look at some of the reasons, and then see whether they can't be eliminated or minimized.

1. "Plays take up entire worship services. We don't have the time."

2. "Drama demands too much rehearsal. Our young people drop everything else for a month and practice every night."

3. "Drama is too cumbersome. With all the lights, costumes, scenery, and make-up, they are always moving the Communion table and taking over things."

4. "To perform, you must pay royalties."

5. "Drama is self-serving. It is not worship."

"Plays take up entire worship services." They can, but they don't need to. If your group would like to perform, and this objection has been raised, you should concentrate on several short plays of five to seven minutes' duration instead of one long one. The longer your play, the fewer places you will have available to perform it. Instead of three or four acts and an intermission, find several one-act plays and build a repertoire suitable for several occasions: banquets, worship services, tours, nursing homes, and the like. If you have a large group, divide the group and rehearse several plays at once, assigning helpers as directors. If you do this, however, you will have to work hard to keep a "team spirit" about the group. Encourage them to attend each other's performances. Be sure to have at least one play involving everyone—perhaps something longer or more elaborate for a special occasion, perhaps one that requires more backstage help.

A group that can't perform, however, is a group without a goal. The way to make your group welcome many places is to have punchy one-act plays. The best of these plays incorporate humor, strong Biblical content, and an ending that brings the message home to the audience.

There are limited sources for such plays. Some of them are listed in the suggested resources at the end of this chapter. You may find, however, after performing a few that you have someone capable of writing plays for your group. Use the same critical eye in examining such plays as you would use in choosing other materials for your group. Ask yourself:

1. Is it Scriptural? Even plays put in a contemporary setting should pass this test. Don't sacrifice content for cuteness.

2. What is the main point? In short plays, the main point should be easily indentifiable, and it should be worthy of performance.

3. Where can we perform this play? A play on materialism might not be the best subject for a nursing home. Then again, it might. Pick suitable material for your group and its audiences.

4. Is it within the capabilities of this group? Some of the easiest plays to write are parables pulled straight from the Bible, using a narrator or two or a choral group to tell the story and actors enacting the story in mime. This kind of play is easy to write, but it is very difficult to perform. It is always good to have some challenging material, but also have something that can be rehearsed and performed in a reasonable amount of time, after no more than two months of regularly scheduled weekly rehearsals.

Is it in good taste? If you are actually in doubt about this, think again. The answer is probably no. If the play meets the test of a strong main point and is solidly Scriptural, you won't likely have any problems here. Sometimes Christian drama should make the audience a little uncomfortable by reminding us that we do silly things and fall short of the things God expects. Don't lose a good point by using bad language. Use drama to show love, not to take liberties.

6. Is the ending powerful? A good one-act play has a good closing line—one that evokes a sigh or a smile or an ouch. Young people love to perform powerful plays, and they will work hard to get that desired response.

"Drama demands too much rehearsal." It doesn't if you use short plays. A drama group can function year-round, or during the school year, using the same regular weekly rehearsal time as a youth choir, bell choir, or puppet theater.

"*Drama is too cumbersome.*" Again, this is not true of small plays. When drama is used in a worship service, keep props, makeup, and costuming to a minimum. Use available lighting. Make yourself welcome in the worship experience. Be cooperative and respectful of other things that take place in the service.

"*To perform, you must pay royalties.*" Royalties are not a problem for plays performed in a worship service where no admission fee is charged. It costs no more money to perform plays than it does to do musicals. You do have to pay for the scripts, just as you have to buy musical books. You may not buy one script or one musical book and photocopy—or even copy by hand—the words and/or music. That is a violation of the copyright law. But that same law allows performance at religious services without further cost or royalties. And if scripts are too expensive, write your own script. You may be able to say something more pertinent to the needs in your area than a published play could anyway.

"*Drama is self-serving.*" Don't allow your group to let this happen, particularly in a worship service. There are ways to avoid it. If the message of your play would be lost if the congregation applauded at the end of the play, as they would a play in the theater, ask the person presiding at the service to lead the congregation in prayer immediately after the play ends. Or choose an appropriate solo that brings home the message again and end the play with the song, delivered in a low-key manner. Or raise the lights quickly for the continuation of the service. There is also nothing wrong with asking the audience not to applaud. Do so in the introduction of the play or the order of worship.

Don't allow your young people to perform and then go home. Seat them with the rest of the congregation so that they may take part, communally, in the remainder of the service.

Drama allows a young person to be, for a short time, someone he is not. Christian drama can afford your young people the opportunity to speak the words of Jesus, to enact His principles, to try on the actions of Christianity. Jesus gave the response, when John and another of John the Baptist's disciples asked where He was staying, "Come and see" (John 1:39). To the question, "How shall we live?" Christian drama answers "Come and see."

Reader's Theater and Youth Work

A unique type of drama technique is reader's theater, also known as choral reading or verse choir. It is the reading aloud of poetry or prose or even a play by a group of people. Reader's theater is choir without music, presenting drama without actions through special arrangements of the spoken word. It is a group of dramatists who work together using the good principles of effective speech and drama to deliver a message that will allow the listeners to visualize in their minds the action of the drama. It is not responsive reading, but is a disciplined group approach just as choral music is. Audiences can be stirred as much by good choral reading as by good music.

The dramatic technique known as "choric reading" was used by the Greeks several hundred years before Christ. Such groups would begin reading together, speaking at the same rate of speed, speaking with expression, and so working as a team that they appeared to be one mighty voice. In a matter of seconds, sleeping audiences would come alive. They sat up and listened and were deeply moved by the messages presented.

The use of reader's theater in the youth ministry is unlimited. It differs from the acting style of dramatics in some very important ways. Choral reading is more structured and rigid in that the group must read what has been agreed to read. Actors cannot ad lib and must remain immobile. There is no need for memorization, however, or for body movement. Scripts are the tool of such a group.

Delivery of Choral Reading

In reading prose, plays, or Scripture, verse choirs approach their drama much as a singing choir. The entire group must determine a common rhythm. They must read at the same tempo. By having certain key words in the script accented, they will read well together without danger of being out of step with one another. The temptation to read the scripts with a monotone sound is ever present. The principle of reading with conversational naturalness must be taught. Have the readers in rehearsals speak conversationally with one another, being sensitive to the range of the voice pitches. Then ask them to read the printed script, attempting to read with the same width of pitch ranges.

Just as singing choirs have their challenge to sing with melody and harmony, so it is in choral reading. In singing, we have soprano, alto, tenor, and bass voices. In choral reading, we have high and low voices, dark and light voices, ladies' and men's voices. Arrange your scripts to take full advantage of these various harmonies. Use solo voices when possible to contrast portions of a play or Scripture. Often, a collection of voices in the same range can speak a narrative part with solo voices presenting those lines that are quotations. If the script calls for a female character, let the light lady voices do the reading. If the script presents the words of a man, then let those lines be read by the darker male voices in group or as a solo. The more important lines of the script should be presented by the theater as a whole.

How to Use a Script in Reading

The dramatic script should be typed, double-spaced, with each line numbered for easy reference in rehearsals. Mark your scripts with musical marking. If the lines are to be read softly, indicate such with the "p" for *piano*. Lines that are to be read loudly should be marked "f" for *fortissimo*. Place accent marks above each word that is important enough to be brought out for notice in the sentence. Indicate which lines are to be read by the ladies, by the men, as a solo, by the entire group, by two people, or by any other special group. Since the scripts are to be used in performances, make the best use of them possible. Don't hide their use, but have the readers place them obviously out in front of their eyes so they can see them very well.

Selecting a Reading

While the Scriptures provide an excellent source for material for your reader's theater, work for expanding your repertoire to include a variety of reading styles and messages. Start your group out first with Scripture readings. The Psalms are the best source. Your original arrangements of the Scriptures, using the dark voices on some verses and light voices on other verses, can allow certain passages to come alive with meaning. Normally, when the Scriptures are used as a reading, the passage should contain between one and twenty-five verses. Avoid using versions with archaic language, since these may prove difficult for youth to read. The New American Standard Bible is an excellent version from which to read, yet it keeps the language beautiful and dramatic. Biblical passages that make for a good theater reading include the following: Psalm 27; Romans 15; John 1:1-14; Psalm 24; Romans 1; Psalm 51; 1 Corinthians 13; and Psalm 23.

The best way to lose the interest of young people in reader's theater is to do nothing but Scripture readings. Be sure to mix your Scripture readings with some full scale dramatic scripts written specifically for reader's theater. Such scripts can be secured from drama companies listed under reader's theater, choral reading, or verse choirs in the publishers' catalogs. One company that publishes excellent reader's theater production scripts is Contemporary Drama Service, Box 457, 1131 Warren Ave., Downers Grove, Illinois 60515. Among their better scripts are the following: "Beatitude Attitudes," "The Paul Call," "Come Alive," and "For the Young Lovers."

What Age Group Should Be in Reader's Theater?

Youth from the ninth grade up through the twelfth grade are most effective in the reader's theater. However, should enough interest be aroused, and if time is available, the art is also good for single young adults. The theater works best with a minimum of ten readers, and could also adequately utilize as many as twenty-five or thirty readers. It is important, whatever the number, that there be a balance between the dark men's voices and the light ladies' voices. This balance is as vital to drama as it is to singing. The theater can often make good use of the harmony in dark and light voices for the sake of variety. Good use also can be made of solo voices throughout the scripts. Good readers can take solo parts, poor readers can be covered up easily in the mass reading parts.

Equipment for Reader's Theater

The first and most important piece of equipment is a good script collection. That is the only essential to the theater. Other good tools, however, are things like choral risers, stools for the readers to sit on while reading, script notebooks, choral robes, and lighting and sound systems. Good equipment takes time to collect. Once it is secured, take good care of it. Young people need to take the responsibility to care for their tools of performance. Give assignments to each member of the troupe to insure that each reader also has a duty for setting up and tearing down the equipment when the group performs.

Some reader's theater scripts may lend themselves to other forms of the arts. For example, if the theater reads the Genesis account of creation, develop a multimedia show illustrating the various periods of beginning. Conclude a Psalm about the greatness of God with the handbell choir playing a song or hymn of praise, such as "Holy, Holy, Holy." Whenever the reader's group performs in combination with other fine arts groups, then additional equipment will be necessary.

Some creative things can also be done with lighting effects for reader's theater. One theater did a black light show on the beatitudes. They colored their faces with fluorescent makeup that illuminated brightly under the rays of black lights. They wore black robes, with hoods over their heads. All that could be seen were their faces glowing in the dark. Their faces represented the faces present in the crowd to whom Christ preached His Sermon on the Mount years ago. At times, those faces became faces in society that heard the words of Christ and ignored them altogether. At other times, they were faces in society that heard the words of the Lord and put them into practice in their lives. The reader's read their scripts in the dark. The printed script was on cotton fiber paper that illuminated brightly in their notebooks when the black light rays caused the words to stand out clearly when everything else was not visible. Be creative and innovative.

Handbell Choirs

There are several things to consider before plunging your church into a fine arts program that includes English handbells. Bells are expensive, rehearsals are time-consuming, and only a relatively small number of people can be involved in a bell choir (which makes the expense per capita even more inhibiting, at least at the outset). Bells involve a considerable amount of equipment. Whereas a youth choir on tour can, if necessary, arrive a few minutes before the time scheduled for it to take part in a service, much more set-up time is necessary for a bell choir.

In spite of the problems, handbells are an excellent addition to your fine arts program. If you are working in a small congregation with a small youth program, they might be impractical because of the expense and because they would require that almost all of your young people be involved in the same specialized art. But if you are working with a program that is large enough to allow for diversity, where a handbell choir could be offered in addition to a youth choir, a puppet group, and/or a drama group, bells are a very good idea.

Not all young people can sing. Some young men who love music might be going through the embarrassment of a changing voice. But almost anyone can ring a handbell. Bells are a good teaching tool for teaching young people to read music, to learn theory, even to learn teamwork. For the young teen and the elderly adult, handbells make a nice substitute for a good choral voice.

You will also find that you will have very little difficulty getting bookings for a bell choir. Many churches would much rather entertain a mediocre bell choir than an excellent singing choir, just because of the novelty of the art.

Buying Handbells

English handbells can be purchased in the United States through such bell manufacturers as Schulmerich Carillons of Sellerville, Pennsylvania; Malmark, Inc. of New Britain, Pennsylvania; and, for the really big spenders, Whitechapel Bell Foundry of London, England. There are others, but these are the most popular. You don't have to deal with the manufacturer, however. Check your local music stores to see whether any of them distributes handbells. Few will keep them in stock, but many will order them for you or put you in touch with a manufacturer or a distributor.

A basic set of handbells consists of two octaves, with G below middle C as the lowest bell. At the time of this writing, the price of a two-octave set from Schulmerich was $2174; from Malmark, $2150. This price includes bell cases and a small tool kit for keeping your bells in good repair. Each additional octave adds a few bells at each end of the spectrum. The third octave brings the full range to C below middle C to two octaves above middle C. The fourth ranges from G to G, and the fifth C to C. The bells have small numerical notations on the handles indicating the octave to which they belong. Middle C is C_5, the C below middle C is C_4, the C above, C_6, and so forth. Therefore, a three-octave set of handbells would contain bells C_4 through C_7.

Presently a three-octave set of bells from Schulmerich costs $3443. Four octaves cost $4975, and five octaves cost $7515. The prices from Malmark are $3415, $4945, and $7420.

You might wish to start out with two octaves and add others later. In that case the additional octaves cost a little more each than when bought as a set, but the difference is minimal, and might even be cheaper than financing to buy them all at once.

Most churches do not have this much money just waiting to be used for something like handbells, especially in the youth budget. You may find, however, that there are people in your church who would like to contribute to a handbell fund, or there may be money left as memorial gifts for such a purpose. Handbells make a very nice memorial gift to a church, and the people who give the money for such gifts are always thrilled to see the money put to use. They don't want those handbells sitting in a closet somewhere, tarnishing and gathering dust.

Some bell companies also have lease programs in which certain portions of the lease money can apply to the purchase price. On occasion, bell manufacturers will have seasonal sales on bells and cases as well.

The Director

There are some things you can do without in a handbell program, but a director is not one of them. If you don't have someone to fill this role, put off the handbell program until you do.

A good handbell director obviously needs musical ability, but it takes more than that. An excellent musician who has no love for your young people, no sense of ministry, and no patience would make a very poor bell choir director.

Your director must be able to read music and to count time. This will enable him to direct the group in rehearsals and in performances. It will help if he can also play the piano, but it is not necessary. When selecting music, however, your director should at least find a pianist who is willing to go through the possible selections so that the director can hear what the finished product should sound like.

Almost as important as these abilities, however, are certain characteristics. A good director must have consistency, patience, preparation, and a sense of ministry. A director who does not put in the proper preparation before rehearsals will waste precious time. The young people will probably waste a good bit of time anyway; so your director needs to be patient enough to deal with that. Your director should always have the same sense of ministry you have. Young people are not just ringing bells when they are part of a church bell choir. They are praising God. They are cooperating with each other. They are fellowshiping. If your handbell choir is not open to non-Christians, if it is not as much an evangelism tool as the other parts of your youth program, or if your young people are frustrated by musical demands made on them in an unloving way, then you have the wrong director.

When you have found that loving, patient, knowledgeable musical director, treat him well. People who deserve praise the most sometimes hear it the least, and you will want to keep your bell choir director a long, long time. As the choir grows and develops, the director will, too.

Bell choir directors are difficult to groom. Bell choir substitutes are almost impossible to find. You might consider having an assistant to your bell choir director. The assistant will keep track of music and all the trappings, and will fill in for the director when the need arises. But remember, your official director needs to be consistent. A bell choir suffers when the director is absent. Nothing can kill your choir quite so quickly as a director who is frequently absent.

Selecting Music

There are some excellent music books available for handbells. Some are strictly two-or three-octave books, others combine options for several octaves. (Some of these books are listed in the Suggested Resources at the end of this chapter.)

For the beginning group and for the enjoyment of those listening to a bell choir, familiar gospel music is best. A beginning group will pick up a familiar tune faster than an unfamiliar one. And congregations enjoy hearing familiar songs played by bells. In addition, because there are no lyrics involved in bells, unless they are played with a vocal choir, the "message" of bell music is sometimes obscure. If your choir plays familiar hymn tunes, the congregation can think the lyrics as the bells play and derive a message that way.

Be sure to start your choir out slowly enough that they not become overwhelmed, but try to keep them moving along fast enough to be challenged. Walk into the first rehearsal with four to six songs for immediate work, and add some each month. That will require you to do a good bit of preparation and selection even before the very first rehearsal; so pick your music early.

You will find it best to pick music that uses the full range of the bells you have available. That will allow you to assign bells to your ringers on a semi-permanent basis from the very beginning. If you have two octaves, try to pick music that uses bells in the higher and lower ranges so that the people who play those bells have something to do. That is much more difficult with two octaves than with three or more, since most two-octave music is not full-range music, but it is a good goal to work toward.

Trappings

All you really need for this ministry are a director, choir, bells, and music. However, the provision of additional equipment will make your bell ringing more aesthetically pleasing, if not actually better. You will probably want to add the following equipment, in this order if you add it a piece at a time.

1. Tables. (This is practically a necessity, but it shouldn't cost you anything. Borrow a table or two from your fellowship hall or a classroom. You will rest the bells on the tables when they aren't being played.)

2. Foam. (Use thick foam at least two inches thick to pad the tables for resting the bells.)

3. Gloves. (The ringers should wear gardening gloves, or any

old gloves, for rehearsal; white clean gloves for performances. Gloves keep the bells from being marked by fingerprints and tarnished by perspiration.)

4. Tables. (You can purchase special bell tables that are easy to set up and take down for rehearsals and performances.)

5. Stands. (You can also purchase small music stands for bell music.)

6. Tablecloths. (For performances, you might wish to drape your foam-covered tables. We have used everything from specially made cotton or velour cloths to king-sized satin sheets. For touring, get something washable and permanent press.)

7. Lights. (You can also purchase special lights that attach to the bell stands. These are very helpful in poorly-lit sanctuaries. Be sure to purchase an extension cord, too.)

8. Custom-made metal racks. (Some choirs with five octaves have their own racks to hold the bells, up to an octave per rack.)

Putting Together a Group

Unlike a youth group, a bell choir has limitations on the number of people who can be involved. You can take advantage of this fact and publicize it when you start recruiting for your bell choir. Tell them you can *only* have fifteen people in the group; don't say, "We have to have fifteen people or we can't play the bells."

The very helpful book, *Joyfully Ring!* by Donald E. Allured (Broadman Press, Nashville, Tennessee, 1974) suggests eight ringers for two octaves, eleven ringers for three octaves (no more than thirteen), and ten to fourteen ringers for four octaves. In our bell choirs, we have used as many as fifteen people for three octaves, ten for two. While we understand the reasoning for having fewer people, considering the expenses involved and the need for young people to be involved in the group, we have sometimes opted for larger groups. There is a limit, however, as to how many people you can put in a group. Two-octave music may use between ten and twenty-five bells, and you want each person to be ringing at least one bell. Ringers who don't have very much to do can become very bored and drop out; so be sure to have enough for each person to do to challenge his abilities. At the other end of the spectrum, however, you simply cannot ring three octaves of handbells (thirty-seven bells) with five or six people, unless they are very talented. Three bells per person is about the standard ratio, but you can make adjustments on that ratio.

It is particularly nice when you are just starting out to have more than one bell choir. You can divide the groups either by ability or by age. If you are dividing by ability, you can put your more musical members in the upper group so they can move along faster, and your slower people in the lower group so they can learn. Then the less-accomplished group will have a model and something to aspire to. If you do not have enough people to merit two choirs (and all it takes is people—you can use the same bells, perhaps the same music, and the same tables for both groups as long as they meet at different times), you can balance out abilities by assigning bells that ring more often to more-accomplished ringers, and bells used less often to less-accomplished ringers.

Advertise that you are starting a bell choir. Ask your young people to register their interest. Then have the bell choir director call each interested party and interview him on his ability to read music (upper or lower clef), whether he plays another musical instrument, and his interest in being a part of the group. Based on the information gathered over the phone, your director may be able to assign bells, unless your young people have grossly over-or underestimated their abilities, even before the first rehearsal. Some changes might need to be made, but a lot of valuable information can be gained through interviews. When the group has been selected, order your music, find a mutually agreeable date and time, and plan the first rehearsal. Be sure your director has informed each member that he is officially a member of the group.

Assigning Bells

Aside from polishing bells that may have been sitting in the church utility closet for a few years, probably the most tedious preparation you will need to make for your bell choir will be assigning bells. There are several methods available to you. Some are quite exacting; others are more general.

You may decide to make your assignments based on the abilities of the people you have in your bell choir. In this case, you would want to give bells that are rung most often to your more accomplished members. One way to determine which bells those are is to count how many times each bell is played in each song you have selected for your group. This sounds like a lot of work, and it is. But in the end, you will have a fair idea of where you need to put your strongest people, and that is a valuable piece of knowledge to have. If you'd rather not do all that counting, there are some basic assumptions you can make to assist you in assigning bells. Generally speaking, bells at the end of the spectrum are not rung nearly as often as those in the middle. Even though you will be assigning more of the large and tiny bells to a player, he will not be playing as often as the person playing in the range around middle C. You will need to weigh this fact against the fact that, although the positions do not play very often, sometimes young people of limited musical abilities have difficulty locating these bells in their music because they are outside their vocal ranges and they are never called upon to read them in vocal music. In addition, a person of limited abilities may be overwhelmed by the four or five bells in front of him. More often than not, however, the people playing the end bells are somewhat bored, since they play most often only at the very end of a song.

Keep in mind, too, the size of the bells you are assigning. A huge teenage boy looks ludicrous ringing tiny bells, and the large bells might be too heavy for a petite girl to handle comfortably.

One piece of excellent information to keep in mind comes from Donald E. Allured (*Joyfully Ring!*): "Assign no more than two diatonic notes to any one ringer. . . . Rare exceptions to the rule can be made in slow passages when the ringer has sufficient time to make the changes required, or in the extremely high or low bells of large sets."

Here are some bell assignments you might consider:

Two Octaves, Eight Ringers

Ringer Position	1	2	3	4
Bells	G G♯ A A♯	B C C♯	D D♯ E	F F♯ G

	5	6	7	8
	G♯ A A♯	B C C♯	D D♯ E	F F♯ G

Three Octaves, Eleven Ringers

1	2	3	4	5	6
C C♯ D D♯	E F F♯	G G♯ A A♯	B C C♯	D D♯ E	F F♯ G G♯
E♭	G♭	B♭	D♭		A♭

7	8	9	10	11
A A♯ B	C C♯ D D♯	E F F♯	G G♯ A	A♯ B C
	E♭	G♭		

Offset line means accidental may be played by either of two ringers

Four Octaves, Ten Ringers

```
                    1              2              3             4          5
G G♯ A A♯ B    C C♯ D D♯    E F F♯    G G♯ A A♯    B C C♯    D D♯ E
                      |E♭          |G♭            |B♭         |D♭

    6          7          8            9         10
F F♯ G G♯    A A♯ B    C C♯ D D♯    E F F♯    G G♯ A A♯    B C C♯ D D♯ E F F♯ G
      |A♭               |E♭          |G♭
```

Once you have worked out your basic assignments, you will need to look over each piece of music carefully even yet. Quite possibly, each song will have one to several exceptions that will need to be made in order to allow every player to play at least one bell, or to help a ringer who has more than he can handle in a given song. The easiest and least obvious change that can be made is to have a bell passed to the next closest person. If one person's normal assignment will not be used at all in a song, instead of shifting all the bells, it might be simplest to move that person for that song to a position where a bell or two could be freed up for him.

Most bell choirs, particularly those just starting out, find it very helpful for each ringer to circle the notes he plays in the song before even playing the song through for the first time. If you have ringers sharing music, they can circle their notes in different color pencils or pens. Some books and bell choir directors will advise you strongly against this. Use your own judgment as to whether your bell choir needs and should be allowed this kind of visual help.

The First Rehearsal

Make sure your first rehearsal is well planned. If you can, make bell assignments immediately, based on the number of people you have in your group and the number of octaves in your set. But before you allow the young people to pick up the bells, you will need to set the ground rules for your choir and give them some tips on how to ring the bells while the room is still reasonably quiet.

Make some rules that are simple, easy to remember, and firm. The three basic rules for bell choirs are to put on your gloves before you pick up the bells, don't miss rehearsal, and don't clang the bells together.

Show your choir how to hold the bells (around the base, not with a hand through the handle). Instruct them to play the bells so that the strike mark can be seen when the bell is tipped forward. The strike mark is a fine line inside the bell. Show them how to damper the bell, that is, how to make it stop ringing. This is usually done by touching the bell to the shoulder. Also remind them not to wear clothing during rehearsals or performances that would have metal pins or buttons at the point where the bell would be dampered.

All this initial lecturing will be necessary before the young people get to the noisy business of handling the bells, but don't be carried away with the lecture. Make sure before the first rehearsal is over that each person has located the strike marks on the bells and has had an opportunity to ring the bells. Have the choir play through a song or two before you dismiss.

Some of your ringers might need some explanation of the notations on the bells. If you have a piano in the room, or a blackboard you can use to draw an illustration, show them graphically that $C^\#$ and D^b are the same note, as well as $D^\#$ and E^b, $F^\#$ and G^b, $G^\#$ and A^b, and $A^\#$ and B^b. Some of the newer bells now have handles with both notations written on each side, but if you have an older set, it will show, for instance, $D^\#$ on one side of the handle and E^b on the other.

The ringers will need to keep on their toes when marking their music, paying attention to the key signature in order to know whether or not they are playing naturals, sharps, or flats. The first few times you rehearse, you may find it helpful to state each position number and the bells played by the person in that position aloud, and have them circle their notes on the staff provided at the top of the song, noting the need for naturals, sharps, and flats.

Some bell music is printed with a number above each measure. This is absolutely necessary for a beginning choir. If your music is not numbered, have your choir members number the measures in addition to marking their notes, and be sure to announce the total number of measures there are in the piece so you can be certain they have not misnumbered. As you rehearse, you will spend a lot of time initially cueing your choir to the measure they should be playing as you proceed through the pieces with those measure numbers.

If you have passed out books and marked music during this rehearsal, also ask your members to put their assignment position numbers on the front of the books. This will allow you to set up music for them before rehearsals, if you like, or them to locate their own music quickly. Numbers are cold; but they are easier to put in order than names.

Be sure you include a prayer or a devotional in each and every bell choir rehearsal.

After the first rehearsal, which, like all rehearsals to follow, should end promptly at the announced time, linger long enough to get to talk with the members of your group. Find out if they have any personal difficulties with the bell assignments you have given. Get to know them a little better. Then shift assignments if you need to. Members will not mind moving to other positions after only one or two or even three rehearsals. Beyond that time, however, it may be very difficult to correct any assignment mistakes without hurting someone's feelings.

After that first rehearsal, one weekly rehearsal of forty-five to ninety minutes should be enough to prepare your group for anything they can handle. Try to avoid longer rehearsals and extra crash rehearsals before performances. They really should not be necessary, and they cause parents and youth unnecessary anguish.

Playing for Worship

Your first performance or opportunity to contribute to a service should be scheduled as soon as possible. This will give your group something to prepare for. Ideally, this should be not more than three or four months after the group has begun rehearsals. Under no circumstances short of death should you cancel this scheduled time to play. Even if the group is not very good, they will need to experience taking part in a service. A group that has nothing scheduled loses interest and motivation. As difficult as it may be, try to impress upon the group that they are playing as a part of worship and as a manner of praise, not to perform in front of Mom and Dad. Pray with your group before they play.

The first few times your bell choir plays in public, they may be quite a novelty. After a time, those who are listening will require more musicianship. Try to observe and vary the dynamics of the songs in your repertoire. Variations in the tempos and styles of the songs your group plays will make the music much more interesting to listen to and will improve the skills of your bell choir members. As you grow and develop, you can investigate variations of bell ringing techniques. (Some books to help you in these more sophisticated areas of bell ringing are listed in the suggested resources at the end of the chapter.) Never lose sight of the bells' main purpose. They are an avenue of praise. Don't let fancy techniques take focus away from the beauty of the music you play and the message it can convey.

Suggested Resources

Allured, Donald. *Joyfully Ring*. Nashville: Broadman Press, 1974.

Baker's Plays and Theatre Bookstore. Boston: Walter H. Baker Co., 1982.

Burger, Isabel. *Creative Drama in Christian Education*. Wilton, CT: Morehouse-Barlow Co., Inc., 1977.

Herbeck, Raymond H. *Bells*. New York: Carl Fischer, Inc., 1972.

Hilson, Stephen. *What Do You Say to a Naked Spotlight?* Leawood: Sound III, Inc., 1972.

Holland, Lois and Kenneth J. Holland. *The Art of Solo Handbell Ringing*. Nashville: Broadman Press, 1982.

Ingrim, Madeline D. *Organizing & Directing Children's Choirs*. New York: Abingdon Press, 1959.

James, Martha. *A Year of Choral Readings*. Cincinnati: Standard Publishing, 1973.

Loveland, Austin C. *Youth Choir*. Nashville: Abingdon Press, 1964.

Maddox, Miriam B. *Dramatized Bible Readings*. Grand Rapids: Baker Book House, 1981.

Salzwedel, James. *A Basic Approach to Handbell Ringing*. Winston Salem: Hussite Bell Ringers Inc., 1979.

Smith, Judy Gattis. *Twenty Ways to Use Drama in Teaching the Bible*. Nashville: Abingdon Press, 1980.

14

Organizing and Executing an Effective Week of Church Camp

Andrew J. Hansen

Congratulations! You have been chosen by the camp program committee to direct a week of junior-high camp! You are elated to be considered for such an honorable position. What an opportunity to serve! The challenge has you spinning with ideas and daydreams of glorious moments that only can be experienced in a week of Christian camp.

However, after the thrill wears off, panic begins to set in with the realization that within a matter of months, you will be in charge of 100 hyperactive junior-high kids for a whole week! The gravity of the situation hits you with full force. The spiritual lives of these kids, all of whom are at different stages of development physically, mentally, and spiritually, will be greatly affected by what is achieved and what is left undone during this week. You are the person solely responsible for pulling it all together. Youth ministry magazines and idea books offer you little or no relief. What should you do? First of all, you should pray.

Pray

Pray for Your Heart

An exceptional week of camp will dynamically depend upon your direction, vision, compassion, and drive. Therefore, before going into the tedious planning and recruiting necessary, make sure you are right before God and that your attitude is set in the right direction. Make sure that you did not accept this position of directorship for an ego trip of respectability, power, and status (for whatever status there can be in being a junior-high camp director). Ask God to give you a tremendous burden for the lives of kids and a deep concern for their spiritual walk with the Lord. Ask God to focus your heart on the need for such a week of camp so you can be irrevocably committed to providing the most excellent week possible for His glory. Ask to be filled with an enthusiasm and anticipation of tremendous joy and satisfaction as a result of your love and effort in this work.

Pray for Workers

The quality of your week of camp will directly correspond with the quality of staff that you have provided for your week. Therefore, you must pray for workers—and not just any workers! You need more than just bodies to fill empty spots! You need mature men and women whose lives are filled with a fervor to serve Jesus Christ, who are willing to pour their lives, energy, and souls freely into the lives of youth.

Sadly I can recall working at a week of camp where the camp fire speaker showed little or no fervor for the week of camp, and especially no desire to spend his time sharing and developing the lives of the campers. As far as he was concerned, once he spoke at vespers, his "duty" was done. His "right" was to sleep as long as he wished and to use the rest of the day in "preparation." This preparation invariably included a round of golf. His greatest worry of the week was what condition the greens were in. He showed little concern for the condition of the souls of the kids at camp. Such a person has no right to be asked to serve at a week of camp, no matter how necessary a function is to your program, how short of people you are, or how talented such a person may be.

On the other hand, I can remember with joy _dozens_ of workers who realized that they were directing the destiny of youth, that they had no right at the week of camp other than to be servants who were investing everything they had into the lives of the youth!

Pray for the Youth

Youth come to camp for all kinds of reasons. Some are forced to come. Others come for motives that are not nearly as lofty as what you would hope for. Then there are those who truly desire to grow in fellowship, knowledge, and service. You must pray for God to open the minds of these youth so they may understand the glory of

Christian living, and to break their hearts so they may be molded and responsible to the compassionate call for growth, maturity, love, and unity of the Spirit.

Pray for Wisdom

When one realizes the awesome responsibility of being a director for a week of camp, he is truly humbled. Beseech the Lord to guide you in the selection of faculty and in the development of a curriculum that will teach timeless Christian truths as well as meet the current needs of teens, to give you the courage to lead with love, and to know how to cope with all the little details that will come your way.

Pray for Stamina, Patience, and Love

Directing a week of camp will be an intense maturing process in these areas of your life. Sleeping hours are precious and few. The well of your patience will be dipped into until almost dry, and the river of love must spring forth in every action and decision.

Seek Wise Counsel

After you have set yourself before God in prayer in order to plan an effective week of camp, you will need to seek wise counsel. Write to a number of people who you know have served well in a directorship position. Ask them to spend an hour to supply you with schedule, curriculum plans, goals, philosophy, hints, ideas, and suggestions that they can offer you as a new director who wishes to provide the best but is working at putting it all together.

As you wait for their replies, recruit one person with whom you relate very well. This person must also love youth. Ask him to serve as your assistant director. Review the materials you receive, bounce back and forth your own ideas, set goals and objectives with time limitations and discuss faculty needs and other issues with him. However, remember that you are responsible for every decision. Therefore, make sure you are comfortable and can give one hundred percent support to every decision you make.

Determine Necessary Positions

Now we get down to the nitty-gritty of organizing for your week of camp! Decide on the positions you will need to fill to make the week of camp run smoothly and accomplish your objectives. You don't want just people; you want people with a mission.

Take a blank sheet of paper. On one side, write down every type of job or position that will need to be filled. Draw a line down the middle of the page. On the other side begin listing people whom you might desire to have serve in the week. Think of those who serve in churches in your camp area. Think of people possibly right within your congregation. Think of those whom you know in Christian colleges and campus ministries. Think of those who have unique talents that will be most beneficial in service to the week, regardless of distance from you.

Below is a list of personnel positions that you would normally have to fill to provide a balanced week of camp:

Assistant director—Someone to dream and develop with, someone able to step in just in case an emergency or illness distracts you from your week of camp.

Dean of men—A man who will challenge the young men, oversee the cabin dads, participate in the line of discipline, help arrange devotions, make assignments for cleaning and pick-up, and inform on rules and regulations.

Dean of women—A woman who will challenge the girls and perform other duties similar to those of the dean of men, above.

Teachers—Make sure these people have a high commitment to preparation and are capable of creatively communicating with the youth.

Recreation director—Obviously someone creative and athletically inclined. More importantly, someone who can design and use recreational activities to build character in the young people.

Cabin dads—Men who are willing to spend time sharing with the youth in their cabins, men who are open to counseling, sensitive to needs, and able to support and fulfill the directions of the dean of men.

Cabin moms—Women who will do the same with the girls.

Team or family leaders—People who will share the desire to have strong personal relationships with the youth and minister to them by getting to know them as friends—knowing their backgrounds, thoughts, bright spots, and needs. They will also lead review and discussion times.

Missionary—Someone who is vibrant for the Lord and can challenge the youth in the area of missions.

Musicians—People to lead the singing, play guitar and piano, and perhaps supply a concert.

Vespers speaker—One who loves to preach but can also relate to youth and work within your curriculum. Must also be willing to be with the youth and serve them during the day.

Bankers—Those who will be in charge of daily distributing the youth's personal money back to them so they may contribute to missions and buy from the canteen. This reduces the incidence of lost or stolen money and helps eliminate wasted spending on the part of the campers.

Nurse, cooks, and lifeguards—Because of state regulations, most camps now provide these personnel on their own. Check with your local camp policy. If you must supply these, make sure the nurse and lifeguards are certified.

Creative activity people—Drama directors, choir director, craft leader, sign-language interpreter, and the like. More attention will be given to this group later in the chapter.

Once you and your assistant have exhausted every possible position, go back through the names of potential workers that you have come up with. Begin to put people into the slots of responsibility. Be especially sensitive to discerning their key gifts and/or talents; plug them into the positions where they can be most beneficial.

An easy way to keep track of all these assignments and to gain an overall view of the big picture of your week is to diagram your plan of action on a grid sheet.

On the top of the grid, list all of the positions which you need to fill. Then, on the side of the sheet, list the names of those whom you wish to serve as faculty for the week. Now mark each appropriate slot with an X to match people to positions. Circle the X's to indicate which persons carry the responsibility for certain assignments or, in a sense, are the directors for certain areas, such as the choir director, craft director, and recreation director. If different faculty are assigned a responsibility for only a certain day (such as leading cabin devotions) you may wish to denote which day they are in charge of beside their X. This way you may quickly verify whether all the days are covered and review with the faculty which days they are in charge of those duties. (See page 211.)

Once you have completed this sheet, you are well on your way to building the teamwork that will blend everyone's talents into an effective week of camp. It would be wise for you and your assistant to go back through and think of alternative people for certain areas. Hardly any camp director receives a one hundred percent positive response to his appeal for staff.

Recruit Your Faculty

This is the do-or-die stage in developing your week of camp, once you have listed the quality people you need.

Do It Early

If you are located in a typical camping region, there may not be an overabundant supply of ministers and workers available. Those who are available are faced with a multitude of demands for their time, including other camp deans. You must challenge them to commit to your week well in advance so they may plan it into their schedules. The earlier you ask, the better your chance to get the best people available.

Get Your Core People First

These are the teachers, missionaries, musicians, and directors. Do not overload your staff with other people—even volunteers—until you are positive you have adequately filled these core positions with quality personnel.

Determine the Projected Size of Camp Attendance

You will be wise to contact the camp manager and ask for the attendance figures for your age group of camp over the past five years. You should also determine how many youth came to camp the previous year that will graduate into your age bracket. While you have the manager on the phone, you may wish to ask if the camp has established a worker-to-student ratio. It is commonly recommended that you supply one worker for every four to six campers. Once you have the figures to establish the estimated number of campers, you can project how many faculty members you will need to organize a smooth week of camp.

Never Shortchange Yourself on Staff

To do so often means that your faculty will have to perform multiple responsibilities. This pressures your workers to do a less-than-excellent job just so the week can run. Even more critically, it means that there will be less opportunity to build close personal relationships with the campers—the ones whom they are to invest their lives in during the week.

Choose a Balance of Relationship-builders and Supporters

You need to provide people who are leaders, people who are outgoing and lively, people who are good verbal communicators. Such personalities can really spark the enthusiasm and interest of your campers. These workers' personalities will have a magnetic effect and pull the youth closer towards their Lord.

However, it is just as necessary to staff your week with people whom we shall term "supporters." These people's talents may not be as visible, yet their steady composure and deep love for youth will provide your week with a strong, stable force. They will give your youth depth. Such a balanced faculty will build and heighten the total efforts of each camper.

Send an Initial Letter

In your letter, express your enthusiasm for the week of camp and your desire to touch the lives of kids for Christ. Make it known that it is imperative that this person attend the week, that his involvement is vital in order to build an outstanding faculty through whom God can minister to the campers. Reaffirm the vital importance of Christian camping. If you already have commitments from a number of key people, you may wish to list their names to encourage others to be a part of the week. (If you are serving as dean for the first time, this may help give your camp ministry the credibility of experience.)

Explain that after you have received their affirmative response that you will be sending a detailed letter stating their responsibilities while at camp, the arrival time, map, and other important data. Enclose a self-addressed stamped response card and urge them to send it back to you as soon as possible. (Indicate a specific date you need it.) Make sure that you boldly state the week, age group, and camp you are directing.

(Notice the sample recruitment letter and return postcard. What would you change? What would you add or delete? Stop right now and write these ideas down. If possible, rough out your recruitment letter and response card.)

Send a Detailed Letter With Complete Assignments

Once you have received a positive response, immediately send a second letter. This one will explain the worker's assignment in detail. The importance of the detail of this letter cannot be overstated. If your faculty member does not completely understand his assignments, then this person will not come prepared to give his best. In order for the faculty members to give their best, you must give your best when explaining what their vital roles will be.

Begin with a word of thanks for the person's commitment. Build a positive image of the potential week. Remind the worker of the price of excellence. State again the date and the theme of the week. Then give a detailed rundown of the individual assignments.

Remind your worker of the need for preparation, prayer, and a spirit willing to give one hundred percent into the lives of the youth that attend. If there are any state regulations that must be met (physical, T.B. testing, character reference, etc.), state this in CAPITAL LETTERS or in **bold type.** Close the letter with another note of thanks, and perhaps personal comments as you sign. Be sure to enclose a map of how to get to the camp, the camp's phone number, a list of what to bring and what not to bring, a curriculum outline sheet, a copy of the staff grid sheet, and any additional guidelines to the worker's responsibility as listed in the camp's policies and procedures handbook. (Acquire one from your camp manager if you do not already have one, and read it thoroughly! Otherwise, you may end up red-faced over an embarrassing situation that you could have avoided if you had adequately informed your faculty ahead of time as to the camp's expectations.)

Obviously, such a detailed letter could take a tremendous amount of effort and time. Therefore, it is best to make the letter as uniform as possible, and then use a code sheet from which your secretary can type in the specific requirements. This will eliminate much busywork, although you will still need to add a written guideline for what you expect of your teachers. To make a code sheet, number the positions across the top of the grid sheet, starting with the assistant director. Then list each in order with a brief job description.

Once you have a detailed code sheet, check each faculty member on the grid sheet. Wherever there is an X, look at the number assigned that activity when making the code sheet, and write the code number on a notecard with that person's name on it. From this card and the code sheet, your secretary will know what assignments to type. You may also wish to add specific information on the notecard.

For instance, Skip Eastman has the following responsibilities according to the grid sheet: dean of men (2), teacher (4), dorm dad (17), camp fire speaker on Thursday night (19), and family leader (21). Therefore, on Skip's card, I put these numbers:

2.

4.

17.

19. Thursday

21.

Beside number 19, I have written, "Thursday" to indicate which day the secretary is to assign Skip to give the camp fire message.

If you assign someone to direct rather than assist in a certain area, you write the word, "Direct," and add an additional paragraph as to what it means to be the director, the goals to be achieved, and the materials necessary.

For your teachers, add an additional page with the encouragement for them to give their best in preparation, state the topic, and enclose outlines and resources. Be sure the curriculum sheet is enclosed so they may observe how their lesson fits into the rest of the week and have an awareness of the other topics being taught.

This is an exhaustive process, but afterward, you can rest assured that your faculty has an excellent handle on their specific responsibility. You know they are going to come better prepared to minister in their respective areas. Just a phone call cannot produce such detailed results.

Send a Reminder Postcard

Even with the best of intentions, you and I often forget to do things until the last minute. This postcard, sent two weeks prior to the camp week, helps to serve as a gentle reminder of the arrival time, time of the staff meeting, special requirements (like the T.B. test), and personal assignments. It also keeps a faculty member from arriving unprepared because he forgot a certain assignment. This may also eliminate no-shows. Hopefully, none of your faculty will back out of their commitments. However, if one must, he may forget to notify you. Receiving this card will remind him to call you, giving you at least a couple of weeks to find a replacement. That's much better than discovering you're short on staff on the first day of camp.

Now that you have secured the best possible staff to work, you also need to prepare a clear purpose for your week of camp and the curriculum that will meet that purpose.

Plan a Well-balanced and Purposeful Program

Before you go any further, answer the following questions:
What do we really want to accomplish during this week of camp?
With what do today's Christian youth need to be challenged?
What should be taught and stressed to present this challenge?
Where are these kids weak?
What issues are confronting them and challenging their faith?
What should be taught and stressed to equip them to meet these challenges?

After listing answers to these questions, you should be able to gain an idea of what your theme and potential curriculum may be. Decide on the theme first. Then determine a curriculum that develops that theme. Here are some possible themes:

Wisdom for Living: a study of Proverbs and related topics.

Caring in a Cold World: lessons on meeting others' needs and affirming others' self-worth in Christ.

Blessed to Be a Blessing: lives that were changed by God and then changed others.

Running the Race: the spiritual disciplines of the Christian life.

Standing on the Rock: today's issues vs. God's man and woman.

Journey With Jesus: people He touched and changed.

Be Bold: witnessing to a world that is lost.

Be the Leader You Were Meant to Become: a study of Biblical leadership characteristics.

The Greatest—the Servant: learning the greatness of servanthood and how to be a servant in my home, school, church, and community.

"God So Loved. . . .": a Biblical overview of God's love to mankind.

Free to Be Me: identifying individuality, gifts, and self-esteem in the light of the Bible.

God's Power: creation (scientific proof for creation), salvation, judgment, love, provision, and protection.

The Ultimate Star Wars: God vs. Satan, who Satan is, Satan's powers, God's power, God's work through Christ, God's work through us.

The best theme is the one you come to after struggling for answers as to your purpose and need for the age of the kids at the week of camp you are developing. The theme for the week determines curriculum: the topics that are taught, Scripture that is memorized, messages that are presented, and devotions that are shared.

As you develop the theme in practical ways, do not neglect the fact that you also need to create a balance of ministry within your week. There are four basic needs that must be blended into your week of camp to create a healthy balance that accentuates whole growth in young Christian lives.

First is *learning*. Young people who come to Christian camp must realize they are there for the essential purpose of learning the Word of God and practically applying such teaching to their everyday lives. Therefore, there should be time for *doctrinal* study, a time to instruct the young people strictly from the Bible. This can take place in the study of a book of the Bible (especially a four- or five-chapter book), parables of Jesus, character studies from the Bible, or word studies. A devotional time should be provided each day in the schedule where the youth can individually and personally dwell upon a passage of Scripture. Creative methods should be used to accentuate the learning process—overheads, videotape, skits, outline sheets, review quizzes. (The latter two can be kept by the youth in a personal packet that they can be encouraged to take home and use to review with their parents what they have learned from the week. This way, they have material to review, reflect on, and refresh their memory with, and the parents will have an opportunity to discover what a benefit Christian camping can be to the educational and spiritual advancement of their children.)

The youth will also need to discover Biblical answers for issues they are encountering and that are challenging their lives in society. Therefore, a *topical* study will also be of great benefit to your youth. They need Bible study, but they must also see how the Bible and Christian ethics affect the questions of society. Some important topics or issues are friendships, getting along with parents, self-esteem, controlling your anger, controlling your tongue, world hunger, drugs, alcohol, divorce, abortion, war, music, and homosexuality.

Once you have chosen the doctrinal study and the topical study for your curriculum, determine how each subject will be broken down day by day. What main points from each section need to be taught, stressed, and applied? Who will prepare outline sheets on each section to give to the youth so they can fill in during the classes? Can application sheets be developed that can be used in family discussion times?

When you have answered these questions, write your curriculum guidelines on a sheet of paper. Describe the classes for each day. What section will be studied each day? What is the main point for each day? How can each main point be illustrated? How can the families apply each lesson during family time? (The appendix at the end of this chapter includes a sample curriculum guideline sheet completed for a topical study—evangelism, dating, servanthood, Christian response, and family.) When the guideline sheets are completed in final form, send a copy to each of your faculty (not just teachers). That way, everyone will have an idea of the main topic and Scriptures to be discussed each day. The faculty can begin preparing early to provide greater input—both in the classes and in family times or even free times—to meet the needs of the campers in these areas.

One item may or may not save you a lot of this work. Many
camps provide a suggested curriculum. Check to see whether
yours does. If so, look it over carefully to see whether you can use
it. Decide what needs to be adapted or changed to meet the needs
of the kids at your week of camp. If you're not satisfied with it,
develop your own curriculum. If it's good, use it freely.

Discover what other resources are available at camp that you will
need. Does the camp have a movie projector, screen, P.A. system
(unless you like yelling at ninety juniors for a week), chalkboards,
and whatever else you need. Be sure you communicate your need
for such items to the camp manager. Check to see what kind of
funds you have available to order movies, support faculty coming
from a long distance, supplement a Bible-college team, or cover
other expenses.

Once you have established the curriculum that will be taught,
determine the method you will use to teach it. There are three
basic methods.

First, there is the method of including every student in the same
class session at the same time. Of course, the camp needs to have a
facility big enough to accommodate such a group. This is a good
method because there can be a theme for the day, and everyone
knows the main purpose of the day's teaching. Family time can
easily be centered on the thought of the day for a unified application time. Following this method, a teacher can give his best shot
once, and the pressure of teaching is off for the rest of the week.
This tends to help the teacher conserve more energy for building
group relationships. Movies or special activities later in the day
can reemphasize the theme of the day.

But there are problems with this method. It is harder to maintain
crowd control when the campers are all together. (One way to curb
this, however, is to have the youth sit in their family groups if they
cannot behave in a general session.) Large groups limit the opportunity for intimate response while teaching. Many youth will not
comment in front of a large crowd. There also is not as close a
contact with the teacher.

The second method is for all classes to be taught every day with
small groups of students switching classes each day. Of course, the
camp must have to have enough indoor facilities to accommodate
several classes simultaneously. Smaller, more intimate classes provide better group control, less goofing off and fidgeting, and more
opportunity to ask a question or discuss an issue.

There are problems here, too, however. The teachers must

repeatedly teach each day or a number of days, which means more energy is expended. You also lose a united theme for each day. Family application time becomes impossible, or at least more difficult. It is also harder to arrange special activities for the rest of the day, because there is no specific topic other than the general theme on which to base such activities.

The third method is a combination of the first two. One class would be taught with the whole assembly in attendance. Another class or subsequent classes would be taught with a small-group method. Obviously this attempts to accomplish the best of both of the previous methods. Also, the variety tends to refresh and stimulate student interest.

Still, there are problems. The teachers still must put forth additional teaching effort. Curriculum becomes more difficult and complex. Group application and a continuing theme can only be based on the one-group class time.

It will be up to you and your assistant to choose the teaching plan most fruitful and convenient for you based on your theme, the number of teachers you have on staff, and the facilities available on your campgrounds.

The second need is for *personal relationships* to be built during your week. There should be time during the week to turn from the fractured, hectic pace of modern society and create within the camp small units—family groups. Hopefully, these small groups will become major support groups for each individual camper during the week. Groups should consist of no more than ten campers, with two adult faculty members. They should have enough interaction materials and time during the week that the members of the group begin to trust one another, share with one another, learn to listen to one another, care for one another, and pray for one another. The adult leaders will play a major role in whether this kind of community can develop. Some young people do not know how to listen or share their thoughts. Such activity will be awkward and uncomfortable at first. Gently, the adult leaders must lead out in such skills. Don't expect much the first couple of days. Disappointments will be numerous and the need for discipline acute in the beginning. Yet slowly, the group will begin to mold together in the Spirit of Christ. Surface relationships will melt away, and rich friendships based on the unity in Christ will blossom. For many, this will be their first real experience of a truly caring Christian community, the church in all her beauty.

However, this will not become a reality unless you, as a director, program it into your week and create activities for the groups to do to help them share their friendship and personalities.

The small group is also an excellent method by which to give a review sheet over the topics and lessons of the day. In this manner, all the youth are challenged to participate in expressing what they comprehended, ways in which they grew in knowledge and discernment, and how their lifestyle will change for the better because of the teaching of the day.

Every day you will need to stress to your faculty to take personal time and talk to their youth and involve themselves in the youths' activity rather than talk among themselves and just relax. Some relaxation is necessary during a week of camp or one cannot survive! However, often we as faculty need to discipline our nature that desires to recreate, and instead turn to a young person. That young person may be greatly affected during the week by our effort to share in his life.

Personal relationships demand a price. That price is one hundred percent investment of our lives into theirs. But rejoice! The rewards are rich!

The third need is for *service/talent development* in the lives of Christian youth. This is an area where we often fail within our churches. In order for a Christian to grow in the Lord, he needs not only to grow in the Word and in Christian friendship. He must also develop a ministry in which he can be a part, where he can serve his Master for the glory of the kingdom, and where he can put his life on the line in giving for the edification and good of others. Therefore, as a camp director, you should always provide some type of creative activity time where your campers are taught skills and get a taste of areas where they may continue to serve their Lord when they go back home to their local congregations. Be as creative as you wish in this area! Below are listed a variety of ideas for creative activity time:

Choir—Teaching youth simple choruses and providing music for them to go back home and teach to the elementary or preschool youth, as well as singing choruses the youth already know and enjoy.

Drama—Learning simple skits that provide Scriptural truths the youth could take back home and teach to their youth groups and then perform during Sunday evening services.

Craft—Making items that can be shared with children or the elderly or can serve as an encouragement to their parents, teachers, or others.

Sewing—Making items that can be sent to a missionary orphanage, such as simple dresses. It would be good to contact the missionary agency ahead of time to discover their greatest needs and sizes.

Balloon Art—Teach youth how to make simple animals and designs with balloons; then let them dress as clowns, put on makeup, and go to the hospital to make and give balloons out to patients, especially children. If at all possible, arrange to visit a pediatrics ward during the week.

Service—Learning the needs of the elderly or some other group. If you choose the elderly, have a director of senior citizens or an active retiree share with the youth on their needs. Take a group to visit in a nursing home. Better yet, make arrangements through a local church for the youth to visit the elderly in their homes (two youth to visit each of the homes assigned). The results of this activity have been dynamic!

Play-Doh Joe—Make characters out of *Play-doh* that characterize a Bible story or portray a contemporary Christian message. Make a backdrop, write a skit, and take slides of each scene. Record the script on tape, and present the show at an evening service. Youth should learn skills so that they could go home and produce another *Play-Doh* Joe.

Mime—Have a professional mime teach the youth the basics and portray a message.

Sign Language—Have a professional signer teach youth the basics of sign language. Then have the youth memorize the motions to a contemporary Christian song, Scripture verses, or theme of the week. Share the need for signers in the local congregation to minister to the deaf in the community.

Preaching—Teach the youth how to write an introduction, illustrations, main message, and conclusion. Have these youth preach in camp and at their home congregations.

Bible Bowl—Conduct a competition among those interested at the camp on questions over the main book or text that is being studied during the week. Have the youth learn how to write simple questions so they can go home and teach quizzing as a learning method for a Sunday-school class.

Computers—This class would be for youth who already have the basic skills in computer programming. They would be taught how a computer could be useful for a church, materials now available, and how to print up quizzes that can be used for Bible lessons for all ages.

The fourth need is *recreation*. Creativity, planning, and good personnel are key factors in providing an excellent and varied recreational activity time.

Traditional games such as softball, volleyball, soccer, and kickball are enjoyable as long as competition is kept to a minimum and total group involvement is stressed. Crazy days (a combination of relays, balloon games, and other fun activities) are excellent for taking serious competition out of the activity and encouraging fun, laughter, and participation.

Keep your own attitude healthy. Ask yourself what model image is being displayed to the campers by your action.

Waterfront activities—like water races, innertube and canoe races, sand-castle building competition, and paddle relays—are a delightful change of pace on a hot day.

An organized wilderness hike in a beautiful natural environment, combined with a prayer walk, could be the highlight of your week. In every aspect of recreation, it is vitally important that all the materials (including nets, balls, balloons, canoes, and life jackets) be on hand and that the recreational director and his assistants be ready to switch the groups from one activity to another with speed and organization. Time delays caused by lack of preparation can cause the momentum to wane, and the crowd will quickly become bored and lose interest. Activity time must be swift, fun, and active!

Whistles for the recreation directors are a must, and a bullhorn is an unbelievable asset. Also, come with backup plans in case of rain. A trip to the local roller-skating rink can provide a great time and a welcome break.

If you plan to award points for the winners of activities, make them minimal to keep competition from being too highly stressed. To help keep competition light, you may wish to dream up some gag awards that can be given out at lunchtime the next day.

If at all possible, spend a day with your recreational director and brainstorm for some unique ideas. At all times, clear your activities with the camp management and safety personnel! Make sure your activities are safe as well as fun. Remember, variety is the spice of life . . . and will keep all the kids looking forward to the recreational period.

Now that you have picked your theme and provided for an adequate balance of ministry for your week (learning, personal relationships, service/talent development, and recreation) you are now ready to set your schedule.

Set Your Schedule

Review the schedules used by other experienced directors. Think of what you wish to accomplish each day with your curriculum, music, missionary, camp fire, family time, and other activities. Even meal times are important.

Keep your lunchtime light after the morning schedule. Include quality jokes you can share, occasional skits, and mail call. Supper time should be a quiet time, with singing of choruses after the meal to set the mood for the evening. Have the youth eat with their families to continue to mold relationships.

Sit down and scratch out a proposed schedule. Talk it over with your assistant. See whether you have left anything out. Is there too much free time? Too long of a day? Be sure that you check with your camp manager for traditions that are expected to be continued (like flag raising, lunch at certain hours, and swimming only at certain times). Listed below is a typical daily camp schedule:

7:30 A.M.	Rise and Shine!
8:00	Flag Raising
8:15	Encounter Time (Personal Devotion Time)
8:30	Breakfast
9:00	Clean-up (Faculty/Staff Meeting)
9:30	First Class Session
10:30	Break (or Missionary Time)
11:00	Second Class Session
12:00 P.M.	Lunch
1:00	Rest Period (required in some states)
1:45	Family Application Time
2:45	Recreation/Swimming
4:00	Swimming/Recreation
5:15	Clean-up
5:45	Supper and singing
6:45	Creative Activity Time
8:00	Free-time/Canteen
8:30	Special Event (Concerts/Movie, etc.)
9:15	Camp Fire/Decision Time/Prayer
10:15	Cabin/Dorm Devotions
11:00	Lights Out!!!

Older youth can take a longer, heavier program. Younger youth need to be in bed earlier and have a few more break periods.

In order to keep from being asked a million times, "What's next?" it is highly advised that you arrange a camp schedule for your workers and youth (guaranteed to cut down the questions *at least* half a million times!).

Include in this camper's schedule (1) a front page stressing the theme of your week, (2) a welcome and challenge from you, the director, (3) the camp schedule, (4) daily devotional readings and Scripture for use during the encounter time, (5) space for addresses of their camp friends, and (6) a "Who's Who" faculty list (helps campers remember names and builds the importance of the faculty).

Have the youth *immediately* put their names on the front page of their schedules, or else you will be forever hounded about a lost and/or stolen schedule!

Set the Tone on the Opening Night

Perhaps the toughest time of your camp week will be the opening night. Everyone is new and on edge. The workers are not secure and in the flow of things, the campers are checking everything out, and the pressure is on you. Therefore, it is vital that you be ready to roll and set the tone and the pace for the rest of the week.

Be at the site as early as possible! You can unpack, check over details with the camp manager, and begin to greet arrivers with a positive, enthusiastic attitude. Have your faculty cabin assignments prepared in advance and ready for them as soon as they arrive. (You must be there ahead of them.) Or send them their assignments in the mail. Make sure that you work at balancing a veteran faculty camper with a rookie. Never allow two first-time faculty members to room together and be solely in charge of a cabin.

If at all possible, have activities such as swimming and open recreation—volleyball, basketball, horseshoes, and more—available and supervised. As you greet your faculty, remind them about the importance of the faculty meeting later in the afternoon, approximately 4:00 P.M., before supper.

The main thrust of your faculty meeting will be to set a tone of teamwork and unity, a tone of enthusiasm, and a dependence upon God to bring results that will glorify His kingdom.

A. Thank your faculty for their willingness to commit to this week of camp and their advance preparation. Stress the need for hearts that are burdened for the lives of the young people attending the week of camp, hearts that are compassionate, kind, broken, and open.

B. Remind the faculty of their main purpose of giving absolutely one hundred percent. They are to pour their lives out as a sacrifice for the needs of the youth assembled this week. This must take precedence over their own desires for fellowship and relaxation.

C. Quickly review with them individually their responsibilities as you have them listed on your staff grid sheet. As you do so, introduce each person to the rest of the faculty. If there are any misunderstandings as to responsibilities assigned, meet with the individuals involved after the staff meeting.

D. Announce how you have divided them into family teams. It is best that you balance your workers, one person of a strong personality with another who has more of a supportive nature. It is recommended to allow husband/wife faculty to stay together so they can have a united ministry and an example of working together for the Lord during the week.

E. Pass out the schedules and quickly review if there is time. Point out daily staff meeting time. Share briefly the plans for the rest of the evening.

F. Answer any questions—sing a chorus together and spend a period of time in prayer.

Schedule supper for 5:30 P.M. Greet the youth enthusiastically. Ask them to remain seated after they have finished eating. After dinner, your goal will be to set a correct attitude with the youth.

A. Let them know how excited you are to have them in attendance and how you have been anticipating and praying for this week and their lives.

B. Pass out the camp schedules. Ask youth immediately to sign their names on the front of their schedules, and stress how important it is not to lose them.

C. Have the campers turn to the "Who's Who" list so they may identify the names of the faculty with faces as you introduce the faculty and explain their main responsibilities.

D. Have the camp manager share a word with the youth. They need to identify who the manager is, and you need to establish the fact that you respect his authority and position in the camp. Have him share what the camp boundaries are, the earliest time anyone is to be up in the morning, and other ground rules for the camp. If you perhaps do not know your manager well enough to trust his dialog during this time, it would be well to meet with him ahead of time and sketch out what you wish for him to share with the youth. You do not want a twenty-five

minute tirade of rules and regulations right at the very beginning. Encourage him to be warm and friendly.

E. Emphasize to the youth that you are going to expect them to
respect people and respect the property at the camp.

F. Stress that this is their week. They need to set the tone and
make the week great! You have a tremendous faculty gathered,
and a sound curriculum, but without *their* effort to make the
week a great one, things will never take off. The direction of
the week is up to them.

G. Let the youth know the chain of authority for problems and
discipline. First there is their family leader and/or cabin mom
or dad. The next step is on to the dean of men or women. If
there is still a problem, the issue is brought to the director's
attention. If he deems it necessary, the director will turn the
matter over to the camp manager, who will immediately contact the parents and make other arrangements available for the
camper. This system has worked with excellence.

H. If a camper feels sick or has injured himself, he should first
notify his family leader or cabin mom/dad if at all possible.
One rule is vital to keep sickness from occurring only during
class times with miraculous recoveries in time for lunch and
recreation. If a camper is sick enough to go to the nurse, and
she allows him to miss a morning class, that camper is too sick
to recreate and will not be allowed to participate in swimming
or canteen time. In other words, if one is sick enough in the
morning to miss class, he is sick *all day!* In my experience, this
rule has eliminated ninety-five percent of the class-time blues.

I. Ask for questions and pray. Dismiss with the understanding
that when the bell rings, they are to meet in the large group
meeting area immediately.

What the youth don't know is that the next main event is to
break them up into family groups without allowing them to form
cliques. You and your recreation director will need to know ahead
of time approximately how many campers there are. If there are
eighty campers, and you planned on having ten families, you will
want to have eight young people in each family. Listed are ways of
breaking them up into families.

1. Have ten different animal names, eight of each kind, written on
pieces of paper. Distribute these papers quickly among the
campers and have them make their animal noise to locate their
group. Each faculty unit will have a different noise. This is a quick
way of splitting the youth up.

2. Have ten different puzzles and take out eight pieces from each puzzle. Put these pieces in a sack, shake it, and let each youth draw a piece out. They then must go and locate the puzzle where their piece fits. Your faculty family-leader units will be holding each main puzzle.

3. Use different colored balloons drawn from a sack to designate families. Or have balloons on a big dart board, with numbered tags inside each balloon (numbered 1—8). Once a youth bursts a balloon, he is automatically assigned a group based on the number in that balloon. Beware of flying darts!

4. Have eight cards made of construction paper of ten different colors. The youth draw the cards from a sack to determine their families.

5. Break the youth up according to the months of their birthdays. (A prearranged computer listing could assist you with this.) You will have to adjust groups to get correct numbers.

Have the youth go *immediately* to their families and have family leaders write down their names before they can switch cards, balloons, or whatever, and therefore switch groups.

Invariably you will have youth immediately come to you and beg to be switched. Usually I refuse to switch or even discuss the idea until the next morning, as it would cause too much confusion. This at least gives them a little time to get used to their new group and discover it is not certain death to be separated from a friend.

If the youth approach you in the morning, give them the courtesy to listen to their appeal before making a judgment. Normally I am only compassionate to those who have brought a friend to camp who is unfamiliar with Christian camping. This is a delicate situation that needs to be resolved. However, if the youth are experienced campers and just want to chum with their buddies, I remind them that they will have plenty of time to be together during the day, but during family time, they should be seeing new friends and working on their own individual growth. Youth need to be split from their cliques and comfortable groups so they can grow. Treat the situation calmly, gently, honestly, yet firmly. Do not be surprised if the youth at first grumble.

Warning! Once you allow switching, especially on the first night, expect the flood-gates to open!

After you are divided up into groups, *immediately* have these groups pick a team name. (This gives the youth little time to think or complain.) You might use one of the following categories: candy bars, pizza companies, cereals, fruit, peanut butter, Bible animals, judges, kings, other Bible characters, gum, or types of tennis shoes. Explain that they must come to you with their team name, and if another family has already chosen it, the second group will have to pick another name. After they have all picked names, have them make an anagram from their team name that has some spiritual significance.

After this small breaker activity, it is usually good to have a big group breaker activity, such as a scavanger hunt, picture charades, or making a symbol for the family group (out of *Play-doh,* construction materials, or something else). If time allows, you may wish to have a contemporary Christian movie that goes along with your theme for the week.

Lead into the camp fire time. Have someone prepared to lead into singing and make it as enthusiastic as possible. After the camp-fire message, have the youth go by families to spend time in prayer. Dismiss the families to their places of prayer one by one the first evening, or you will have lost youth, noise, and chaos. After prayer time, ask them to go quietly to their cabins. Make sure all cabins have a short devotional time planned.

After the first night of camp is over, your balanced program will be scheduled and flowing. Feel free to vary your opening evening, but be sure to keep it moving and somewhat fun and light.

The first night of camp often presents several cases of homesickness. If possible, never allow a youth to go home on the first night! Explain that it is too far for the parents to come back, that they are surely tired and have to go to work the next morning. Encourage the youth to stay the night, and you will discuss this with them in the morning if they still want to go home. Then, if the subject is brought up to you again in the morning, try to get the camper to wait until the afternoon so his parents can come after work. If by afternoon the child is still unhappy and not in tune with the program, it is in his best interest, as well as your own, to send him home. Otherwise, his mopiness will soon affect his cabin and family, and become disruptive to your group unity, vision, and enthusiasm. A whiny camper can also sap the strength out of your camp workers. However, ninety percent of all homesickness is temporary, due to the new territory and the unsettling aspect of the unknown. Once a camper has survived a day, his fears usually vanish, and Christian camping becomes a joy.

All week, perhaps from the first night, decisions will be made. Camp decisions are often viewed as emotional and pressured. Ethically, we need to do all we can to relieve the fears of such a decision. However, in such a Christian atmosphere of learning and love, decisions are to be anticipated, prayed for, and expected. Publicly encourage the youth if at all possible to speak to their family leaders or cabin moms or dads before outwardly making a decision. During a mid-week staff meeting, you may wish to mention those whom you know (from their registration cards) that have not made a commitment for Christ. Have the faculty pray about these campers and, at a good time, gently approach the subject with them.

If a camper does make a public decision, rejoice! However, it is strongly advised that you receive parental permission before you proceed to baptize a camper. Accept his confession of faith, give him a hug, and praise God. But do not step around parental authority. It is not your place to do so. In fact, most camps expect you to receive permission before proceeding with a baptism. If it is late at night, wait until the next morning to contact the parents. I prefer to contact the home minister and ask him to get in contact with the parents. His is a more familiar and friendly voice than mine, and he will be able to have a follow-up contact with the family. A parent will often be much more responsive to this type of contact.

It is also good to encourage family leaders to step forward when a camper makes a decision. Turn over the sharing of the decision, the confessing of faith, even the baptism, to them. After all, they are the ones who have been investing the time and energy and love into this youth. They ought to experience the joy and responsibility of the youth's response to the gospel message. Keep a record of each decision that takes place at your week of camp. Most camps will desire such a report at the end of the week.

Daily staff meetings *ARE A MUST* to provide the unity so necessary for a faculty to function! If there must be a few adults on the grounds, have a couple different volunteers each day. At each staff meeting, review the goals of the day, review those responsible for activities, have the faculty share exciting things that are occurring, bring up any needs or concerns you may have, and then spend a time in worship together by singing and praying together. Such times have often thrilled my soul and prepared our hearts and minds for the service of the coming day. *This is a must!*

Always have with you a pad of paper and a pen to write a running list of needs that you should tend to or find the correct person to do so. As you approach this glorious week of ministry, and as you live daily through it, remember to do your best for the Lord, but then allow Him to do the rest!

Follow Up After the Week Is Finished

Before you allow your faculty to leave, be sure they give you a camp evaluation sheet. It is best to give your faculty these sheets on Thursday. This allows them to have a little more quality time in responding, and also gives you time to remind them of the necessity to fill it out and return it. (See the Appendix for an example of such a survey.)

It would be a shame to consider that we have touched lives for a week and then, after the tears and the good-byes, it is over. Now we send them off like sheep to the slaughter, sometimes to apathetic churches, to poor home backgrounds or to unhealthy friendships!

This need not be so. Strongly encourage, in fact, *insist,* that the faculty members get the addresses of the youth that are in their families and write these youth an immediate follow-up letter, and then to continue to write them notes of encouragement throughout the coming year. If another big event takes place later in the year, such as a state-wide rally, encourage these youth to attend so that there can be a reunion of the family. Through such an extension ministry, you and your faculty can continue your camp ministry and encourage a much more lasting result of the efforts poured into a week of camp. It is also a joy to see these youth with which you have worked continue to grow in the grace of the Lord! You as the director may also wish to send material, such as additional lessons, a group picture, or a note of encouragement two to three months after the week.

After you have received the evaluations from your faculty, compile the listing of the results and send a copy to each one. Enclose a letter of sincere thanks for the talent and individual effort each faculty member put forth to make the week what it was. Share your love for them with the promise of prayer and an anticipation for the next year of camp.

Finally, send a letter to all churches whose youth made a decision. It would also be good to send a letter of thanks to the camp manager and his staff for their cooperation and support. And be sure to take time to thank your Lord for seeing you through and using you as His vessel to touch the lives of youth for His name's sake.

Appendix

R. L. C. A. '83 Junior Hi Week August 7-12	Director	Assistant Director	Dean of Men	Dean of Women	Teachers	Choir	Craft	Bible Bowl	Service	Play Doh Joe	Drama	Mime	Preaching	Sign Language	Recreation	Ass't Recreation	Bankers	Dorm Dads	Dorm Moms	Camp Fire	Dorm Devotions	Family Leaders	Special Events	Camp Fire Music
Andy Hansen	X				X																			
Brett DeYoung					X					⊗				X				X		X (SUN)		X		
Skip Eastman			X		X													X		X (THU)		X		
Rob Rodebush					X					⊗								X				X		
Bud Holmes												⊗						X		X (WED)		X		X
Mike Humm																X	X	X		X (SUN)		X		
Larry Bryant							X											X		X (WED)		X	X	
Pat Miles								X										X		X (TUE)		X		
Scott Hoag									X						X			X		X (MON)		X		
Mark Coffey		X			X					⊗								X				X		
Rich Mullins					X	X												X		X (MON)		X		X
Chris Rollston		MEMORY VERSES											X					X		X (THU)		X		
Tim Nawrocki					X													X				X		
Mike Pierce					⊗													X		X (TUE)		X		
Laurie Zehr								X											X			X		
Lisa Bryant					X														X			X		
Becky Disbro		MEMORY VERSES												X					X			X		
Marlene Eastman				X	X														X			X		
Candy Hunkins								X								X			X			X		
Robbie Ingraham								⊗											X			X		
Shelly Gilpin								X											X			X		
Susan Rodebush									X										X			X		
Sandy DeYoung										⊗									X			X		
Cindy Murphy		MEMORY VERSES						X											X			X		
Kathy Monroe							X												X			X		
Cindy Hammond							⊗												X			X		
Becky Winburn								X					X						X			X		
Becky Waldon								X											X			X		
Lorna Garton														⊗					X			X		

Assignment Grid Sheet

Recruitment Letter

Dear _____ ,

Hi! I hope the Lord is allowing you to see great fruit as a result of your faithful ministry and is blessing your life as you serve Him.

Presently I am looking out my window at the thirteen inches of snow on my lawn, trying to convince myself that the first activity at Rock Lake Christian Assembly actually takes place in five months!

I know it's hard to believe, but YES, summer is on its way, which once again signals a *dynamic* year of Christian camping.

It certainly has been busy camping, especially with the increase of attendance to our camps—but what a blessing!

This year the skeleton staff already forming insures our 7-9th Grade Week, August 8-13, of another great week of ministry. Some of these people are Kent Odor—St. Louis, Rob Rodebush—Cincinnati, Rich Mullins—Nashville, Terry Fisher—Cincinnati, Larry and Lisa Bryant—Nashville, and the unforgettable Dean of Men, Skip Eastman.

HOWEVER, with the large week we always have, I need you to serve in order to provide for a well-balanced, excellent week of camp. You are a very important person! Please seriously consider this week. Enclosed is a postcard, already addressed, ready to send. PLEASE fill this out *within a week.*

Our theme for this year is "Wisdom For Living." Thanks for your consideration. I pray you'll say yes to being one of this year's staff at the 6-8th Grade Week—August 8-13. A detailed letter describing activities and how you will serve will be sent to you within a couple of weeks of your reply by April.

Again, if possible—say YES!

Response Card

Dear Andy,

After a time of prayer and consideration, I have the following response to your invitation to share in the ministry to the seventh, eighth, and ninth-graders coming to Rock Lake Christian Assembly.

_____YES, count on me to serve with you! (More information will be sent to you regarding the details of faculty responsibility.)

_____I really want to but have to make arrangements first. I can let you know by _____ .

_____Thanks for the offer, but _____
_____
_____

Signed: _____

Assignment Letter

Dear _____ ,

GREETINGS IN THE NAME OF JESUS!

I am thrilled that you have consented to be one of this year's faculty for the 7th, 8th, and 9th grade week of camp at R.L.C.A. August 7 -12. I can honestly state that the Lord has provided an *outstanding* faculty! I anticipate nothing but the best in ministry with such quality.

However, our prayers and commitment to hard work are the main ingredients for success. The kids God will allow us to minister to and share our lives with need to see spiritual purity, joy, compassion, love, servanthood, unity, and faithfulness from us. Well-prepared lessons, devotions, activities, and recreation must be continuously blended with a strong development of personal concern and relationship between the youth and faculty. Such a week will be blessed with challenged and changed lives, as well as the knowledge that God deeply used you for His kingdom.

So we are honored to have you on staff, and we'll need your best to help create a dynamic week of camp.

We would like you to participate in the '83 program with the following responsibilities. (See the attached page.)

PLEASE!!!

1. Remember to obtain a T.B. test before coming to camp (required by State Law for all staff).
2. PLEASE, PLEASE, PLEASE be at the Assembly campgrounds by 3:00 P.M. on Sunday, August 7. The camp manager needs us there to be in the cabins and dorms BEFORE registration can begin. We will have a most important faculty meeting at 4:30 P.M., if at all possible. Camp will end Friday night at 6:30 P.M.
3. Be mentally prepared to lead discussion and listen during the family times (your small group of ten youth and two or three faculty). Be constantly sensitive to needs and allowing the Holy Spirit to use you in meeting those needs.
4. PLEASE BRING A TAPE RECORDER.

Please be in constant prayer that God will prepare your heart for ministry during August 7-12. Your input could greatly make the difference for a young soul.

To His Glory,

Andy

Staff Survey

Thank you so much for serving on the staff for this week of camp. Your comments on this questionnaire can help us prepare for another week of camp. Please take time to think over each question thoroughly before answering.

1. What did you like best about this week?

2. How do you feel you grew spiritually?

3. Where did you think you served the most, or with the greatest effect?

4. Give your evaluation of the Creative Activity Time. Any suggestions for other activities in the future?

5. Give your evaluation of the Recreation Time. Any suggestions for activities in the future?

6. What did you feel about our Instruction Time? Any suggestions for topics in the future?

7. What did you feel about our Illustration Time? Any suggestions for the future?

8. We tried to program more time for personal relationships and sharing such as Application Time in small family units. Any comments?

9. Evaluate the Camp Fire Time.

10. What would you like added to the schedule? Taken away?

11. Would you be willing to work next year?

12. Is there anyone you would suggest for this week next year?

13. Any other comments—

15

Creative Camping Ideas

David Wheeler

Discipling has become a powerful tool of ministry over the past few years, but one of the biggest frustrations seems to be the lack of time. We often wish that we could arrange to have some of the youth we work with come and live with us for a while. That's usually not possible, but the church camp setting provides a variation of that situation. One is actually able to live with several young people for a few days and concentrate on the Christian life. Let's make the most of those few days. The purpose of this chapter is to give you some practical ideas for making your week of camp significant.

The main purpose of a week of camp is to present God to the campers and allow them to make intelligent decisions concerning Him. Everything that is done during the week should aim toward that goal. Even the more crazy activities should help to achieve it.

It might be noted that these ideas are aimed toward the senior-high age group. Many could be adapted for younger groups, but put some thought into it first. Be careful about giving big kids' activities to little kids too soon.

Planning a creative week of camp takes time and work. I wish I could take credit for all the ideas contained in this chapter, but I honestly can't. These ideas have been collected and adapted from so many sources over the twenty years that I have been involved in camp that it would be impossible to give credit where it is due. I humbly thank all the creative people who allowed me to work with them and learn from them.

As you prepare for your week, plan in detail. Collect ideas wherever you go. Ask others what they are doing at camp. Get together with several of your staff and brainstorm a few times during the year. A boring week of camp is easy to organize—you simply show up with a volleyball, five sermons, and teachers for four classes. Putting together a creative week involves a lot of trivial detail work. But the results are worth it.

Involved with the planning should be a lot of prayer. God will give you some great and creative ideas on how to communicate Him! It is a thrill to see Him taking part during the months leading up to camp.

As the week begins, it is important to get the kids on your side. Help them want a good week of camp as much as you do. See that you and your staff make your love for the campers unquestionable. "Kids don't care how much you know until they know how much you care." Once they see that you haven't just thrown a week together, but that a lot of work has gone into it, they'll start moving to your side. And when they see that you're not there simply to put on a show, but that you have come to love them and move them closer to the Lord, they'll be solidly planted on your side.

Why do we go to so much effort to put variety into our camp program? Someone has said, "It's a sin to bore kids with Jesus." I agree. The God who created aardvarks, cacti, thunder, sex, ladybugs, sunsets, and Howard Cosell deserves to be presented in an honest, creative, and exciting way! I acknowledge that the Christian life isn't always fun. However, at church camp, whenever it is possible to make learning and living the Christian life fun, we do so!

Many of the details of the actual planning of the week are contained in the previous chapter in this book and in my chapter on camping and retreats in the first book of this series, *Ministering to Youth: A Strategy For the 80's* (#88582). In this chapter, I am covering the five functions of a week of camp and giving a few ideas on how to implement them more effectively. I call them the "E-I-E-I-O" of Christian camping: Education, Inspiration, Entertainment, Involvement, and Outreach.

Education

The church-camp setting offers a near-perfect situation for learning. Role models, in the persons of the staff, actually live with the students so that their lives can be examined as the teaching is taking place. The lesson isn't limited to an hour a week—the entire week is a lesson. Lessons are learned on the ball field, at the lunch table, and in the pool as well as in the classroom. Remember the phrase, "More is caught than taught."

Our classes followed a holiday theme for several years. During the week, we went through the life of Jesus using holidays. Sunday was Christmas Eve, with carols, a decorated tree, a visit from Santa, and the hanging of stockings. Monday was Christmas, with classes on the birth of Jesus, on the prophecies concerning His birth, and on incarnating Christ in our daily lives. The day included more carols, Christmas dinner and Christmas cookies, sharing homemade gifts, and a yule log at the camp fire. Tuesday was Halloween, with classes on the temptations of Jesus, dealing with the devil, fear, and guilt. The evening included a Christian movie on demonic activity, a Halloween party with a haunted house, and a camp fire that presented God as the great exorcist. Wednesday was Labor Day, and we studied the life and ministry of Jesus. Classes were in the area of the Holy Spirit, His gifts and fruit, and finding one's personal field of service. The afternoon or evening involved a labor of love. The Outreach section later in this chapter will present that material. Thursday was Maundy Thursday, with classes revolving around the significance of the Lord's Supper. Friday was the peak of the week, Good Friday. Classes touched on the sacrifice of Jesus, facing grief and death, and dying to self. The evening featured "The Way of the Cross," a re-enactment of the events surrounding the crucifixion. Saturday was Easter, with an exciting resurrection appearance and celebration. The Great Commission was delivered just as the campers were ready to return to the real world.

The holiday theme takes a lot of work! For example, we decorated the dining hall differently every day. But it was an effective way to take the campers through Jesus' life in a context they would remember.

One could also use the holiday theme simply to add color to the week. For example, one day could be Valentine's Day, with classes on love, sex, and marriage and a banquet in the evening. Another day could be April Fools' Day, with everything backwards on the schedule and classes on peer pressure, living contrary to the world's standards, and being "fools for Christ's sake."

Speaking of classes, I must encourage the use of electives. Offer a wide variety of classes and let the campers choose the ones that "scratch where they itch." Of course, you'll probably need more teachers, but you'll be meeting needs. Present a variety of Bible studies, plus topical studies such as the Christian and the media, handling emotions, the family, dating, and others.

We have also offered what we called "mind-stretchers"—sessions devoted to making the campers think at a deeper level. We bring in people who will challenge the kids' thinking, but we do it in a controlled environment. We have had an atheist, a Roman Catholic priest, a pro-abortionist, a bio-geneticist, and an undercover drug agent. We've had sessions on homosexuality, rock music, and sexuality. (We considered bringing in a homosexual, a rock musician, and a prostitute to lead them. We didn't, but it's still an idea.)

The strength of these sessions is that even if the outsider is forceful enough to boggle the kids, you will have several days to help them recover, examine his arguments, and point out weaknesses and falsehoods. The kids discover their need to be better equipped to do battle with the world.

One final idea: use your camp phone. It's very easy to hook up the camp phone so that the conversation is amplified and the entire group can listen. A few years ago, we had a series of lessons on cults. As a part of the study, we viewed Mel White's film Deceived. I had previously contacted Mel and made arrangements so that after viewing the film, we gathered around the phone and called him. Several of the campers had questions, and we all listened to the conversations. Mel informed us of new developments in the Jonestown tragedy and gave us a delightful forty-five minute phone visit. I suggest that if you are in a study and there is an authority you would like the kids exposed to, call him or her. Arrange details in advance and offer to pay for the time together. It's an intense and exciting learning situation.

Inspiration

The opportunities to involve campers in worship are golden! By offering some meaningful worship times at camp, the worship experiences at home become more meaningful. We try to make sure that the campers understand what real worship is: attributing worth to God. It helps if they can view it as a performance, with God as the audience and the congregation as performers. It is made clear that a worship service is just that—service. We are present to give, not just to receive. Once this distinction has been made, it's time to involve them in worship.

If it's possible, consider starting your week of camp on a Saturday afternoon, or even Friday evening. This not only provides valuable extra time, but it also allows the camp family to share in the Sunday-morning worship together.

Music naturally plays a significant part in our worship. We try to get "worship leaders," not "song leaders." That doesn't mean that our praise times are always sedate. On the contrary, at times they have been extremely exuberant! But we always make sure that God is at the center of our attention.

The most effective way we did this was by graphically depicting His presence. On Saturday evening, we gathered the campers together and practiced several praise songs—songs addressed directly to the Lord, such as "I Love You, Lord." We told the campers that we were going to have some special guests on Sunday morning, and we were going to do a concert for them. The next morning, as we gathered for worship, the campers were led to a hillside and arranged as a great choir. As they began singing in the bright sunshine, a friend dressed as Jesus came strolling out of the woods and sat in a chair facing the choir. He nodded, tapped his feet, smiled, and applauded after each song. The kids sang their hearts out! Afterwards, he shared the Sermon on the Mount with us. The worship songs during evening vespers for the rest of the week were much more joyful and intense because of the memory of that experience.

"Confrontations with Jesus," as we call them, have become some of the most inspiring and worshipful times of our camp weeks. We have had Jesus appear and preach on mountaintops and during picnics at lakesides. During each evening camp fire, we have taken several campers, one at a time, to a room where they shared juice, bread, and conversation with Jesus. As mentioned earlier, we have re-enacted the Lord's Supper, betrayal, denial, cross-bearing, and crucifixion. At the end of the evening of the crucifixion, the campers wrote a list of their sins and burdens and actually nailed them to the cross at the feet of Jesus. We have also had a variety of resurrection appearances which have led to some very spontaneous celebrations.

As you may guess, this involves a lot of work. You need to find someone with dramatic ability and a sensitive heart to portray Jesus. Lights, music, costumes, and grape juice don't just appear magically, either. But the purpose is to make Jesus a bit more personal to the kids so that as they enter into worship, whether privately or corporately, they will do so with a heart full of love. After these types of experiences, the campers definitely feel that there is much worth to attribute to God!

One note of caution, though. Our camp program is not aimed toward producing emotional experiences, but these types of dramatizations are emotional. We don't offer any type of invitation after a program like this. We simply let the campers experience and absorb it. Don't take unfair advantage of the emotional points of your camp week. Motivate, don't manipulate.

Preaching is another vital element of leading the camp in worship. There are all types of creative things that can be done in place of a sermon. However, I still suggest that you find the most Christlike preacher you can and turn him loose!

Make sure that the campers have some quiet time for private worship. I'm not talking about thirty minutes in the bunk after lunch! After some moving confrontation with Jesus, exciting praise in song, and preaching full of God's power, they need some time to put it all together. I've discovered that the best time is right after the evening vespers. Let them scatter all over the camp, find a spot totally alone, and then spend fifteen or twenty minutes reading the Word, talking with the Father, and watching the sunset. (Make sure that the faculty is involved in this time, too.) It may be that your week will fulfill the vital function of teaching kids that time alone and without interruptions isn't something to be afraid of.

Entertainment

Entertaining just for the sake of entertainment isn't actually a function of church camp. But there are definitely times when entertainment fits into a week of camp and can still help in the role of pointing kids to Jesus. If the campers are going to have a significant week, they simply must get to know each other. Most of the things mentioned in this section are used to help the campers to feel comfortable with each other. It is a process that continues all week, even though the crazy activities may be diminishing as the week progresses. There are those who feel that these types of activities are frivolous, but I have attended weeks without crowd-breaker activities, and the depths of relationships weren't as profound. It simply takes longer for quieter kids to initiate friendships without the crowd breakers.

I strongly recommend the use of initiative games. These have been used for years at scout camps and wilderness camps. They are beautiful for building teamwork and cooperation within a group.

These include such things as getting your entire team over a four-teen-foot wall or getting across a swamp by swinging from tire-swing to tire-swing. Some expense and preparation is necessary, but if it's done properly, there is no more danger of being hurt in these activities than there is on the ball field. The mutual encour-agement and thrill of achievement is a joy to watch.

Closely related are "New Games." "New Games" books may be ordered at most bookstores. These are non-competitive games that require cooperation but not winning. Playing the game and having fun is most important. That's a nice lesson to teach our campers who are living in a nation that places such strong emphasis on competition and winning.

A messy alternative is "Fight Night." The *Ideas* books from Youth Specialities are good resources for these activities. The pos-sibilities are endless: water relays, old tire relays, mud pits and mud fights, shaving cream and water balloon wars, flour and mo-lasses attacks, Crisco wrestling, and block ice relays. It may sound silly, but I've seen groups of 150 strangers become a mass of gig-gling friends within ninety minutes with activities such as these.

Some camps require morning exercises, but these have been presented in such a lifeless manner that they're often worthless. So we spiced them up at one camp. We filmed our own version of Jack Lelane on video. We had representatives of different nationalities come in on different days to lead "Ethnic Exercise," such as the Mexican hat dance, the French dip, and the Afro walk. One year, we had an obstacle course. "Rocky" led exercises one year with his theme song playing in the background. Aerobics are always fun, and "non-jogging" went over big one year. We discovered that it is difficult to plan anything significant for the early morning time; so we decided to use it just as a time for the campers to have fun together.

Lunch is a prime time, too. Games such as "Let's Make a Deal" or "Hollywood Squares" have added a lot of smiles to our camp and allowed several campers to be up front who might normally get left in the background. These are also creative ways to make an-nouncements, pass out mail, pass out awards for "worst bunk," and get rid of silly songs like "The Order of the Fork"!

Keep in mind that Jesus is to be at the center of our fun, too. Don't allow cruelty or humiliation to enter into these activities. Keep the purpose of these activities fresh in the minds of your faculty. They may be a minor part of the camp program, but they can add so much.

Involvement

As you plan, try to avoid putting together a week that makes spectators of the campers. They need to be as involved as possible. Here are some ideas to help accomplish that.

The concept of dividing the campers in families rather than teams has gained wide acceptance and popularity over the past few years. Just calling each group a family adds a note of warmth and caring. We let the families decorate their tables however they please. They do the initiative games together and, in general, spend as much time as possible with their parents, brothers, and sisters. The family concept also helps the staff to center in on a few campers rather than spread themselves too thin trying to get to know all the campers.

Role plays and simulation games have been very successful in involving the campers in a very active way. For example, the "Persecution" game is a three-hour simulation that recreates the Roman society of 2000 years ago—a society that was hostile to Christians. During the game, the "Christians" are harrassed, arrested, and even "killed." They are faced with some important decisions: do they hide, do they reject Christ, do they evangelize? Our camp manager claims that it is the most effective teaching experience he has seen in all his years at the camp. Years later, campers still talk about the "persecution." The major contributing factor is that they are actively involved, not passively sitting and listening. Role plays and simulations are available commercially at most Christian bookstores, but are even more effective when written especially for your situation. It's not difficult; so try it.

A related experience we often use is the "dependency meal." At a mealtime, usually lunch, the campers are handicapped in some way so that they will be forced to depend on each other if they are to eat. They may be blinded by taping over their eyes; they may be made deaf and dumb, denied the use of their hands, allowed to only feed the person on their right but not themselves, or tied at the wrist to the person on either side of them. It's a lot of fun, but the idea of the "body of Christ" strikes home in a powerful fashion.

We also leave the camp property at times in order to get the kids involved. Don't feel that everything has to occur on the camp-grounds. We have taken the campers off-campus for activities such as caving, rappelling, white-water rafting, hiking, and tubing. The relationships that are built during these experiences strongly reinforce what goes on during the rest of the week. Once again, the campers are actively involved, actually functioning as the body of

Christ, rather than sitting in a lecture hearing again that they need to function as a body.

Outreach

At times, it seems, we have almost forgotten that it is Christian *Service* Camp. The original idea was to take youth away for a period of training and inspiration in order to return them to the congregation better equipped to serve. Unfortunately, in many cases, they have been kept busy and entertained, and even inspired, but when they returned home, they were faced with a big question, "So what?" Nothing that had happened at camp was applicable to home, school, or church life. Here are some ideas to help you as you work toward preparing your campers for service.

For several years we have enjoyed putting together a performance-worthy program featuring the campers. We then took the program to an area church on Wednesday night of the camp week. We would have one or two practices a day before the performance and worked on a simple musical such as "I Am a Promise" (upgraded for older kids). The program usually involves music, drama, puppets, instrumentals, and multi-media. Campers who are not comfortable performing operate the tape players, lighting, and projectors or work as stagehands. Absolutely everyone, campers and staff, is involved. If you have over 100 campers, you may want to consider breaking into two groups and going to two different churches. The kids are excited about the idea of reaching out, and it gives them some skills and confidence they can take home with them. It's a lot of work, but the enthusiasm generated is more than worth it. Do a lot of publicity about this. We often had more onstage than were in the audience. Presenting the program at a mall or a city park is an exciting idea, too.

We have also reached out through work projects. Often there were jobs that needed to be done at the camp itself: painting, minor repairs and construction, brush clearing, creek cleaning, and the like. Other projects were directed more toward the community. We spent a day at an orphanage painting, cutting grass, and washing windows. Some groups have picked up trash at parks, picketed adult bookstores, and conducted surveys for local churches. Just find a job to be done, make arrangements, and do it. It's nice to do the work anonymously and thereby teach the campers that they don't have to receive praise to enjoy a job well done.

We have also offered the campers opportunities in various areas of personal ministry. In one week, they were allowed to choose between jail ministry, nursing home ministry, ministry to juvenile delinquents, rescue mission work, or hunger relief. On Monday, Tuesday, and Wednesday, the campers attended classes relevant to the ministries they chose. These classes were taught by people involved in the actual ministries, some of whom came each day just for the class. On Thursday, the campers were loaded into vehicles and visited the ministries: the jail, the detention center, the courtroom, the nursing home, and the Salvation Army. The reports that came back from these visits were exciting. Campers realized that they could be involved in significant ministries, even if they decided not to attend a Bible college. Our hope was that they would be motivated enough to return home and become involved to some degree in one of these ministries. Levels of commitment, maturity, and compassion took great leaps during these experiences.

Conclusion

There you have it, the "E-I-E-I-O" of Christian camping. I have tried to pick some of the best ideas, but much more has been done than is included here. It is gratifying to know that committed and creative minds are constantly churning to find more effective ways to communicate Jesus to our youth. Please take these ideas, add your own creativity, and spring out into new areas of ministry through church camp.

Always keep that central purpose in mind. "Does it help in presenting Jesus to kids?" That is the final test that must be given to every idea you plan to incorporate into your week of camp. Don't do something creative simply because you want to be different. Do it because it will help the campers see God in all of His awesome majesty and love.

16

Working With a
Camp Manager:
What the Manager Expects from the Dean

Gary E. Brown

In every camp, there is someone to whom the ongoing care of the facility is entrusted. He may act only as a caretaker for the weeks the camping program exists, or he may be the head of a staff that maintains a program all year long. Whatever the status of each one is, they all have something in common. They care about the camp.

A camp is a system of trustees, directors, faculty, deans, campers, summer staff, programming, facilities, supporters, churches, and much more. The one person who touches every part of the system is the manager. His phone rings when there is a question, a complaint, or a comment on any part of the system.

His first responsibility is to have the camp in shape for your arrival. Everything from food to medical supplies must be ready. He provides a staff to meet the needs of your program. He oversees every aspect of the office work, from promotion to record-keeping and registration. It is he who must answer to the powers that be for whatever happens during your week of camp. The parents are trusting him to provide a safe, effective, and spiritual experience for their children. Christian parents do not just send their children to camp; they invest them. The camp manager is one who oversees that investment. He is committed to those children's lives. Because of that commitment, the manager expects certain things from the dean, not the least of which is a sharing of that commitment.

Every manager wants a high level of commitment from the dean.

He wants a dean who desires to serve and to be a servant. A dean that does not take his week seriously can be maddening. The dean should consider everything he is doing as groundwork for doing a better job next year. Each week that a dean is both serving a week and preparing for another week the following year excels! When he asks someone to join his faculty, he should be asking for a continual commitment on an annual basis. Preparation for a week at camp should be an ongoing process twelve months a year. The dean must realize what is at stake with the children whom he is going to live with and lead.

Programming

That commitment should express itself in the program that is set for the week. The dean must realize the vast amount of time for which he is responsible for the campers. And he must plan to use every minute of that time constructively.

When a dean fails to fill the minutes and hours of a week of camp, he very often resorts to more free time. But extensive free time is really what I call "cheap time," and kids don't handle cheap time very well. Most of the injuries, vandalism, homesickness, and horseplay at camp happen during cheap time. Cheap time does not yield the return on investment that parents are expecting—not by a long shot! Free time—a short, occasional break from the activity—is nice, but cheap time—extensive amounts of time with nothing to do—is boring. The program must be filled with constructive activity.

Positive, Christ-centered programming that brings everyone closer together and closer to God is our goal. The week should warm the heart and whet the appetite for future encounters. Don't bring the world into camp with you. Camp has no room for worldly attitudes, speech, concepts, actions, or relationships. For one week, campers get to live in a far-away, strange, and wonderful place, a place so unique that once they leave it, it can never be found quite that way again. They each will take part of it with them and keep it as a memory. Make sure no part of your faculty or program is a Trojan horse that will bring the world in upon them. Make every part of your week special, and let nothing and no one contaminate the experience.

There are three special areas of your program that affect the manager and his staff directly. They are bedtime, mealtime, and the canteen. The manager also needs information regarding the supplies you need to run your program.

Bedtime

Bedtime is one of the most important times of the day. Not only do young people need their sleep, but so do you, your faculty, and the camp staff. Often the deans and the faculty seem to live under the curse of the vampire: only coming alive in the fog of late night, and rendered useless with the pending dawn of the new day. If your people are doing their jobs, they need their sleep. Those campers who are crazy about staying up will wilt and lose their drive and appetite right before your bleary, bloodshot eyes.

Mealtime

Another part of the schedule that affects the manager and the dean is mealtime. Fun and games in the dining hall is a standard at most camps, but it can get out of hand. Once you start to play and the commotion heats up, all eating stops, and food is wasted. If playing at mealtime is part of your program, then wait until the campers are done with their food. Never allow the food to be a part of your play. When the campers slide by mealtime and tank up at canteen, a lot of behavioral changes begin to emerge. Make eating your top priority at mealtime. Encourage them to fill up for the next four-or five-hour marathon.

Canteen

One of the great centers of any programming day is the canteen. The camp manager needs to have fixed canteen times with definite openings and closings. He cannot afford to hire a lot of staff to run it for hours on end, and he can't afford the dean's faculty to run it at all. The canteen is one of those items that chips in to help pay the bills around any camp where it is managed correctly. Also remember that when you decide to have canteen before mealtimes, they bag the wasted food in fifty-gallon bags after the meal. When you decide to have late-night canteens, remember that some of the camp staff have been working since 6:00 A.M. They are getting a little bleary-eyed and would like to go to bed. Please give the manager advance notice of such canteens so he can organize his staff to fill the positions.

Supplies

It takes a lot of equipment to service a week of camp. Between class times, games, special activities, and sports, the items could fill a catalog. The dean may take for granted that the camp has many of the items he needs readily available. Maybe you have seen or used certain items at camp before, or someone else told you the camp has certain equipment. Please don't trust your eyes, your memory, or the testimony of others. Some items are just borrowed for a short time. Some items have been long-since destroyed or replaced by another type. Some items succumb to the pressures of the summer and disintegrate. Some items are borrowed and are never returned. Some items never existed at your camp, but did at another camp where you once worked.

Please check in advance before planning on the existence of any supplies or equipment. If the manager doesn't have a certain item, maybe he knows where to get it or can suggest something else. Try to provide as many specialty items as you can yourself, and never leave any of them behind if you have no idea of donating them to the cause.

You will need to check with each of your faculty on the subject of supplies. Check for special teaching aids or equipment that they will need to work in their areas. Remind them that five minutes before they need an item is not the best warning for the camp staff to produce it out of stock or thin air. Make sure everyone gives you a written list of what they need and when they need it, and get these lists as early as possible.

If you need some big-ticket item to make your camp week work and need for the camp manager to acquire it, you and he need to talk about it much in advance of your week. First of all, he has a budget to maintain. If an item is important, and he has enough warning, he may be able to raise special funds and get with other deans who might find the same item beneficial.

Remember: take nothing for granted, write it down, and get your requests in early.

People

Faculty

As soon as your program begins to gel in your head, the process of faculty selection begins. You need to get people who share your commitment to young people. You want people who can work well with you and with each other. You need people who are prepared.

The camp manager can help, and he would like to. Often, he should be the first one you contact. Share with him the program ideas you are developing. He not only can tell you whether or not the camp is equipped for your activities, he can also tell you about some people who can or cannot help.

Camp magnifies people and events one hundred times in the eyes of children. You must select people who are truly spiritual and team oriented. Most of the problems that the manager has to mop up after a camp week is over, involve the faculty. Sometimes it is what one of them has said or done. Sometimes it's what was not said or done. But in some sense, they have failed someone.

The faculty have close contact with the children. Some people with personality problems or deep insecurities like that situation because it makes them feel needed. Perhaps their whole reason for being at camp is to get their act together. Year after year, these people return to strike again and again. Even though the deans who have used them know better than to use these people again, there are always deans who don't know them—especially first-time deans. But the manager has seen them all!

You want a strong faculty, a group of people who go to camp for what they can do for the cause, not what the cause can do for them! You want a staff that believes and teaches the truth without having any axes to grind. So as you select your faculty, contact the manager. Many times he can warn you of, or commend to you, a prospective faculty member's past performance. He can share strengths and weaknesses of some individuals, and help you find out such information about others. Sometimes he has met some really sharp people in churches he has visited. Many of them would be an asset to your program.

When your faculty is taking shape and you begin to correspond with them regarding assignments, remember the camp manager. Put his name on your list when you send letters to your faculty telling everyone who is serving and how. The manager needs to know what each faculty member's responsibility is. (He especially needs to know the assistant dean in case the dean should become unable to continue his responsibility.)

You should also begin meeting regularly with your faculty as soon as you have a significant number confirmed for your week. At least one of these meetings should be at the camp itself so your faculty—especially new faculty members—can get acquainted with the facilities. (Naturally, such a meeting will have to be arranged with the camp manager to be sure the camp is available.) If an on-site meeting is not possible, arrange a time when your rookie faculty can meet with the camp manager to tour the camp.

One really sharp thing to do is to gather all your faculty at camp prior to the arrival of the children for a retreat. This will get them acquainted with the facilities and each other even more. It is a time for polishing the last-minute details and gathering spiritual strength from each other. It will give the camp manager time to go over the rules and the reasons for the rules in camp, also.

When you have a pre-camp retreat, you are assured that all faculty members will be in their places and ready to serve when the first camper arrives. They will be physically, mentally, and spiritually prepared at the onset. So many times faculty members arrive late and in a fog, and the campers are moved in, dug in, and three steps ahead for the rest of the week!

During the retreat, the dean can go through each day of the week, quarter hour by quarter hour, to make sure that everything that is needed to supply and control the program is available. Each member of the team can again see the program as a whole and where his specific ministry will fit.

Please be sure to notify the camp manager of your desire to have a pre-camp retreat several months ahead of time. This is necessary to make sure the grounds will be available for you.

Special Faculty

There are usually three loose threads on the faculty tapestry: the evangelist, the missionary, and the college team. Many times, these people are brought in from the outside and arrive only as the week begins. Both the manager and the dean need to spend special time with them to tune them in to the week. If at all possible, you need to keep a running correspondence with them so they know the nature of the week and know of some of the people they will be helping. They need to know their jobs specifically, and the manager needs to know what they will need from his staff to do those jobs. If there are any special requirements as to housing, diet, materials, or equipment, the manager needs to know as soon as possible so he can be prepared.

It is very important that the manager know who is coming in these special areas as soon as possible for another reason, too. In many cases, mail will arrive for them or messages will need to be stored or forwarded. In some cases, money and necessary supplies will be shipped in advance to the camp. The manager needs to know when they will arrive so he can answer inquiries from interested supporters or friends. If they plan to stay over, the manager needs to make special arrangements for that, too.

Camp Staff

Those people whom you find waiting on you when you arrive at camp are called the camp staff. These plucky servants have signed on for the duration of the summer. Each of them feels that a ministry can be performed through even the most humbling of tasks surrounding the care and feeding of the facility and the program. As long as they feel a part of the team and have a sense of being a link in the chain of ministries that are being performed, they are happy to serve.

When they are transformed into "motel people," they grow restless, complaining, and discouraged. "Motel people" are those shadowy, anonymous lackies scurrying in the shadows performing their various mundane tasks. When you begin to view them as some foreign contingent of nameless clerks, cooks, and custodians, you rob them of their spot on the team and, therefore, of their full ministry.

Before you arrive, make sure your people know who the staff is, what they do, and just why they are there. As you assign prayer requests, remember them. When you are at camp, try and fit any talents that they might have into little pieces of your program.

The greatest, single-most devastating condition that can befall one of the staff members is tunnel vision. They only see your program in the light that it touches their specific area. Many times I have had a great week of camp in residence and was overjoyed with it until I heard it discussed by staff members with tunnel vision. To the cook who works hard to feed your group, hot meals are a failure when you arrive late and her food is cold and then tossed into the garbage. When you arrive too early and chant to speed things up, you become a rude and inconsiderate mass. To those who are assigned to clean, you may become sloppy bums. To those who run the canteen, you may be greedy, pushy people. Tunnel vision is usually at the base of all faculty and staff relationship problems.

Be aware of tunnel vision on the part of the faculty as well as the camp staff. Teach your faculty to be understanding of staff members who work long hours week in and week out. Kind words and praise will do wonders to blend your staffs together. Remember that the staff is here to remove from your shoulders the routine tasks a camp needs to survive. They have dedicated themselves to be ready for you and have been in anticipation of your arrival for months. Please realize that both the faculty and the staff minister the best when they minister together.

The best way to make sure you minister together is to keep in mind the two chains of command at camp. The faculty answers to the dean and the staff answers to the manager. There should be communication and cooperation at all levels between faculty and staff, but when problems arise, the dean and the manager are responsible for working things out. If the manager must intervene in a faculty matter, he does so through the dean. If the dean has a problem with a staff member, he goes through the manager.

Campers

That brings us past all the preparation and to the week of camp itself. And that means there is one more group of people to consider—the campers.

The manager will let you run your own program as you see fit. He will not interfere, but he needs to be kept informed. Each day the dean and the manager should get together four or five times to check schedules, compare notes, evaluate progress, and locate weak and strong points. Are the campers growing? Are they becoming more committed? What can be done to accelerate or maintain that growth?

If the dean is having trouble with a faculty member, the manager also needs to know about it. If something comes up and the dean will be gone or unable to serve, the manager needs to know that, too, and get with the assistant.

If a discipline problem arises, the dean should always be brought into it—even in minor cases. This keeps the discipline fair and consistent. The manager should not be involved in discipline unless there is a serious problem. Then he must be!

The manager wants to be involved because he is cautious. He wants to be prepared the next year if the child returns to camp. He also needs to know the true nature of the problem and the dean's course of action so he can answer questions raised later by parents or a church. It's not fair to leave him a time bomb waiting to explode without telling him. Keep records of any disciplinary action to assist in defusing such threatening situations when they occur.

The Facility

In most camping programs, seventy-five to eighty percent of the time, energy, and money is devoted to maintaining and developing the actual campus. Just as surely as you have searched for volunteers to staff your program, the manager has searched for volunteers to help him launch and maintain the orbit of the facility you will be using. If you would sit in on the board meetings and trustee meetings that surround any camp program, you would find the major topics of conversation are money, manpower, maintenance, and expansion. The largest aspect of the manager's job lies in the area of stewardship. He only has so much time and money allotted to keep the campus in top shape, and he needs you to help.

First, he needs you to realize that he can only afford to maintain a limited staff and must rely on you and the campers to police many areas. Keeping the campground clean, the sleeping areas tidy, and the meeting areas neat are essential to keeping the whole facility glued together. Once the campus begins to assume a trashy personality, then vandalism starts to grow. You and everyone else who uses the facility must realize that you are not borrowers or renters, but part owners. The campus is yours—yours to show proper stewardship.

One of the most interesting phenomenon of camping is the mountains of great clothes left behind each week. After you leave, the camp staff will spend hours on the phone trying to get the right items back to the right owners. They have to clean, store, save, and return countless items. Sometimes clothes are left because parents send unfamiliar clothes to camp with their kids. Sometimes clothes are stuffed into nooks and crannies, or borrowed by other campers. If you keep a neat and organized cabin, most items will leave with the campers and save the staff a lot of work. This is especially true on the last day of camp as everyone packs up. Make it a mission to gather up all items floating around unclaimed and restoring them to the owners so it doesn't have to be done later. Some child may be spared an ugly scene at home when his mother asks him, "Where is all the stuff I bought you for camp?"

Trash gathers more trash. As soon as any area shows the first sign of being a dump, then the lid is off and more is piled on. Allow several times each day for cleaning and straightening up the sleeping areas, grounds, and recreational equipment.

Also remember that the camp staff expects breakage. The natural tension that exists between a child and any physical object will create it. When something breaks or is about to break, let the manager know. In this way, he can maintain a safer camp and possibly rescue valuable property before it, too, becomes trash. Those things that are saved do not need to burden the budget, allowing more money to buy new and potentially useful equipment for your program.

One of the most sensitive areas to any manager is the timing between your week of camp and the next camping activity.

Because of the current popularity of camping, the next group will probably be a retreat that will arrive just as you leave with little or no break to allow for repair or cleaning. That is the reason that, on the last day of camp, you and the staff need to work very closely to make sure that time and energy are applied to the right places and that you leave the camp in great shape for the group right on your heels.

Closing Thoughts

Every camp manager and every camp dean must realize that camping is a total team experience. It is a blending of faculty, staff, program, and facility with children to create a physical, social, and—most vitally—spiritual harmony. It is through this special harmony that the ministries of the dean and the manager are joined to change lives. No amount of time, energy, or money can stand against the reality of putting the Christian experience into the hearts of young people. You will be a part of warm memories that will last a lifetime. It takes a great deal of courage and commitment to set oneself up as an example to the children. But the rewards so vastly outweigh the risks that you will return year after year to the steamy dorms and the camp fires that glow forever.

Suggested Resources

Ball, Armand B. And Beverly H. *Basic Camp Management.* Martinsville, IN: American Camping Associaion, 1982.
Camp and the Child, Martinsville, IN: American Camping Association, 1979.
Camp Staff Application. Martinsville, IN: American Camping Association, 1980.
Camp Staff Job Description. Martinsville, IN: American Camping Association, 1980.
Evaluating the Camp Experience. Martinsville, IN: American Camping Association, 1979.
Knowing the Camper. Martinsville, IN: American Camping Association, 1979.
Johnson, C. Walton. *Unique Mission of the Summer Camp.* Martinsville, IN: American Camping Association, 1973.
Pick, Diane. *Camping Strategies for the 80's.* Martinsville, IN: American Camping Association, 1981.
Rodney, Lyn S. and Phyllis M. Ford. *Camp Administration.* Melbourne, FL: Robert E. Krieger Publishing Co., 1984.

17

Wilderness Camping

John Yates

Powerfully
I am drawn to that which grows slowly
and drives its roots deeply
which has permanence
and knows the pain of growth.
To grow is my wish
but am I prepared to receive the wounds of life?
Am I ready to give shelter to many
yet to seek shelter only with You?
I want to be radiant from the inside.
I want to stand firm and to mature,
to grow into You,
to live through You ...
But I know
that the price is high.

Ulrich Schaffer[1]

Wilderness camping means growth and maturity achieved by standing up to the stark realities of God's creation. In some ways, a young person is much like a new sapling on the ridge of a mountain. All successful trees started as saplings, and the testing of their strength and stamina never ceases from season to season. Wilderness camping becomes the eye-opening beginning for some kids to deal with the often harsh realities of life in the Christian faith.

Why Wilderness Camping?

Resident camp managers have told me that there are primarily two things necessary to please the people who come to their camps: good meals and a hot shower. Neither of these are on the wilderness program. So why would anybody want to be involved in a wilderness camping program?

If challenge, difficulty, hardship, and adventure are not among the needs of the individuals you desire to reach, then you probably can't give a good affirmative answer to that question. Perhaps a different type of ministry is where you should focus your attention. But you must answer the question, "Why wilderness camping?" or, "Why aren't roller-skating parties enough?"

Motivation and purpose are the roots of any new venture and dictate the direction that venture will take. If you plant a tree, you should know whether it is intended for bearing fruit or firewood.

It is important at this point to define some terminology to build a foundation. One of the biggest struggles among camps using the wilderness environment has been the establishment of terminology that truly defines the intents and purposes (philosophy) of their various programs. Let me suggest that there are two major schools of thought. For lack of better terminology, I will call them "recreational" and "educational" styles of leadership. I refer to "styles of leadership" because that is the difference between these two camps. They both employ many of the same activities, like backpacking, canoeing, and mountaineering, but they differ greatly in their purposes and in the methods employed to conduct these activities.

The recreational school of thought uses the wilderness as a unique environment in which to play while developing skills and building teamwork and camaraderie within groups. Skills are often emphasized as stepping-stones toward higher levels of involvement in the wilderness environment. Hardships are minimized, either through becoming adept at skills or selecting wilderness areas well within the grasp and abilities of the participants. The unexpected is usually avoided, as it complicates the leader's ability to maintain a leisure atmosphere. Challenges are often sought purely for their ability to excite people.

On the other hand, the educational approach, or more specifically the experiential education approach, regards the wilderness as an ideal classroom to test a person, assess his needs on the basis of those tests, and attempt to meet those needs through various activities that require the person to deal with problems and work out solutions in that area of need. In light of this philosophy, I offer the following definition: "Wilderness camping is a temporary means of dwelling in a foreign environment where the participant is a visitor functioning as a learner." The key to this definition, and to the philosophy it purports, is the emphasis on the foreign environment and the visitor-learner concept. In the recreational philosophy, familiarity and feeling comfortable within the environment is very important. That doesn't mean that the ground has to be any more comfortable or the sky any clearer or the mountains less steep, but the participant does not want to have to deal with the unexpected. He reads the guidebook, follows the signed trails, stays within close proximity to the camp parking lot, and brings with him as many of the comforts of home as possible, or has developed sufficient skills, over time, to be at complete ease despite the circumstances. On the other hand, the experiential learner cannot anticipate the environment he will face. He purposefully puts himself in unpredictable environments to achieve the pioneer experience of discovering answers and developing skills as the need for such knowledge manifests itself. The participant has to be willing to strip himself of the accoutrements of home and step out as a visitor into this foreign environment to discover his fears, his selfish ambitions, his need for other people, and, most of all, his ability to be taught. The newness of a foreign environment creates hardship that must be endured and enjoyed. Once a person gains the realization that he can face hard truths through interaction with others and God in an environment that amplifies his need for them, he gains the ability to seek learning. He no longer passively waits for learning to happen or to be done for him.

Recreation and leisure are essential in an age where busyness is the next thing to godliness. Hardship and struggling are essential in an age of hedonism. I have presented these schools as divergent philosophies concerning wilderness camping; however, it is the blending of these two ideals that meets the needs of the whole person.

Carmen Poulos Bergman stated in a poem, *The Liberation of Leisure*, "Somewhere in the depths of conscience, wisdom pleads for the time when jobs had to be done and one did them to survive." The youth of today have that same longing in their souls to be needed and useful. They want jobs that have to be done, jobs without which their group cannot succeed, jobs that lend

significance to their personal worth. Kurt Hahn, one of the found-
ing fathers of Outward Bound, described what young people hunger for: "All they ask of us is this, demand much of us, and make
use of us." Tim Hansel stated it this way,

> The need for adventure has never been greater. Young people
> especially need large doses of adventure in order to change, dis-
> cover, and grow. If they aren't sufficiently challenged by real life
> adventures, they will seek and find other fictitious adventures of
> significantly less value. I'm not at all surprised when I see youth
> explore drugs, sex, or delinquent behavior. I don't condone it; I'm
> simply not surprised. They are often seeking their idea of new-
> ness and adventure. It is their means of breaking, what Paul Tour-
> nier calls in THE ADVENTURE OF LIVING, "the deadly monot-
> ony of a society which to them has become over organized,
> fossilized and impotent."[2]

Wilderness camping is not a cure for anything. It can, however,
provide a diagnosis. I am thoroughly convinced that the need for
wilderness camping is greater today than it has ever been before.
The nature of our affluent society, with its throw-away answers for
everything from milk cartons to unwanted births, stands too much
in contrast to the demands of the gospel, where the only thing
disposable is one's own life. But wilderness camping doesn't solve
this problem. It doesn't require a person to give up his life—or
even to be willing to. It only makes a person more aware of the
kind of life he is living. Only Christ requires our lives.

The Essence of Wilderness Learning

Stress in the wilderness is not a marketable idea among most
Christians. Nobody likes to hurt, but it is hard for us to deny that
growth often occurs through struggles. If you have ever tried to
present the idea of an experiential education course to a youth
group, you have found that kids hate it, and so do adults. Suppose
someone asked you to go without food for three days, spend that
time in prayer and the reading of Scripture, and do it totally alone
without a sleeping bag. No wonder Jesus was hanged. He asks us
to do things even harder. Need it? Yes! Love it? No! Wilderness
camping is not a drawing card to expand your youth group.

Not all wilderness trips begin with or include as challenging an
experience as I just mentioned. The level of intensity for each trip
must be geared to the needs of the participants as well as the
abilities of the instructors. A wilderness trip should always begin
from the basis of real need. Much of youth ministry is structured
around blanket needs that pertain to an age group or a segment of

society with all its stereotyped behaviors. But individual needs vary greatly, and the development of philosophy, leadership, and the entire wilderness program must be based on these needs.

At this point, I suggest a thorough researching of the book of Exodus. Within this part of Scripture, human relationships in all their frailty and inconsistency are brought to light as God leads His people to the promised land. Everything from going without water (Exodus 15:22) to being bountifully supplied with meat and bread (Exodus 16:12) is shared in this book, demonstrating to us how God taught the children of Israel to overcome a bitter and grumbling spirit.

Neither the attitudes nor the learning process exhibited in the book of Exodus have changed in dealing with people's demanding ways and selfish desires. The general need to overcome bitterness in the face of hardship is as important to conquer now as it was then, but it is essential that the wilderness leader dig deep and assess the specific needs of the learners. God's solution for what we see in His diagnostic tests in the book of Exodus was to raise up a whole new generation to go into the promised land. The youth minister and Christian educator have the opportunity to help facilitate the growth of a new generation that will be recognized by God as His good and faithful servants.

A wilderness program should always begin with a need-assessing phase. This stage is a testing ground to determine much of the structure of the trip.

> The modern teacher continues to find testing of value. The efficient pedagogue begins to teach by finding out where his pupils are before he undertakes to lead them elsewhere. He needs to measure past achievement to guide him to the proper material and methods. It is fully as important to make the pupil aware of his own needs.[3]

We will discuss the specifics of this testing process later. The beauty of the wilderness experience is that it deals with real-life situations; there are pots to be scrubbed, beds to be made, water to be collected, and the anatomical essentials of life, all of which are compounded in their difficulty to achieve in the new environment.

> In order to raise all of life to a spiritual plane, God's method is ever the spontaneous vitality of actual life. There is no need of artificial stimulation of interest when inner urges are being utilized, when the sources of material are direct and primary. It is true that experience is the best teacher provided it is the right kind of experience, provided it is skillfully guided.[4]

It is this skillful guidance of the learner that makes the difference between a quality wilderness experience and a mere walk in the woods. Just as Moses had no easy task cut out for him, the wilderness instructor has the awesome responsibility of assessing needs and promoting an environment to help individuals achieve the goals to meet those needs.

Leadership

Many church people believe backpacking is basic, and there are hundreds of ex-Boy Scouts and camp crafters available to go out with the kids. "In fact, we have a guy in our camp (church) who does rock climbing. I'm sure he'd do a great job with the kids." Unfortunately, he won't, and neither will 1,000 Boy Scout leaders. If hiking out to the back forty of the camp or traveling the signed tourist route in your local park is what you are shooting for, that may be okay. But wilderness camping requires people with years of experience, not only as mountaineers, but in dealing with interpersonal struggles inherent with living in the wilds of God's garden.

Speaking of the garden, the tender care of the wilderness environment also requires special skill and, above that, a special attitude. Of course, the more technical the program, the higher the requirements for the leader as well as the participants.

Spiritual maturity and insight are essential ingredients in a good leader. An associate instructor with Discovery Expeditions incapsulated the Biblical roots of leadership when he said, "He who seeks to lead must first seek to serve." The servant-leader concept permeates the New Testament. Through the washing of feet and dying on the cross, Jesus exemplified perfect leadership, the kind of leadership that makes others want to follow your example.

Tim Hansel coined the expression *holy sweat* in reference to this servant-leader concept:

> The term, "Holy Sweat," emerged almost accidently. It serves to remind me that we are called to obedience with calluses and salvation with dirt under our fingernails. Holy sweat is grace with blisters on its hands and feet, and perspiration running down its forehead. It is holiness that believes in hard work. It is commitment with talent, courage, and tenacity, and it is faith that has come to realize that sanctification is a process and not just an event.[5]

Though hardship is unmarketable, and people almost unanimously avoid pain at all costs, there is something attractive deep in the spirit of a Christian about the kind of suffering that Christ endured. We desire to love in the way He loved and to endure for the hope of the same resurrection. I know of no greater classroom than the wilderness to witness and experience struggles that so closely resemble the ones God used to teach His disciples through Biblical history.

The Course

> Every gate to the inner man was besieged from without by the lessons to be learned in the wilderness. Every lesson was re-enforced, emphasized, strengthened by the senses. No door to the soul was untouched.[6]

This statement was made in reference to the Exodus, but it really makes reference to God's curriculum. The curriculum of the wilderness learning process must involve the tools that God has given man to learn with. Activities need to encompass the use of all of our senses, many of which have been dulled by television and other immediate-gratification types of stimuli.

Phase one of the course involves moving people out of their familiar environment into the unfamiliar. For some, this is easy and may only require driving twenty miles into the country where there are no sidewalks and street lights. For others, such as the experienced backpackers, removal of toothpaste, toilet paper, and shampoo is all that is needed to put them in a real wilderness. For others, more drastic measures must be taken. To know how far to go with your group in this process of moving into a foreign world, you will need to assess and test the areas of comfort they cling to for security.

Phase two brings on the testing process. The participant begins to develop an understanding of self and the real needs he will want to deal with throughout the course. This phase often involves the use of group initiatives, ropes courses, and various other activities that cause people to let their hair down or make it stand on end. An instructor can learn a great deal about the participants and himself through this phase.

Giving groups and individuals problems to solve was a tool Jesus demonstrated throughout His time with the Twelve. John 6:5-14 shows Jesus using a test to bring His disciple Philip a little bit farther down the road of trust and faith. Jesus used the teachable moment of a hungry crowd to increase the disciples' faith by first frustrating them with a revealing test that showed their spiritual inadequacy.

Phase three is the preparation phase. Specific skills necessary to accomplish tasks and to use the wilderness environment properly must be mastered during this period. The intensity and time taken during this minor expeditionary segment of the course will vary depending on the length, environment, season, and goals of the trip.

Phase four is the expedition. At this point, the leader has facilitated within the group some goal-setting. Goals have been set to meet needs that have been assessed through the first three phases of the course. Specific objectives are presented and achieved. These objectives may include peak assents, solo time, early morning run and dips, pinecone baseball games, days of rock climbing, river travel, and caving. Each day concludes with a debriefing and an assessment of the process for meeting needs and achieving goals. Eight days into a fourteen-day trip is a good time to ask how the participants are doing spiritually. On the third day of the trip, they may have proclaimed lofty goals for reading their Bibles daily and spending time with the group in prayer. A leader must be willing to allow people the opportunity of experiencing spiritual starvation in order to open their eyes later with the question, "How are you doing spiritually?" Often the answer will be, "We blew it. We didn't pray. We didn't read. Why didn't you lead us in some Bible studies?" The desire for participants to point the finger at the leader will be overwhelming as they are faced, often for the first time, with being personally accountable for their lives spiritually, emotionally, and physically. The expedition is the consummation of being taught through our senses; it is the time when "no door to the soul is untouched."

Phase five is what I call "the trip that never ends." Participants must realize that wilderness camping experiences are only the beginning of a learning process that never ends. Because it deals with real-life activities, there is no reason that the learning should cease. The willingness to choose foreign environments in order to facilitate one's own growth should become attractive as the learner transforms seeking into serving.

Some Essentials

You must realize at this point the magnitude of developing and implementing a wilderness experience. My desire is to encourage you to use this tool, yet realize that the hazards and risks of its use are great. Therefore, the responsibility for trained leadership is extreme. This chapter is intended to be an exposure to the essence and basic structure of this ministry tool. I encourage you to begin planning how you might facilitate making a wilderness experience available to the people you minister to, either through existing ministries or through the development of yourself and others as qualified leaders. In the suggested resources at the end of this chapter, you will find some places to start asking questions to further this process.

The ministry through wilderness camping is often misunderstood, or at best misinterpreted. Therefore, it is very important for someone aspiring to facilitate the beginning of such a program to find out first the full scope of what is involved. Of course, that will not accomplish the task any more than researching routes up a mountain will enable you to climb that mountain. More often than not, it will convince you to climb elsewhere. But with a proper perspective, good decisions can be made.

If you decide the need is great enough, and wilderness camping can meet the need best, then consider the following questions.

Who will administrate it? After all, what comes first, the foundation or the house? Organize and coordinate. Set rules and standards. Be flexible in structure. Delegate and evaluate. Set up systems for communication and, above all, plan not to plan.

Where will we run it? From where will you draw participants? Consider costs of travel to and from tripping areas. Should you own your own wilderness land or not? Are there camps or organizations ready to help establish a wilderness camping program? What about the city as a wilderness? Never let places precede people.

How and where do we find leaders? Look for the spiritually mature and those with good judgment. Remember that skills are always subservient to those two qualities. Can you give experience or do you need it? Don't look for born leaders, look for born servants. Do they know and admit their weaknesses? Find motivators and not manipulators. Christlikeness must be their goal, and seeing Christ develop in others, their vision.

What activities should we do, and how do we pull them off? Know what kind of demands are placed on people by specific activities. Choose activities with a purpose in mind. Activities mixed in a good way keep people alert, whether the purpose is fun or struggle. Don't conduct activities beyond or too near the limits of an instructor. Coordinate your logistics to be economical and safe, and still fit your philosophy. Learn about margins of safety and leave large ones. The goal of specific activities is to put a person's problem within their grasp, whether it be fear, interpersonal relationships, or a poor self-image. Don't expect anything to happen just as you planned, but plan it as if you expect it to happen.

How do we stay safe? Remember there are two ways to end a rappel. Set up margins of safety. Instructors should have a thorough knowledge of activities, rescue, and first aid within the environment they are using. Use quality maintained equipment, and know its limits. Have a plan before things happen. Measure the panic level of participants in a controlled setting first. Build real confidence, not false security. There are real dangers, and human error is the greatest.

What equipment do we need? Learn from the success and failure of others. Buy for durability with margins of safety as your prime consideration. The more technical the program, the more expensive the equipment. Buy only what you need. Don't ever count on campers to bring their own equipment and have the right thing.

What about insurance?

Most wilderness camping will take place off your campgrounds. Insurance people call your campgrounds "premises." Properly written LIABILITY insurance would cover your camp's (a) premises and (b) operations. A legal action resulting from alleged negligence taking place on your camp premises would be insured under the policy's premises (a) portion. Alleged negligence taking place OFF your grounds should be covered under the policy's operations (b) portion—if you don't have it excluded!

Insurance underwriters are concerned about adequate certification of staff, but they are more concerned for the screening and preparation of the campers.

BEST BET: (1) Supply your company with a narrative explaining your credentials and your program. (2) Request a written memo stating you have this protection in your policy.[7]

What needs to be known about the environment? How crowded is the area you wish to use? Have a full knowledge of no trace and minimum impact camping. Remember that good hygenic practices make the water taste better. Christians should be in the forefront of proper instruction in the use of God's garden. There are important lessons of life to be gleaned from the discipline of caring for creation.

It is sad but true that many church groups have scarred the image for Christian groups backpacking in national parks, wilderness areas, and national forest land by bringing in large groups and using very poor standards of conduct in their use of the resources.

You have the opportunity to help change that image by developing good relationships with local authorities and by maintaining a sound wilderness ethic.

Know your limits and don't hesitate to work within those limits. Desire first to serve, avoid pride at all costs, and take to heart the words of Helen Keller, "Life is . . . either a daring adventure . . . or nothing at all."

---

[1] Ulrich Schaffer, *Searching for You* (New York: Harper and Row, 1978). Used by permission.

[2] Tim Hansel, "Holy Sweat," *Journal of Christian Camping* (Vol. 14, No. 3, 1982), p. 10.

[3] Lois LeBar, *Education That Is Christian* (Old Tappan: Fleming H. Revel Co., 1958), p. 95.

[4] LeBar, p. 91.

[5] Hansel, p. 11.

[6] LeBar, p. 93.

[7] Richard Castor, "Insurance Words," *Journal of Christian Camping* (Vol. 14, No. 2, 1982), p. 10.

Suggested Resources

Books

Angier, Bradford. *Home in Your Pack: the Modern Handbook of Backpacking.* New York: Macmillan, 1972. (Basic backpacking and woodcraft)

Fletcher, Colin. *The Complete Walker.* New York: Knofp, 1984. (Basic backpacking)

Mitchell, Dick. *Mountaineering First Aid.* Seattle: The Mountaineers, 1975.

Peters, Ed, ed. *Mountaineering: the Freedom of the Hills.* Seattle: The Mountaineers, 1982. (All aspects of basic climbing, mountaineering, and leadership)

Rohnke, Karl. *Cowstails and Cobras.* Hamilton, MA: Project Adventure, 1977. (Details for use of ropes courses and group initiatives)

Wilkerson, James A., M.D., ed. *Medicine for Mountaineering.* Seattle: The Mountaineers, 1977.

Agencies

Christian Camping International
P.O. Box 646
Wheaton, IL 60187
(*Journal of Christian Camping,* workshops, seminars, books)

Christian Wilderness Leaders Coalition
Ken Kalisch, Research Coordinator
Honey Rock/High Roads
Three Lakes, WI 54562

Colorado Outward Bound School
945 Pennsylvania
Denver, CO 80203
(Instructor's manuals, general resources on concepts and methods)

Discovery Expeditions
P.O. Box 1022
Grass Valley, CA 95945
(Newsletter, consortium of wilderness leaders, training programs)

The Mountaineers
P.O. Box 122
Seattle, WA 98111

Project Adventure
775 Bay Rd.
Hamilton, MA 01936

18

Youth Mission Trips*

Paul Borthwick

The Motivation for Youth Mission Teams

Over the past few years, we have had the privilege of sending over two hundred people out on youth mission teams. Teenagers have traveled a hundred thousand miles as they have gone out to paint camps, schools, churches, and private homes. They have constructed log cabins, led Vacation Bible Schools, built stone walls, and participated in church services in ten different countries.

While being favorably impressed by these youth missionary teams, some people invariably ask us why we are doing this. Why do we spend thousands of dollars to send students—most of whom are at least four years from making career decisions—off to areas that they may never again visit? What is the motivation?

Modeling

Jesus' discipleship ministry might be summarized in the command "Follow Me." He built His ministry to His twelve chosen ones on the principle that experience is the best teacher. He never told them to do something that He did not exemplify before them.

Missionary teams for young people are an excellent opportunity for modeling. The older adults who lead the team and the missionaries who work with the team have unparalleled opportunity to model both the Christian life and Christian compassion for others to students. Such modeling leaves lasting impressions on the spirits and hearts of the student participants.

Memories

Ralph Keyes[1] suggests that the high-school experience is the most important period of time for forming memories. The intensity of adolescence creates an atmosphere in high school where the most memorable experiences occur.

When we started doing youth teams, we postulated that these service experiences could be a place for positive memories to be formed. This we have found to be entirely correct. Large numbers of our students, upon applying for college, list the youth missionary teams as their most important and memorable experiences of their high-school lives. That is what encourages us to keep making these teams a priority in the youth ministry.

Missionaries

The 1980 Conference in World Evangelism in Pattaya, Thailand, set a goal for 200,000 new missionaries by the year 2000. What an incredible goal! How can it be achieved?

It is the assumption and principle motivation of the youth mission team concept that such experiences will plant seeds of desire in students that will bear fruit in the form of cross-cultural servants of Jesus Christ.

What We Have Done

Whenever mission teams are discussed among youth workers, there is always excitement and a feeling of, "Let's do this in our church." Discouragement sets in a few days or weeks later when the youth leader realizes that the preparatory work for a project has to be done *in addition* to all of his normal responsibilities. It's not easy!

I want to encourage youth workers to go the extra mile and pursue these teams. Every youth group is unique, but the reader should know that our projects started off with a lot of hesitancy— even opposition. The first two years of projects were coordinated by a part-time, seminary-student youth worker. Nevertheless, we overcame time constraints and opposition and now the projects are not only an acceptable aspect of our youth ministry, they are expected!

To prepare for discussion on the concept of youth mission teams, let me outline what experiences we have been able to provide in just the past four years. These experiences should demonstrate both the variety of tasks that can be accomplished and the costs of potential projects.

Destination	Date	Length of Time	Cost	Working With	Number of Participants	Project
Casablanca, Morocco and Krefeld, W. Germany	1982	3 weeks	$1050	North Africa Mission and Christ Camp	13	Morocco—tour & gain exposure to Islam W. Germany—building at a Christian camp
Mexico City, Mexico	1982	2 weeks	$600	Latin American Mission	13	Painting at Camp Kikoten
San Jose, Costa Rica	1982	2 weeks	$700	Latin American Mission	14	Painting at Camp Roblealto
Oranjestad, Aruba	1983	2 weeks	$750	TEAM	15	Paint at Radio Victoria
Kijabe, Kenya	1983	3 weeks	$1250	Africa Inland Mission	14	Construction at Moffat Bible College
Paterson, New Jersey	1983	2 weeks	$150	Africa Inland Mission	7	Work with day camp for city kids
Beverly, Kentucky	1983	2 weeks	$150	Red Bird Mission	10	Participate in work camp
Farmington, New Mexico	1983	2 weeks	$550	Navajo Missions	14	Work at the Indian Reservation
San Cristobal, Venezuela	1983	2 weeks	$750	TEAM	14	Paint at the Christiansen Academy
Palmer, Alaska	1983	2 weeks	$800	Arctic Missions	12	Build at the Victory Bible Camp
Krefeld, West Germany	1984	2 weeks	$800	Christ Camp	12	Physical labor at the camp
Cartagena, Colombia	1984	2 weeks	$800	Latin America Mission	14	Build at the Colegio Latino-americano
Paramaribo, Surinam	1984	2 weeks	$900	International Missions, Inc.	14	Build and paint at Maranatha Bible Institute
North Pole, Alaska	1984	2 weeks	$900	Radio Station KJNP	10	Physical labor on the station grounds and buildings
Waxhaw, North Carolina	1984	2 weeks	$250	Jungle Aviation & Radio Service	10	Participate in the "Jungle Jump-Off" program
Port-au-Prince, Haiti	1985	2 weeks	$600	New England & World Missions	14	Participate in child-care ministry; paint
San Cristobal, Venezuela	1985	2 weeks	$900	TEAM	9	General maintenance at Christiansen Academy
Kaoma, Zambia	1985	3 weeks	$1600	Africa Evangelical Fellowship	15	Build at the Manna Bible Institute

The projects we have done are primarily designed to give students experience outside of their usual cultural environment. Because our group comes from the middle-class suburbs of the United States, experiences in urban, rural, and international settings offer students a small example of what cross-cultural work is like.

How can all this be done? The following three sections are designed to encourage youth workers from churches with any size membership and any size budget to consider youth (and *adult*) missionary teams for their groups and their churches.

Planning

Although a successful youth project will be a consolidated team effort, the bulk of the planning for such projects is done by the youth leader(s). The amount of time required to plan a mission trip varies, but it is wise to consider planning anywhere from eight to twelve months in advance. For those who are part-time or volunteer workers, a longer time period may be required.

Step One: Decide What You Want

After learning about our youth missions program, many youth leaders respond enthusiastically, desiring to do the same in their own group. The problem is that each group is unique. Therefore, each project needs to be tailor-made to the needs, abilities, and financial means of the students and the church. The following questions should be answered as you decide what you want:

1. What are your objectives? Do you want to build your leadership? Will you work only with students who have an expressed interest in missions? Do you want to give cross-cultural exposure or simply exposure to serving others?

One of our principle objectives each year is to give students first-hand experience in urban, rural, and international settings. This objective determines where we will go and who will go with us.

2. Where will you go? How far can you travel? Can you afford to fly? Does the church have a bus or a van that you can use? Where are your contacts?

3. What type of work can your group do? Painting? Construction? Evangelism?

4. How long will you go? One week? Two weeks? All summer? The fact that a majority of young people are trying to get jobs will limit the time. Also, leaders are hard to find, and many of them will be forced to sacrifice a vacation. Be realistic.

5. When do you want to go? During school vacation? Over the summer? Can you travel mid-week and save on airfare?

6. How much can your group afford? The socio-economic background of your church and your students will determine where you can go. Be cautious and sensitive not to shoot too high. Offering a project that is out of the financial reach of the families of your church could discourage your students from missionary service.

7. What will you offer the people for whom you work? Will you pay for your own food? How about lodging? Such questions should be answered before you approach missionaries about working with them. Our policy has always been that we will pay for our food, our travel, and at least part of the cost of our supplies. We expect the hosts to arrange for lodging and to arrange for the preparation of our food.

Step Two: Look for Opportunities

After making basic decisions as to what you are looking for, begin pursuing opportunities. Some of the most obvious options are the missionaries supported by your church family. You might also contact friends or ministers from other churches.

Correspondence with these potential opportunities will get initial results. Many will be negative, but this is to be expected. Missions organizations are often hesitant to do projects with high schoolers; so they may shy away from your suggestions. To give an example, our ratio of projects completed to projects considered is about 1:5. This figure, however, goes down with experience. Positive reputation and recommendations from other missions groups will lend credibility to your work for future projects.

Step Three: Recruit Your Leaders

The most basic question for youth missionary teams is, "Who will lead the team?" Opportunities to serve and enthusiastic high-schoolers are all for naught if there are no adults to lead the team.

Go first to men and women in your church who are interested in missionary service. Members of the missionary committee are often the best prospects. Even if they are not personally interested or able, they may know someone who is.

Although it may be difficult, it is best to get commitments from these leaders early. This will give them adequate time to associate with and befriend the students. The most effective missionary teams will be those with leaders who have long-term relationships with the students. It is a rare individual who is able to develop quality relationships with students on a short, one- to three-week project. Aim for at least one adult for every four students. Young couples or singles are some of the best possibilities because they will be better able to keep pace with the high-schoolers' metabolism.

Development

While there is some overlap between planning and development, I have chosen to separate the two because the development section is the momentum-building time. It is during this period that the project begins to fall together and the excitement builds in both the youth group and in the church family.

Step One: Planning the Budget and Raising the Money

While it is not wise to propose a project to the youth group or to the church that will be far above the financial limits of the families, it is wise to ask people to stretch their faith and trust God to provide.

"How much will it cost?" will be the parents' first question. Early in the development stage, the youth leaders need to have some financial information. There must be early contact made with the missions committee to propose that funds be allocated for the youth project. Because many budgets cover an entire year, it is wise to make proposals as soon as possible.

How much will it cost? Before approaching the youth, the parents, or the missions committee with the project, the youth leader must have an idea of the cost. Every project will differ, but the main costs are usually for travel, food, and supplies. To estimate travel costs, include tolls, gasoline, fares for air travel or land travel, visa charges, and any other expenses likely to be incurred. Figure food costs for the whole trip, both on-site and on-the-road costs. Your supplies (paint, cement, etc.) will vary with the project. Check whether it will be cheaper (if feasible) to bring supplies with you or to buy them on location. A budget may also need to make allowance for lodging (either on-site or on-the-road), depending on the nature of the project and the means of transportation. Students should be held responsible for their own passports, spending money, film, and clothing costs.

The following principles and ideas have helped form our policies in budgeting and fund raising.

1. When presenting the monetary needs of such projects to the missions committee of your church, be a little generous in your

estimations. The price of travel, gasoline, and food will increase; do not get shortchanged by being too conservative.

2. Ask the missions committee to budget certain funds for the project. Specifically, ask the committee to budget a certain amount per project to help pay for supplies. Ask also for scholarship aid if it is to be made available to students.

3. Make sure students are not given the trip. One of the most growing experiences is trusting God to provide the needed cash. We instruct parents to donate only a portion of each student's cost. The student is then responsible to trust God for the rest.

4. Make special allowances for your leaders. To expect a person to give up vacation time, lead a youth team, and then pay full price is not very fair. It must be decided how much leaders will pay, and, assuming that this is only part of the cost, it must be decided how the balance of the money will be provided. Will the cost of leaders be divided evenly over the student fare? Or will the missions committee offer the balance as a scholarship?

5. Information can also be made available for students and parents as to other potential monetary sources. Some individuals or organizations may make money available for student aid, and this can be part of the fund-raising procedure.

Step Two: Promotion

Early in the development stage, the youth leader needs to begin promoting the youth missionary team idea to the youth, their parents, and the church. Promotion might include bulletin announcements, general informational brochures, and posters that will help generate interest in the church family.

The purpose of the promotional phase is to get people interested and thinking about a project. Promotion does not need to be supported by a great number of details. Promotion should happen four to eight months before the targeted date of the project. The youth leader should be cautious and use words like, "We might," or, "We hope to." Don't make promises that will not be fulfilled.

Step Three: Recruitment

The recruitment phase is the time when a definite decision is reached. This is the time for the presentation of the exact details—how much, how long, when, how many, where, and what will be the task?

The recruiting process is often difficult because the young people may be hesitant to commit themselves, especially to a new idea. It is wise to have the support of the other youth leaders (or sponsors), the parents, and especially the minister. If the minister endorses what the youth leader is trying to do, it will increase the credibility of such a project to the church family.

To accelerate the recruiting process, it is wise to abide by the following principles:

1. Inform people of as many details as possible. People fear the unknown, and a dissemination of the facts will answer many questions before they are asked.

2. Emphasize commitment. Non-refundable deposits, official applications, and official letters of acceptance are a few ways to emphasize to students the fact that they are committing themselves to serious work. Requirements will add to this emphasis. (See the suggested list below.)

3. After a person registers interest in a project, give him personal attention. Such attention is often an affirmation to the student. It serves to calm his fears and answer the doubt, "I do not know whether I could do it."

4. Emphasize limits and deadlines. A group limit will communicate to students that they had better register before all the spots are filled. A registration deadline (and possibly a penalty fee) also serves to prompt decisions.

Step Four: Requirements

High-school students are aware of the principle that if a program demands little of them, it must be worth little. For this reason, preparatory requirements are very important to the students who are considering a youth missionary team.

While the requirements will differ with each project, all projects should demand something from the students. The following requirements are suggested.

1. *Essays.* This includes an introductory essay with the application. This essay describes the student's relationship to God and details the student's hope in going on the project.

Another essay (or research project) should focus on either the region to which the team is going or the people whom the team will serve. Short reports on geography, history, and culture will help prepare the team and will force them to learn.

A third essay should be required as an evaluation after the youth missionary trip. While this cannot be written during the development phase, it should be stated that they will be expected to write it after the project is over.

2. *Meetings.* Team meetings are the best way to prepare for teamwork. Because we are working with high-schoolers, team meetings should include some discussion of the project, but relationships will grow more rapidly if the team goes bowling or out to get pizza together.

3. *Other requirements* might include Scripture memory, reading, or language study. All the requirements should seek to affirm to the students that the project is serious enough to require work.

Step Five: Training the Leaders

Experience has taught us that the relative success or failure of a youth missionary team is *directly* dependent on the leadership. The adult leaders are the glue that holds the team together. For this reason, their training is essential in preparing for a youth team.

Specific training should be offered in relational and practical matters. Leaders should be instructed as to how to deal with crises, how to rebuke a complainer, how to encourage communication, how to listen, and any other relational skills that will help for better team spirit.

Leaders should also be instructed in practical matters such as travel tips, how to go through customs, and financial management on the trip. Training the leaders may require the importing of outside speakers or instructors. Offering training for the leaders by someone who is an expert in small group dynamics, giving these leaders an hour with an experienced travel agent, or providing training by a building or painting contractor will be keys for a successful project.

Step Six: The Practical Details

The momentum builds as students register for the project. Leaders are trained and team members begin to fulfill their requirements. While all this is happening, it is easy for the team leader to think all is well. This is not necessarily so; there is an abundance of nitty gritty details that have to be worked out in the few months before the project gets underway. While there are many responsibilities, they fall under three general categories.

1. *Travel Details.* For a local trip, this includes arranging for cars or a van, deciding on what routes will be taken, and arranging for lodging if over-night travel is required.

For an international trip or any trip that requires flying, the travel details are more extensive. Ordering tickets, getting visas or visitor cards, making sure students have passports and necessary shots, and staying in touch with the travel agency requires organization and diligence.

2. *Host details.* While all the preparations are being made at home, there must be consistent communication with the people to whom you are going. Letter writing and an occasional phone call will enable you to find out cultural factors, climatological oddities, and situational changes that may have an influence on the trip.

Correspondence with the host group is the best way to find out what clothes the group will need, which shots are required, what the people are like, and what are the cheapest means of travel.

3. *Financial matters.* The details prior to the project will include a good deal of financial management for the team leaders. Finances for a local trip involving cars or vans will be much simpler than those for a trip that includes air travel. The least expensive air tickets will be the "Advance Purchase" variety, most of which will be written and paid for at least thirty days in advance. For convenience and ease of planning, it is wise to collect all money at least sixty days in advance for air-travel projects and at least thirty days in advance for land-travel projects.

What about *insurance?* This is one financial matter you had better check into. There are two possibilities. Either the church policy will cover the team (or can be extended to cover you) or you can make each team member responsible for his own coverage. Whatever the choice, it is wise to get something *in writing* before you depart. Accidents can happen, and it is wiser to be safe than sorry.

Step Seven: Building Church Awareness

One of the most important functions of the church in sending out youth missionary teams is affirmation. It is the members of the church family who give the youth the special sense of being sent out in service. The best affirmations can come from a church family that is aware of the project and the specific youth involved. Building this awareness is an essential part of the development phase.

Each church has a different organizational set-up; so the means of building this awareness will differ from congregation to congregation. Every church, however, has some type of general publication (such as a weekly bulletin) that can include information about the youth missionary team. This information should appear more often as the departure date gets closer.

Perhaps the most important way to build the general awareness of the church family is a commissioning during one of the major services of the church. This commissioning should involve a recognition of the team, a description of what will be done, and a specific prayer of commissioning. The purpose of this commissioning is not only to inform the church, but also to build the students' sense of being representatives of the church.

Step Eight: Planning for Pictures

It may seem overwhelming to be forced to think about reporting back after the project even before you have left, but such thinking must be done. Poor photographs will severely limit your ability to describe to others what has taken place. To insure the best pictures, we assign at least two people as team photographers, and they are responsible for specific pictures. Taking two or three shots of the same sight will insure that there is at least one shot good enough for reporting to the church or other group. We advise that all shots be slides; this is less expensive, and the best slides can be chosen and processed into prints.

Leading

The myriad of details have been fulfilled, and the team is ready to go. You meet at a central location for prayer (and, if possible, a mini-commissioning from the minister), and you load up to start driving or to go together to the airport. The days ahead will be some of the most exciting and memorable you may ever have.

Step One: As You Travel

The travel experience may be the most significant time to build anticipation of the upcoming work and service. It is very important to emphasize the following while traveling to or from a service project:

1. *Team pride.* The way a team dresses will influence how they feel about themselves and how they will behave before others. Since 1980, we have required, when possible, the men to wear suitcoats and ties and the women to wear dresses or skirts. While many have complained about this requirement, all are grateful after the fact because it builds a camaraderie between team members, and it causes most of the young people to stand tall because they are proud of how they look as a team.

2. *Team witness.* The excitement of travel sometimes causes students to forget the Lord whom they serve. For this reason, the

leaders should emphasize that the team's behavior, attitudes, and language will be a witness for (or against) the glory of Christ to fellow-travelers and other people that the team encounters.

3. *Team courtesy.* Related to team witness, courtesy toward gas station attendants, stewardesses, or food-service workers will, in most cases, have to be taught. Courtesy should also be exhorted for intra-team relationships. This means helping each other with baggage and being conscientious in looking out for the needs of others.

Step Two: After You Get There

After arrival, there will be a time of adjustment for all of the team members. New people, new surroundings, and in some cases, a new language or culture will take some getting used to. Be patient.

1. *The leaders' example.* Upon arrival, the leaders will be consulted often by the students. Students will watch the leaders for their responses to the new setting and for a model as to how they should behave.

The leaders must fulfill three important roles. First, they immediately become the counselors of the team and need to listen hard and long to the students to find out who is hurting or who needs a special word of encouragement.

Second, the leaders must be the pacesetters. If the leaders are excited about the people, the culture, and the joy of discovery, the students will be, too. Being the pacesetters also requires that the leaders work the hardest and pray the most often.

Finally, the leaders operate as mediators for intra-team relationships and between the team and the host group. At various times, team members will get on each other's nerves, and bitterness will arise. Leaders should be the mediators who prompt communication to work out the problems. It is very rare for a seven-to twenty-one-day project to occur without every team member's (including the leaders) having to ask another for forgiveness at one time or another.

As mediator between the team and the hosts, the leaders must speak up if the team is being driven too hard. The youth missionary team members are servants, but they should not be abused. The leaders need also to interact with the hosts as to how the students perceive them. If the host missionary is always giving orders but never doing the work, the youth team is sure to notice.

2. *Student exposure.* While serving, there are four distinct areas to which students can be exposed to provide a full educational

experience. First, students should be exposed as much as possible to the hosts. Exposure to missionaries, local or national leaders, and their families will be the best opportunity for students to discover that servants of Christ are normal people who hurt, get discouraged, yet triumph in Christ.

Second, students should be exposed to the culture, and they should be helped to see their own cultural biases. If they notice that people look funny or drive on the wrong side of the road, the leaders should inquire as to the basis for their judgment. Cultural exposure will be the best way for students to learn that cultures and people can differ without being right or wrong.

The third exposure students need on a well-rounded project is that of hard work for Jesus. Keep in mind that many high-schoolers (especially those in ninth or tenth grade) will have never worked an eight-hour day or a forty-hour week. Diligent teamwork will stretch students and teach them that they can work harder than they ever thought possible. Reminding them that they are there to serve Jesus will provide some of the needed motivation.

The final exposure from which students will benefit is to the leaders. With the exception of parents, most students will have never lived with an older Christian person for any significant length of time. Living with, watching, and emulating the leaders will be the best training in discipleship that some students will ever receive.

Step Three: The Work and the Play

The experience of a missionary service project has many facets, the two most important of which are the work and the play. Because most of the waking moments of the project will be spent in one of these two functions, it is important to make the maximum use of this time. To make the entire experience a learning adventure, it is important to consider the following.

1. *Measurable results.* High-schoolers are pragmatists. They do not think conceptually as well as they think practically. For this reason, measurable results will be the most positive way for them to know that God has used them in His service.

Although their presence and enthusiasm will be a great encouragement to those for whom they work, this will not register in the students' minds as a measure that God used their lives. They prefer to see some project completed, some wall built, or some house painted. Such a tangible result will demonstrate to them that God did indeed use their efforts to achieve a visible goal.

2. *The leaders' excitement.* Because high-schoolers are often inhibited in front of each other, they will hesitate to show enthusiasm or excitement at a new discovery. A high-school guy will usually hesitate to register excitement over an extremely beautiful flower or a colorful butterfly. If the leaders are uninhibited and excitable, the students will experience greater freedom to learn, discover, and enjoy themselves and their surroundings.

3. *The journal.* To state that high-schoolers are impressionable is one matter, but to help them remember their impressions is another. The intensity of a service team—with all the experiences and discoveries—may provide team members a host of valuable experiences, but they may not remember any one of them. Recommending or requiring daily journal entries helps students articulate what they learn. This writing and recording will fix the experiences in their minds to remain long after the project is over.

4. *Fun activities.* When missionaries report back to supporting churches, they sometimes give the impression that all they do is work. While this may be the case for some missionaries, it is not typical. Most people, no matter what type of cultural setting they live in, have some sort of recreation. To give the students on the youth service team a full experience, you should include some of these recreational experiences. This might include swimming in a stream or hiking up a mountain. It might be something unique—such as feeding a wild deer or snorkeling on a coral reef. Whatever it is, make sure to include it during the project.

Step Four: Feedback

During the project, the most crucial relational tool needed to keep the operation running smoothly is feedback. The students and the leaders need time to talk together. This is very important.

1. *It helps the team deal with disappointments.* One of our teams went to Alberta expecting dog teams and scenes from Jack London. They found expansive plains and oil derricks. As a team, they needed time together—apart from their hosts—to voice their disappointments and to decide together to work at overcoming these feelings of disappointment.

2. *It allows time to cope with problems or complaints.* The mediatorial role of the leaders come into play here. Allowing for feedback will give opportunity for the leaders to find out what things are bothering the team members.

3. *It allows the team to let down.* Because the students come from a certain culture, they will see or hear things in a new setting

that will seem odd or silly to them. Team feedback time allows students time to work through their reactions without hurting the feelings of the hosts or embarrassing the team.

4. *It allows for confrontations.* There will be times when one or two people will need to be exhorted for being too lazy or too secretive. There will be other times when those who are ill or tired will need encouragement. Team feedback time is the most appropriate time for these confrontations.

Step Five: After the Trip

The most difficult adjustment for most students (and leaders) will occur after the trip is over. From an intense, highly growth-oriented, deeply spiritual time, the students will separate and return home to life as usual.

Upon returning, some students will feel extremely lonely, thinking that they are misunderstood by their family or friends. They will wonder whether the experience was just a dream. They will question why no one is as excited about this trip as they are.

Others will crash spiritually after the trip because of the sudden removal of intimate fellowship. Still others may even be emotionally affected—particularly manifested by depression.

To deal with these problems, consider the following:

1. *Deprogramming.* Time after the project must be provided when students can have a reunion. Only in their own group will they find others who are as excited as they are. Deprogramming times should include an honest discussion about the real problems that they face now that they are home. Confronting the problems directly will help students resolve the issues.

2. *Affirmations.* A variety of sessions should be planned to help students feel a sense of the affirmation of the church family who sent them out earlier. Meeting with the missions committee, the minister, and the entire church body will enable students to report what they have learned. It will also reconfirm to the students the specialness of the work they accomplished. The team needs to know that the church appreciated their work.

Step Six: Follow-up

Lord willing, the effect of these projects will be felt long after the project is over. Assuming that one of the goals of the project is to stimulate the students' interest in missions, there should be careful follow-up of the team members (both leaders and students) after the project.

Following up students might include either of two options. The missions committee may want to follow up individuals. If there are twelve people on the missions committee, and there are twenty-four students who, as a result of some projects, have a desire to consider or pursue missions, then each member of the committee should specifically pray for, befriend, and reach out to two of these students.

A second option for follow-up might be the awarding of certain trophies. A picture of the team in the church lobby or a T-shirt (for each team member) that reads, "I painted a house for Jesus," will act as further expressions of the church family's affirmation of these students.

Epilogue: The End Results

It would be nice to say that all of the students and leaders who have participated in our projects are now pursuing missionary service. This is not the case. Some are, but most are still too young.

So then, what is the outcome? If your church decides to plan and execute a youth missionary trip, what will happen?

While the exact outcome is impossible to predict, the results we have observed in students and leaders include the following:

1. A greater understanding of servanthood.

2. A working knowledge of and desire for teamwork.

3. An increased world-awareness. Specifically, the youth have gained a better perspective on their own church and their own problems because they understand that the world and God's people are larger and more varied than they ever knew before.

4. An intensified desire to pursue God's will for their lives.

5. An increased willingness to consider missionary service. The most significant outcome is that participants on these teams have a new perspective on missionary service. Rather than considering the call to missions as extraordinary or as a special call to a few unique spiritual oddballs, our students look at missionary service as a normal option to consider for their future.

---

*Adapted from *How to Plan, Develop, and Lead a Youth Mission Team* by Paul Borthwick (Lexington, MA: Grace Chapel, 1980). Used by permission.

¹Ralph Keyes, *Is There Life After High School?* (Boston: Little, Brown & Co., 1976).

19

Planning an Effective
Youth Retreat

Paul Schlieker

Getting away for a weekend retreat is an excellent way to build character into the lives of junior-high and high-school young people. The success of any retreat takes a lot of hard work. Good retreats don't just happen. As you plan and prepare for a retreat with your youth group, please consider some of these ingredients. They will help make your retreat everything that it can and should be.

Purpose

It is essential that you identify the purpose for your retreat. Why are you having it? If this is not clear in your mind, it will never be clear to the students who attend. One reason to have a retreat is for the purpose of building relationships within the youth group. Another purpose for a retreat is to focus on the students' relationships with the Lord. Some retreats focus on a combination of these two. Retreats that are for the purpose of service are sometimes called working retreats or work weekends.

Though the purpose for your retreat might vary from one retreat to the next, it must be clear in your mind and in the minds of the students attending. It is essential that you say one thing well in a weekend retreat. Don't try to meet every need of your youth group in two and a half days. Focus the retreat on one idea, book of the Bible, issue, concern, or problem.

Generally, the best retreats focus upwards during study times and focus outwards toward friends, at meals, recreation, and free times. Often, a retreat is planned for the purpose of bringing a youth group together, and the youth leader is tempted to dismiss the upward focus. But if there is a lack of love in the youth group, the real problem is a problem between the students and God, not just between students. Because the average retreat has so many relational opportunities built in naturally, it is still usually best to focus on the students' relationship with God during study times. These decisions call for careful judgment by the leadership.

Place

After deciding the purpose of your retreat, find the place. Often a church camp, resort, lodge, or cabin facility will be available on a rental basis for your retreat. It is important to find a place that is affordable for the young people. Retreats in a rustic setting offer a special atmosphere where students feel that they are getting away from it all. If cost is a concern, retreats can be held at the church building, though sleeping accommodations may be poor. The key concern is to find a facility that is close to your church building and is adequately equipped to meet the basic needs of life. If you are holding your retreat in the mountains, where it is especially cold, inform your young people so they will be prepared. If you are ambitious and use tents, take only the finest equipment, which can endure various types of weather.

Planning

There is an old saying: "If you fail to plan, you have planned to fail." Trite as this may sound, it is true. The more details you anticipate in advance planning, the better the retreat. A checklist is given on page 265 for your consideration as you plan.

Feel free to adapt this list to fit your purpose and accommodations. Good retreats don't just happen. You must plan ahead and take care of details.

When you plan, you must set the right date. Weekend retreats for junior-high and high-school young people must take into consideration their school schedules. If you are planning a fall retreat, check the high-school football schedule, the homecoming date, and the dates of other school activities before you set the retreat date. True, it is impossible to work around every school activity, especially if you are in a church with several high schools represented. However, checking ahead always helps. Most towns have

CHECKLIST FOR RETREAT

_____Bus/Driver
_____Movie
_____Movie discussion
        questions
_____Movie projector/spare
        bulbs
_____Take-up Reel
_____Screen
_____Extension cords
_____Adapters
_____Overhead Projector/
        spare bulb
_____Transparencies
_____Transparency pens
_____Pencils
_____Discussion questions
_____Funny skits
_____First-aid kit
_____Communion
_____Games/Mixers
_____Football
_____Speaker's sleeping bag/
        pillow
_____Junk food for party
        Saturday night
_____Frisbee

_____Volleyball
_____Popcorn/Oil/Salt/Butter
_____Popcorn popper
_____Big containers for popcorn
_____Paper bowls
_____Paper cups
_____Kool-Aid /Cooler/Ice
_____Stopwatch
_____Whistle
_____Checks for speaker/and
        retreat site
_____Song books
_____Extra vehicles/drivers
_____Inner tubes
_____Camera/Film
_____Tapes and recorder
_____Discussion groups
_____Sound system
_____Music stand
_____3 x 5 cards
_____Napkins
_____Paper towels
_____Can Opener
_____Christian music tapes
_____Substitute teacher for
        Sunday-school class

one key football or basketball game each year with a rival school.
Schedule the retreat away from those popular games.

Publicity

You may have the greatest retreat planned in the history of the
world, but what good is it if no one knows about it? It is important
to tell the students the important details. Be sure to publicize the
following:

*Date. Let the students know the date of the retreat at least two
months in advance. This will enable them to rearrange jobs and
other commitments so they can attend.

*Place.

*Cost per person.

*What to bring. Making this a *detailed* list will eliminate some problems at the retreat. Many students do not know what is appropriate to bring or leave at home.

*Departure and arrival times.

*Transportation information.

Use your church paper to publicize your retreat. Take two-minute spots in Sunday school and youth meetings to remind your young people about the upcoming retreat. Try using a special letter to the young people and their parents for publicity. Try publicizing this year's retreat by showing slides from last year's retreat. If you don't have slides, prepare for next year by taking a camera this year. Don't forget the old stand-bys of posters, phone calls, and word of mouth.

Outside Speakers

An outside speaker (someone outside your church family) is a great way to build enthusiasm for a retreat. Naturally, the concern here is the speaker's travel expense and paying him an honorarium. It is important to pay your outside speakers well. Don't take these people for granted. They are sacrificing their own church and family commitments to be with you. It is rarely appropriate to pay only the travel expenses. Discuss the honorarium with the speaker before the retreat. It is preferable to pay your speaker on the day he arrives.

Junior-high retreats generally do not need outside speakers. High-school and college retreats tend to attract more young people when there is an outside speaker. This enables the youth minister or youth sponsors to play an administrative role rather than a heavy teaching role.

I would suggest that the youth minister do the primary teaching at junior-high retreats and ask an outside speaker to teach at the high-school and college-age retreats.

Adult Leadership

No person can lead a retreat by himself. It takes a team of adult leaders. If the retreat will be attended by both boys and girls, there must be an adequate number of both male and female counselors.

The best way to recruit your retreat leaders is to write the responsibilities for each leader and then present to them the job description. If you cannot write why you want them to go, you can't expect them to be enthusiastic about accepting. Make their role at the retreat as clear as possible. A variety of adults is desirable, including different ages. Young married couples with no children are excellent candidates for sponsoring a weekend retreat. However, they might not have as much effectiveness in discipline as would adults who are in their forties. Use your judgment and enlist the help of a variety of adults.

The best ratio for a retreat is generally one adult for every seven young people. This allows a number of opportunities for small groups, with each group having an adequate adult leader. A helpful thing to do with your adult leadership is to meet a few days before you leave and discuss the entire schedule and their role. Inform your adults as to the nature and purpose of the retreat, the focus of the studies, the application that will be made, and other important details. Adults going on the retreat are more enthusiastic when they know what is going to happen before they get there.

If possible, subsidize the expense for your adult leaders. A good rule of thumb is to take the cost per student and divide it by half. Have every adult leader pay half of the cost and have the church pick up the other half.

The Schedule and Program

The schedule for any given retreat will vary according to its purpose. But there are some things that will be true in nearly every retreat. For most retreats, there are six major programming areas to keep in mind.

1. Group study and discussion times
2. Breaks/recreation
3. Meal times
4. Group singing/worship
5. Group prayer times
6. Sleep

If your retreat begins on Friday evening and ends on Sunday afternoon or Sunday evening, let me suggest some practical things to keep in mind.

One of the best ways to get your retreat off to a good start is to eat right after you get to the retreat site. If you have time, you can unload your cars or church bus and then eat, but it is not necessary. If you have traveled very far to get to your retreat site, the group will be hungry. Meeting this physical need will make them more receptive to the spiritual teaching that will come later. Some groups travel so far to their retreat sites that they lose most of Friday evening in transportation. This is unfortunate, but at sometimes unavoidable. But if possible, plan to arrive at the retreat site in time for supper on Friday evening.

When planning the schedule, remember that young people and adults are tired at the end of a long week. If you're going to lead a Bible study on Friday evening, it must be very interesting to keep everyone awake. One good way to kick off a retreat is to show a film on Friday evening as the major study for that night. The film should be selected according to the theme for that weekend. The rest of the program on Saturday and Sunday can then be built around the thrust of Friday night's film.

It is important to have breaks through the weekend where young people can stand, stretch, use the restroom, and get a snack (mainly something to drink). Listed below is a retreat schedule that we have used for a number of our junior-high, high-school, and college retreats.

Friday—   4:00—Load bus
                  4:30—Leave
                  5:30—Arrive at camp
                  6:00—Supper
                  7:00—Mixers/Games/Get acquainted
                  8:00—Study session #1
                  9:30—Camp fire
                 10:30—Get to bed

Saturday—   7:00—Up
                  8:00—Breakfast
                  9:00—Study session #2
                 10:30—Free time
                 12:30—Lunch
                  1:30—Free time
                  4:15—Study session #3
                  6:00—Supper
                  7:00—Study session #4
                  8:30—"Saturday Night"
                  9:30—Camp fire
                 10:30—Get to bed

Sunday—   7:00—Up
                  8:00—Breakfast
                  9:15—Study session #5
                 11:00—Leave
                 11:55—Arrive home

Probably the most neglected area on the average retreat is the importance of sleep. Young people who are allowed to stay up as late as they want on Friday or Saturday at a retreat generally don't get very much out of the spiritual studies the following day. Sleep is one of the most important activities at the retreat. If the young people and adults are not well rested, the impact of the rest of the weekend is greatly limited. It is important to expect them to go to bed at a reasonable time. This includes adults as well as students. The adults must enforce this among the entire youth group, or a few loudmouths will keep everyone awake. Make your expectations in this area clear and stick by it. This will make a much better retreat.

Student Involvement

It's important to convey the idea that this is the young people's retreat, not your retreat that they attend. Involve the students in as many areas of planning and preparing as possible. Let them pick the games that will be played. Involve them in publicity, phone calling, selection of parts of the program, and other planning. Young people who feel that they have had a chance to buy into the program from the very beginning are young people who will be more enthusiastic about the retreat.

Another good way to involve students is to allow them to lead the devotion times in the evenings. If you have a camp fire setting or a fireplace in a cabin, this is a great way to have different students share what Jesus means to them and lead their peers in a time of prayer and praise to God.

Registration

When planning your retreat, set a registration day when the students are asked to pay for the weekend in advance. Consider no person registered until you have received his money. What a young person would like to do, and what he really does are often two different things. If needed, have a late registration fee that you apply to students who don't register by a certain date. See page 271 for a form that would be easy to adapt to your church's retreat.

Scholarships

Some young people are simply not able to afford $30.00 (or whatever your cost) for a weekend retreat. If that is the case, make sure everyone knows that financial help is available through the church or individuals in the congregation. Often, a young person can raise half the money if the church can supply the other half. While your method may vary from others, make sure that no person is eliminated from attending on financial reasons alone. There are always adults who are willing to help.

The Day You Leave

There are some final things that you need to do on the day that you leave. One is to make sure that you have a final checklist of every person going. Often students will call up at the last minute and either want to go or not go. Anticipate these last minute interruptions as you are scurrying around gathering up supplies, food, and materials. Probably the most helpful thing that you can do is to get all of your work done on the night before you leave. Then the day you leave can be devoted to last-minute details, troubleshooting, answering questions of students and parents, and simply allowing you to go into the retreat more rested and with a more relaxed state of mind.

Rules

Rules should never be the focal point of a youth group or youth event. However, good rules provide a structure that can enable a positive atmosphere—especially at a retreat. Here are some guidelines for setting effective rules.

1. Be positive. Don't assume that the young people's primary goal is to break the rules.

2. Have enough adult supervision. A large team of adults working together goes a long way in preventing discipline problems before they begin.

3. Take time at the beginning of the weekend to explain some practical guidelines that will help the retreat be a success. Listed below are some guidelines that could be used at almost any retreat.

  a. Do not leave the retreat grounds without permission.
  b. Cars will not be used during the retreat.
  c. No boys in girls' rooms; no girls in boys' rooms.
  d. No puffing, no chewing, no spacing out on pills or drinks.
  e. Report any injury immediately to a sponsor.
  f. Be present at all activities on time.
  g. Everyone must be at every meal whether he eats or not.
  h. Be careful with the property at the retreat facility.
  i. Love conquers all. Let's work together and build each other up.

You need to anticipate potential problems at the retreat. The following is a list of situations that might occur:
1. Young people arriving later.
2. Young people leaving early.
3. Special health problems of certain young people (diet and medical needs).
4. Having to share the facilities with another group.
5. Two young people who are not getting along and are making the weekend unpleasant for everyone.

Prayer

This item is not listed last because it is least important. Prayer must provide the support for every activity. "Unless the Lord builds the house, they labor in vain who build it" (Psalm 127:1 NASB). A retreat is both demanding and exciting. As you plan, prepare, program, and pull off your weekend retreat, trust God's power to work through you to produce supernatural results.

Suggested Resources

For an excellent step-by-step retreat planning guide, there is none better than the *Retreat Book,* by Arlo Reichter. It is published by Group Books, P.O. Box 841, Loveland, Colorado, 80539. This four-hundred-page book costs $16.00 and contains a detailed answer to nearly every question you would ever have regarding retreats.

Registration Form

1986 SENIOR-HIGH WINTER RETREAT
HIGHLAND CAMP
JANUARY 3, 4, 5
Cost $30.00

NAME_____GRADE_____

ADDRESS_____CITY_____ZIP_____

PHONE_____AMOUNT PAID_____

MORE RESOURCES
for Youth Groups

Ministering to Youth: A Strategy for the '80s (88582). A practical source book for developing a total approach to youth ministry. Compiled by David Roadcup and written by leaders in youth ministry, this book is one of the best available.

"Good Stuff" (3 volumes: 3403, 3407, 3411). Here's a series of resource books for use with Junior- and Senior-high teens. Each book contains four topical studies loaded with resource materials, learning activities, worksheets, and transparencies. The studies are useful for youth meetings, retreats, camps, and a variety of other settings.

Dating and Waiting: A Christian View of Love, Sex, and Dating (39972), by Les Christie;
Christian Ways to Date, Go Steady, and Break Up (39949), by John Butler. Here are two books to help young people set Christian standards for dating. These books cover virtually every aspect of dating relationships.

A History of the English Bible (39974). This book explains the nature, authority, and relevance of the Bible and helps your young people understand why we rest our faith in Jesus on this wonderful old Book.

Available at your Christian bookstore or

STANDARD
PUBLISHING